TYPOGRAPHY 42

The Annual of the Type Directors Club

The 67th Annual Communication Design Competition

The 24th Annual Typeface Design Competition

The World's Best Typography°

© 2021 Type Directors Club

First Edition
published in 2021 by:

verlag hermann schmidt

Gonsenheimer Str. 56
D-55126 Mainz
Phone +49 (0) 6131 / 50 60 0
Fax +49 (0) 6131 / 50 60 80
info@verlag-hermann-
schmidt.de www.typografie.de
www.verlag-hermann-schmidt.de
facebook:
Verlag Hermann Schmidt twitter:
VerlagHSchmidt

ISBN 978-3-87439-961-6

Type Directors Club
The One Club for Creativity Carol
Wahler
450 West 31st Street
6th Floor
New York, NY 10001
Tel: 212-979-1900
E:tdc@oneclub.org
W:tdc.org

Printed and bound in Turkey
ÖMÜR Printing

ACKNOWLEDGMENTS

The Type Directors Club
gratefully acknowledges the
following for their support and
contributions to the success of
TDC67 and 24TDC

Design
Juan Carlos Pagan
CarlosPagan.com
SundayAfternoon.us

Production
Adam S. Wahler
A2A Studio
a2a.com

Editing
Dave Baker
Super Copy Editors
supercopyeditors.com

TDC67 Competition
(call for entries)
Design
Juan Carlos Pagan
(Sunday Afternoon)

Principal Typefaces
Donated and used in the
composition of The World's
Best Typography,
TYPOGRAPHY 42

Geograph designed by
Kris Sowersby and
distributed by
klim type foundry
klim.co.nz

° Signifies TDC member

The World's Best Typography® (Typography 42) is the only awards annual devoted exclusively to typography. It presents the winning designs for the Type Directors Club's two respected annual competitions: the 67th annual communications design competition (TDC67) and the 24th TDC Typeface Design Competition.

This beautiful 372-page book features over 500 full-color images of international graphic design and type design in a wide range of categories, including books, magazines, corporate identities, logos, stationery, annual reports, video and web graphics, and posters. The World's Best Typography was designed by Sunday Afternoon in New York.

Type Directors Club members throughout the world receive this publication as part of their annual membership, and everyone is encouraged to join the TDC.

RUBÉN
Fontana
TDC Medalist 2020

Rubén Fontana was born in Buenos Aires in 1942.

His interest in the letter started when he was 10 years old. On his way to and from school, two blocks from his house, he noticed the way a fileteado lettering artist was working. Fileteado is a type of artistic drawing and lettering with stylized lines and flowered, climbing plants. It adorns all kinds of beloved objects: signs, taxis, lorries, and even the old colectivos, Buenos Aires' buses. Young Rubén would often stop to look at the evolution of the artist's daily work over two years.

After a year of high school, Rubén started working as a messenger for an advertising agency, and then he moved to a larger agency. During the deliveries and pickups, he would study the street posters and banners. During the agency's calm moments, he spent his time in the art department, where he learned a lot just by looking at the lettering artist. Rubén remembers very well drawing his first original—but it did not work because he drew it with blue ink and so it couldn't be reproduced. That was the first big lesson of this job.

Over the years, he was asked to help with some of the lettering, and at the age of 17, with a polished craft, he became the art department's assistant. From that moment on, without realizing it, he had started specializing in hand-drawn lettering for headers. Before 1959, all of these, as well as posters, were done by hand.

That was the beginning. More and more assignments were coming his way, and in 1964 he started collaborating at the Instituto Torcuato Di Tella (ITDT) with his artistic idol Juan Carlos Distéfano. At the Di Tella is where Rubén had a learning phase and a ratification of his profession.

"The ITDT was an extraordinary place where I met people essential to my training," he says. "There was an effervescence to Buenos Aires in the '60s, which allowed me to start my craft in design with the surrounding art and culture as my principle. It was the moment in which graphic design forged its own identity in our country, distancing itself from advertising and fine arts. At the ITDT, I had the opportunity to meet the most important designer of the time, Juan Carlos Distéfano. Together, we developed the vocation to communicate with the letter, a specialization to which I had dedicated myself by natural inclination, when everything was done by drawing. With Distéfano and Juan Andralis, another of the extraordinary beings who contributed to my typographic training, we developed a joint work methodology that resulted in a very particular style."

In 1971 after the ITDT closed, in association with his dear friend Distéfano, he started his own design studio. The studio continued to hire

new designers in the generations that followed. The team grew in size and in quality of clients. Editorial design was added to the already existing corporate identity design.

"Since 2001, the studio has been experiencing its third evolution. It has fewer designers but at the same time, a deeper level of experimentation. Since then, I have shared the strategic and production of FontanaDiseño projects with Zalma Jalluf, a partner and co-director of the team. Also with a group of full-timers and freelancers with whom we agree in trust, passion for design, typography, and a certain work methodology, which for us is very significant."

FontanaDiseño has designed some of the most important branding in Latin America, including the Central Bank of the Argentine Republic, YPF energy company, La Nación daily newspaper, Disco supermarket chain, Freddo ice cream (retail), Telecom telecommunications company, Havanna alfajores, Banco Ciudad, 1882 Fernet bitter herbal tonic, Morph home furnishings-décor, and John Foos rubber shoes.

While running his studio in 1985, when democracy had returned to the country after seven years of military rule, the public University of Buenos Aires (UBA) invited Rubén to participate as a teacher of the new graphic design chair. He was also chosen to create two elective classes for the third year, and he developed Editorial Design and Typography.

"The urgency to cover that necessity— we only had one week to create the typography program—brought me to make a practical decision," he says. "I remembered my visit to Basel in 1971, where I had met André Gürtler. He showed me his process for students to understand the typographic signs. I took the main concepts and tried to adapt them to the Latin American student's idiosyncrasy."

His daughter Soledad says, "My dad, who has never been a student, in his adult life now turned out to be teaching classes. The electable class became a chair, and that chair wrote a book, Typographic Thought, on how typography was taught at the University of Buenos Aires. And it served as inspiration to other universities."

The class was a big success, and it became and open seminar for all the students (during those days, 900 of them). Based on the students' response, we created a program for the first and second year and an optional for the third one. Today every single student in the Design Chair takes Typography.

"Today, if I could," Rubén says, "I would apply the experience of all these years of teaching typography. I think I would make an emphasis, at least similar or more, on editorial education—in other

1
Andralis. This font, more than a little tribute to him, is a profound offering of gratitude to his memory.

2
Distéfano. This type family bears the name of the most notable argentinian designer.

3
Fontana ND. Received the certificate of excellence from the TDC and winner of the type design Bukva:Raz!, sponsored by ATypI in Moscow, Russia.

4
Olivetti: design and products. Poster 1969.

5
Chaco. Chaco originated after testing the deficiency shown in road signs in Latin America.

6
Polesello. Poster 1969. Rogelio Polesello's retrospective show.

7
Lutero. Poster 1965. John Osborne's Lutero. Theater play.

8
Palestina. Palestina is a sans serif font designed for reading texts and inspired in the condensed Trade Gothic font, which features a strong influence from the time of metal foundry-based typography.

4
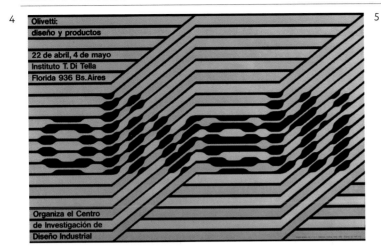

5

6
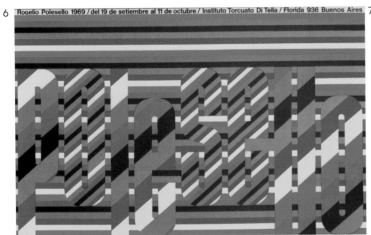

7

8

words, on how typography affects the word. Because the letter is a tiny part of the word, a component of the word, but it does not have an influence on the outcome of the word. Beautiful fonts have been designed that do not work with the word, and not-so-interesting fonts have been designed that 'put' a word together, in order to be well understood and assimilated. Every day I ask myself, 'If we are not focusing too much on the role of typography in a word, then what it is the role of the word in understanding the meanings of texts?' I think I would try to promote more awareness in that specific aspect. Typography is efficient as a vehicle to generate words. The 'problem' of communication is the word, not necessarily the letter."

With the Typography and Editorial Design classes becoming an important part of the students' design community, Rubén realized that most of the publications being read during those times were in a foreign language. Thus he decided to start a magazine, tipoGráfica, to support the Design course of the UBA, and at that time it had no other objective than to develop a bibliography in Spanish.

The magazine became widely popular and spread throughout the subcontinent. Its specialization in typography topics contributed to its recognition and value among professionals and teachers who needed current topics written in Spanish. However, the publication was globally relevant as most of its articles were created by recognized professionals and advisors from various countries and continents.

The Typography classes and tipoGráfica happened at the perfect time. There was a need in the design community, and those two things sparked a new movement. Typography became a very popular movement. tipoGráfica started sponsoring all kinds of typographic events: conferences, exhibits, Letras Latinas (the first typographic competition within Latin America, now known as Tipos Latinos), professional gatherings (T-convoca), and more.

During the 20 years of tipoGráfica, readers became acquainted with the articles and the "voice" of its typography. Rubén designed the typeface Fontana ND for the magazine, based fundamentally on the Spanish language as its natural and cultural context. Among other typefaces, he designed Andralis, Chaco, Distéfano, and Palestina. Fontana ND received a Certificate of Excellence from the Type Directors Club and was one of the chosen winners in the international competition of type design Bukva:Raz!, sponsored by the Association Typographique Internationale (ATypl), in Moscow.

In 2009 he began to direct the Specialization Career in Typography at UBA. Between 2015 and 2017,

he directed the master's degree in Typography, the first in Latin America, always from the context of public education. What started as a three grade-level course became a typography design postgraduate course that took about 400 hours and consisted of 80 students broken out into three groups. Due to the continued success of this class, realizing that this wasn't enough, UBA under Rubén's direction created the master's degree, which covers 776 hours of teaching and is attended by students from all over Latin America.

"I believe that today one could think, design, and produce typography all by yourself," Rubén says. "Before, the person who developed the idea could only get to the final artwork—from that point on, other trades and techniques would take over to develop a font, and each of those who intervened contributed their knowledge to the work. But in the peripheral countries this work, due to lack of technology, could not be done; it was only possible to aspire to originals of the drawn letters. In this sense, the new digitalization technologies democratized the experience of typography throughout the world."

The Spanish quote "Nadie es profeta en su tierra" (no one is prophet in their own land) doesn't apply to everybody. This self-taught lettering artist, designer, type designer, professor, and educator is living proof of that. Not only did he start the typographic tsunami in Buenos Aires, but its characters flooded the whole Latin American "continent."

Rubén Fontana is the first Latin American person to receive the Type Directors Club's highest award, the TDC Medal.

—Diego Vainesman

10

11

9
Banco de la República Argentina.
Central Bank of the Argentine Republic.

10
1882 Fernet.
Bitter herbal tonic drink.

11
Telecom.
Telecommunications company.

12
tipoGráfica magazine.
The leading typographic/design magazine in Latin America (1987-2006)

12

TipoGráfica

comunicación para diseñadores

Revista de diseño.
Número 1, julio 1987, Buenos Aires.

nueve australes

TipoGráfica

comunicación para diseñadores

Revista de diseño
Número 2, setiembre 1987, Buenos Aires.

doce australes

TipoGráfica

comunicación para diseñadores

Revista de diseño.
Número 3, diciembre 1987, Buenos Aires.

15 australes

tipoGráfica

comunicación para diseñadores

Revista de diseño
Número 4, abril 1988, Buenos Aires.

20 australes

Few have contributed as much to the modern history of the typographic arts as Ed Benguiat. He drew over 600 typefaces. That's a lot of letters – especially when you consider that they were all drawn by hand. He was also an extraordinary teacher. He held no secrets about his work, and was keenly dedicated to sharing his passion and knowledge.

Benguiat designed typefaces for International Typeface Corporation (ITC), for PhotoLettering Inc., and for corporate clients such as AT&T, Estée Lauder and *The New York Times* newspaper. He created revivals of old metal faces such as ITC Souvenir and ITC Bookman. He drew absolutely new, and original designs such as ITC Benguiat, and ITC Barcelona. And long before sophisticated software and type interpolation programs became available to the type design community, Benguiat was drawing large typeface families and combining two and three different typefaces into one design. ITC Tiffany and ITC Lubalin Graph are just two examples of his ability to combine multiple typeface designs.

And every typeface, from Benguiat's first, Norma Spenserian, (which he said wasn't very good) to the ensuing wealth of his designs were drawn with pencil, pen, ink and brush. Sometimes, he would use French curves, he had modified to suit his needs. Sometimes, he would use a #16 X-Acto® blade to carve a perfect curve out of photographic film emulsion, and sometimes he would use a photocopier to create the beginnings of a new weight or proportion of a typeface family. But these were the limits of Benguiat's technical tools. He was a craftsperson of the highest order. While some of his early typeface designs, which had rudimentary character-sets, were dashed-off quickly, his later typeface families, could be a year-and-a-half in the making.

Benguiat was often asked about this best, or favorite, typeface design. He would, almost always, say that it would be his next one. "I've never been satisfied with my work," he'd confess. "I want each typeface, each piece of lettering, every logo I design, to be better than the last. No one climbs a mountain in a single leap, but rather step by step. My work has been as simple as that: one design, then another, with the goal to make each new design better than those that preceded it." Once, when pressed, however, Benguiat looked around to be sure that none of his other typeface designs were listening, and coyly answered, "I'm pretty fond of ITC Benguiat."

And well he should be. It had the most difficult gestation period of any of his designs. When he was working at Herb Lubalin's design studio, a friend asked Benguiat to create a new logo for a store that he was opening. Price was no object – because the friend had no money.

Letting his sense of friendship override prudence, Benguiat provided his friend with a few ideas at no cost. But none of these free designs were accepted. Benguiat submitted several more ideas, and these suffered a similar fate. More were provided – still no success. Finally, after virtually hundreds of trial efforts, a design was chosen – but it wasn't the basis for ITC Benguiat. That was a submission about halfway back in the submission process.

Benguiat liked these earlier letters, even if his friend didn't – and began to draw additional characters in the same style. Over several months he many characters were added to the mix: the full alphabet in caps and lowercase, an exceptionally large number of ligature letters, and an equally large complement of alternate characters. Drawing the letters became something of a hobby. For weeks most of the Benguiat's free time was spent creating, and re-creating, characters that would eventually make up the ITC Benguiat family.

The trouble was, Benguiat's definition of "free time" was not the same as Lubalin's, and one day his boss officially declared a moratorium on the hobby. He told Benguiat that if he didn't find some practical justification for his letterform doodles he would have to quit doing them. The drawing stopped for a few days, but Benguiat soon decided that he had too much invested in the unwanted typeface, to just drop it.

He sorted through the stacks of drawings and found the necessary letters to provide a proper design submission to ITC's Typeface Review Board. Unfortunately, the board initially found as much love for the design as Benguiat's friend. But a simple "We don't think so," wasn't going to stop Benguiat. As a result, he mounted – with the help of Lubalin – a full scale promotional campaign to convince ITC's Review Board to give his design a chance. Tenacity won out, and the board finally agreed to release the previously rejected typeface.

Obviously, Benguiat's very choosy friend, and the initial reactions of the review board were wrong. ITC Benguiat became one of ITC's most popular designs, and a staple of graphic communication for over 20 years. Recently, young designers have rediscovered the design, and it can be seen in a variety of places.

Benguiat didn't limit his designs to typefaces. As long as the project had letters in it, it was fair game to him. When he said that he used Garamond for al logo he drew for AT&T, he didn't mean that he typed it into a computer and simply printed it out. "I took ITC Garamond, redrew it, changing the proportion, weight, and countless other little details," said Benguiat. A process he called "tailoring."

Benguiat loved to draw letters. In one way or another, letters were always

1

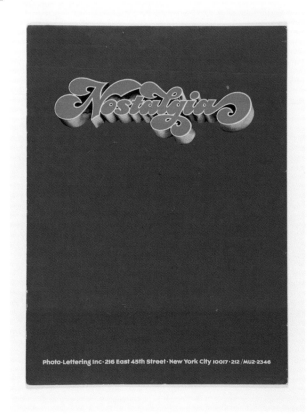

2

1
Benguiat's wood carving for the brochure cover

2
Nostalgia brochure cover

3
Benguiat's Custom French Curves

4
Benguiat Charisma typeface

5
Script Sketch

6
Script Final Art

7
Letterform Nomenclature Chart Designed and Lettered by Benguiat

3

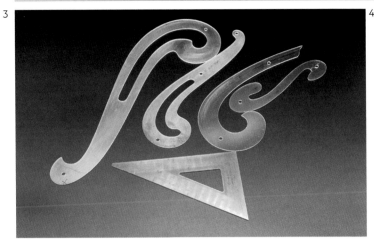

4

5

Screenshot

6

7

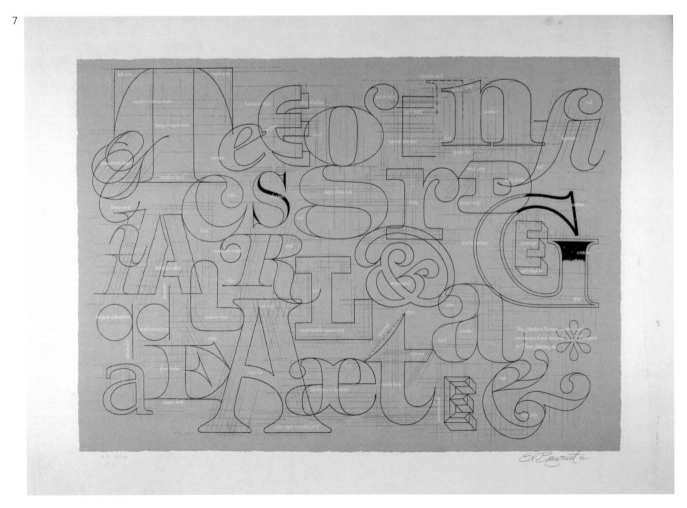

in his work. And every once in a while, they weren't even drawn. The cover of a booklet promoting a suite of his script typefaces has a delightfully winsome bit of typography that looks to be an illustration – but is actually a photograph of something he carved from a block of wood and painted by hand.

Benguiat designed or redesigned logotypes for Esquire, The New York Times, Playboy, McCall's, Reader's Digest, Photography, Look, Sports Illustrated, The Star-Ledger, The San Diego Tribune, AT&T, A&E, Coke, Estée Lauder, Ford, and many, many others.

Even when he wasn't working on a project, Benguiat would amuse himself – and others around him – by sketching letterforms. In restaurants, he would draw letters on table clothes or napkins, in meetings he often doodled in Spencerian and his greeting cards and "thank you" notes are always hand-drawn. "I play with letters," was how he described his work.

And then, there was Benguiat the teacher. He often said, "Teaching has been the most rewarding thing I do. It gives me the opportunity to pass on what I've experienced and what I know." Benguiat taught at the School of Visual Arts for fifty years. (Let that sink in for a minute.) Thousands of students owe success in their careers, in part, to Benguiat. And they all owe their love of the typographic arts to his energy and charisma. When he worked in New York, he taught design after hours. When he began working out of the studio in his house, he drove into the city to continue teaching. When he could no longer drive, he took a cab. Only when he could no longer do that, did he stop teaching. "It's about payback" he said. And Benguiat paid back with interest. He would often stay after-class for hours, working with students and sharing tricks of the trade. At type events and conferences, he was happy to provide impromptu design critique and guidance to any who asked for it.

Ed Benguiat was born in Brooklyn, 1927. The son of a display director at Bloomingdale's, and got his hands on his father's pens, brushes, and drafting sets as a small chile. An early project was forging a photostat of his birth certificate, so that (the under-age) Benguiat could join the Army. He also wanted to learn to fly, but color-blindness precluded this dream – for a little while. Memorizing the correct answers to the color-blindness test, however, got him over that hurdle. Benguiat was accepted into the Air Corps. After fulfilling his dream of learning to fly, Benguiat became responsible for photo reconnaissance flights over Nazi occupied Europe, in a camera equipped P51 Mustang. His love of airplanes and flying stayed with him for the rest of his life.

After serving in the Air Corps in Italy, Benguiat made a name for himself

as a jazz drummer under the moniker "Eddie Benart," playing with bands led by Stan Kenton and Woody Herman. Downbeat magazine declared him to be the third best drummer in the United States.

But Benguiat was married – with a child on the way. Weeks-long tours, with big bands, became out of the question. He picked up gigs in local New York jazz clubs and restaurants, until one day he saw an advertisement in a window on 5th Avenue for The Workshop School of Advertising Art. He enrolled with the intention of becoming an illustrator. Letters, however, crept into Benguiat's life again and he ended up studying under the famous calligrapher, Paul Standard. Benguiat's love affair with letters was never to cool.

He said his first break as a lettering artist was basically a fluke. According to Benguiat, he was working at a studio, doing photo touch-up, and the person responsible for lettering called in sick. The studio needed a lettering job done. Benguiat said he'd take on the project – and never looked back.

Benguiat continued to work as a freelance designer and art director in several New York ad agencies and studios until 1953, when was hired as a designer by Esquire magazine. Nine years later, he joined PhotoLettering Inc, a ground-breaking type setting service. His association with PhotoLettering and Herb Lubalin, who Benguiat says he knew since his Bar Mitzvah, brought him to the forefront as one of the major contributors to ITC's growing list of juggernaut designs.

His first typeface for ITC was ITC Souvenir. Originally, just a single-weight face hand-set font of metal type, first shown in 1914, Benguiat redrew it, adding additional weights and italics. ITC Souvenir soon became, along with ITC Avant Garde Gothic, one of ITC 's most popular typefaces – a position it held for years. Benguiat went on to draw, or collaborate on, over a dozen other typeface families for ITC – all of them used with gusto by graphic designers.

Benguiat once said, "Doing something a long time does not mean you're good. It just means you've done it a long time." Benguiat not only worked in the typographic arts for a long time, he brought unwavering passion for type and typographic design, life-long dedication to teaching, relentless commitment to creating the best possible lettering and typefaces, and hundreds upon hundreds of typefaces, while doing so. Benguiat was more than good – way more.

Special thanks to Elisa Benguiat, Ilene Strizver and Dr. Steven Galbraith, Curator Cary Graphic Arts Collection at Rochester Institute of Technology. Their help was invaluable.

—Allan Haley

8

9

10

8
Benguiat Barcelona

9
Early Benguiat Typeface for PhotoLettering, Inc.

10
Stranger Things Logo

11
ITC Souvenir. Benguiat's first typeface for ITC

12
Poster for jazz concert. E.D. Benart is Ed Benguiat.

13 Sketches for Photolettering, Inc. logo

14
ITC Benguiat

11

12

13

14

17

Chair Statement
Meet the Judges

This competition, and annual could have only come together because of the work and detection of many individuals.

Carol Wahler, the executive director of the Type Directors Club who brings her thirty-seven years of experience and knowledge of the TDC to every meeting.

When I joined the board of directors of the Type Directors Club in 2019, I was both eager and excited to learn as much as I could about the inner workings of an organization I care so deeply about. I had been a member for a few years, which meant I was already very familiar with the TDC's annual competition. I have had the good fortune to participate in the annual competition from the outside, as an entrant. It has been and continues to be my favorite annual design competition. I am always excited to have my work seen and judged by the very best practitioners of design and typography. Now, as a newly minted board member, I was able to pull back the curtain to see how it all comes together.

At my first board meeting, we discussed the competition that was then underway: TDC 66, co-chaired by Liz DeLuna and Douglas Riccardi. It became immediately apparent to me the scope and weight that goes into being selected chair of the annual competition. This was also openly communicated to me by both Liz and Douglas. So, when I was asked to chair TDC67 a few months later, I was both humbled and admittedly terrified. This also happened to coincide with the outbreak of COVID-19 and subsequent shutdowns, which added to the stress.

All that said, I was thrilled to put together an annual competition that reflected the changing voices within design and typography. This started by assembling an incredible jury of some of the world's best designers from all over the planet. Melissa Deckert, Jason Ramirez, Jason Sfetko, Leandro Assis, Joyce N. Ho, Leland Maschmeyer, and Marta Cerdà Alimbau all said yes to my request. Many of these designers I have admired from afar for years, and I was honored to have the opportunity to learn from and listen to them as judging began. We received over 1,500 entries from 66 countries, and only 254 were selected as winners.

It was also my responsibility to appoint a design studio to develop the identity system, the call for entries campaign, and the annual book that you are holding, showcasing The World's Best Typography. During one of our board meetings, Bobby Martin jokingly, or maybe not jokingly, suggested that I take on the task of doing the design work for TDC67 myself. I immediately sprang into action, fueled by excitement—and a tight deadline. This did make sense. After all, I had a very specific idea of how I wanted the call for entries campaign to look and feel like. What came out was a campaign rooted in the simple idea of connecting: the way we connect with our work and the work of others we admire; the connections we have with typography, and, most important, the connections we have with each other. To that end, we developed a system and a funky custom geometric sans

serif with letterforms that embrace one another in all sorts of interesting, quirky ways.

This competition and the annual could have only come together because of the work and dedication of many individuals: Carol Wahler, executive director of the Type Directors Club, who brings her 37 years of experience and knowledge of the TDC to every meeting. The rest of the TDC board, who offered insight and supported me in this process. Adam Wahler, Bertram Schmidt-Friderichs, and the rest of the team who came together to help create and produce this annual. Kris Sowersby, who generously donated his beautiful typeface Geograph to use in this book and for the campaign. Ksenya Samarskaya, for sitting as chair of the Typeface Design Competition. I would also like to personally thank all of the judges for participating and giving us their precious time and contributing to this wonderful typographic tradition. Sixty-seven years and running.

Juan Carlos Pagan
Chairman,
TDC67 Communication Design

Juan
Carlos
Pagan

JUDGES

Marta Cerdà Alimbau

Leandro Assis

Melissa Deckert

Joyce N. Ho

Leland Maschmeyer

Jason Ramirez

Jason Sfetko

Marta
Cerdà
Alimbau

Leandro
Assis

Melissa
Deckert

Joyce N.
Ho

Leland Maschmeyer

Jason
Ramirez

Jason
Sfetko

Marta Cerdà Alimbau

@MartaCerdaAlimb
martacerda.com

1

Marta Cerdà is a Barcelona based independent Letterer, Illustrator and Graphic Designer. Her main body of work is focussed on the boundaries between typography and illustration. While Marta's style is strongly eclectic, she believes that the separation of these two disciplines into specialized activities is a limitation for her work.

She graduated in Graphic Design in the University of Elisava, Barcelona. At the end of 2008, after working in agencies and studios between Barcelona, Düsseldorf and Munich, she won the ADC Young Guns and decided to found her own studio. Since then, she has worked globally, based in different cities like New York, Los Angeles, Amsterdam and Barcelona, working on projects which call for Art Direction, Design, Illustration and Custom Typography for Arts, Culture and Advertising Clients.

Marta has been awarded by major Design competitions like The Type Directors Club, The Society of Publication Designers and the Art Directors Club Young Guns, among others. She also lectures about Design at creative conferences and Universities internationally.

2

3

4

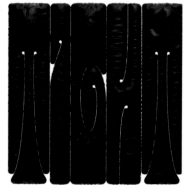

1
Barcelona Poesia
Poster of the campaign
for the International
Barcelona's Festival of
Poetry.
Client: Ajuntament
de Barcelona

2
Roller
3D Type exploration
based on
Alfred Roller's letterings.
Client: Offf Vienna

3
Razing Cane
Opener for *Afar*
Magazine
"Razing Cane: To taste
Haiti's artisanal
rum is to cut to the heart
of what makes
the island so magical".
Client: Afar Magazine

4
Ad Algea
Book/Album for the
theorist
Josep Maria Martí Duran
Client: Cultura Temporal

Leandro Assis @lebassis
lebassis.com

1

Leandro Assis, aka LEBASSIS is a brazilian artist, art director and letterer based in Rio. Lebassis is known for super bold letterings, colorful palettes and playful illustrations, drawing the attention of global brands and agencies. Lebassis also uses his creativity and designs as a tool to promote positivity for black culture and LGBTQ+ rights.

2

3

4

1
Poster for Chobani's
Our Food campaign for
Black History Month
Lettering: Lebassis
Art Direction:
Chobani Design Team

2
Nike Remix Pack
Letterings + Illustration:
Lebassis
Art Direction: Eric Peet
and Lauren Lindstroom

3
Rock the Mountain
Festival 2021
Art Direction and Design:
Lebassis

4
Snapchat Lit Collection
Art Direction and Design:
Lebassis

Melissa Deckert   @melissadeckert
melissadeckert.com

1

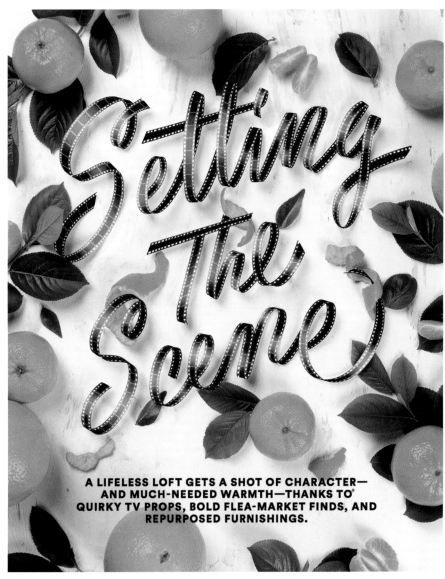

Melissa Deckert is a multidisciplinary designer, art director and co-founder of Party of One Studio. Formerly the Senior Brand Designer at Etsy's in-house Brand Studio, her work spans a variety of disciplines including branding, book covers, lettering and murals. In 2018, Melissa co-founded Party of One with Nicole Licht, a collaborative creative studio based in Brooklyn, New York. Combining traditional design principles with handmade elements, colorful set design and unusual styling, Party of One creates compelling, story-driven visuals for brands, products and publications. Their clients include The New York Times, Mercedes-Benz, Playboy, The Washington Post, and Random House. Melissa's work has been recognized by the Society of Illustrators and Art Directors Club. Independently she has been a guest critic at Pratt Institute, Rhode Island School of Design, and The New School.

2

3

4

1
AirBNB Magazine
Setting The Scene
Type Opener
AD: Lisa Lok
Party of One Studio

2
Columbia University GSAPP
Fall 2020 Lectures & Events
Series
Poster Design
Party of One Studio

3
The Washington Post
11th Annual Spring Cleaning
Edition
Cover Design
AD: Chris Rukan
Party of One Studio

4.
Foreign Policy
Who Will Save the World?
Cover Design
AD: Lori Kelley
Party of One Studio

Joyce N. Ho @joyce.n.ho
joycenho.com

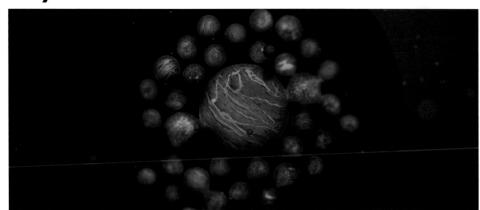

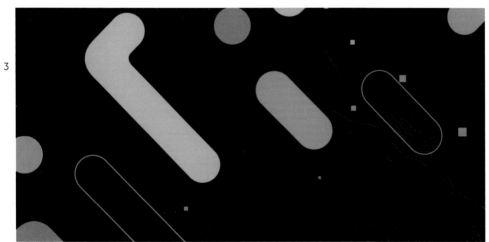

Joyce N. Ho is a Hong Kong-born Australian designer. With a decade's experience, there's nothing she enjoys more than storytelling through motion and bringing ideas to life through design. As an art director and motion designer, Joyce's work is textural and expressive. Her approach is design-led and she's always excited to learn, experiment and explore uncharted territory whenever possible. Now based in Brooklyn, Joyce continues her obsession with all things motion and freelances in-between befriending all the cute dogs NYC has to offer. She has directed numerous noteworthy projects, including 'Semi Permanent 2018' titles, 'The Expanse' opening titles and was design director for "Volume 3" of Netflix's 'Patriot Act with Hasan Minhaj'.

Joyce has been a finalist at SXSW Film Awards three times and her work has been recognized by The One Club, The ADC, The ADCC and the Australian Production Design Guild, among others. She was named one of "10 Women of Title Design" by Art of the Title in 2018 and was recently a Young Guns 17 winner.

1
Semi Permanent 2018
Opening Titles

2
The Expanse
Main Title

3
Likeminds 2017
Opening Titles

4
Resonance
Short Film

Leland Maschmeyer @leemaschmeyer
leemaschmeyer.com

1

In 2016, Leland joined Chobani as its first Chief Creative Officer and led its lauded brand transformation. In 2020, he became the company's Chief Brand Officer. He is a Board Member of the One Club for Creativity and Advisory Board Member of NOMI Networks – a global organization dedicated to ending modern slavery. Leland is also the Co-Founder, Board Member, and former Co-Chief Creative Officer of COLLINS, the globally renowned design firm. His work has defined "the next big design trend" (AIGA Eye on Design), produced "the future of music videos" (Forbes), influenced federal climate legislation, federal childhood nutrition policy, presidential candidate platforms, and won every major global creative award.

His re-launch of the Chobani brand earned nearly 9 billion media impressions and praise as "literally and absolutely perfect" (AIGA Eye on Design). His global re-imaginations of Spotify, Instagram, and Chobani were each recognized as "Best of the Year" (Fast Co, Wired, Brand New). He has won recognition as "Global 30 under 30" (Campaign), "Young Influencer" (Ad Age), "Most Influential Designers Today" (HOW Magazine), "Design Thinking Leader" (IBM), "Master of Marketing" (Assoc. of National Advertisers), "Tastemaker" (PDN Magazine), and "Designer to Watch" (Graphic Design USA).

2

3

4

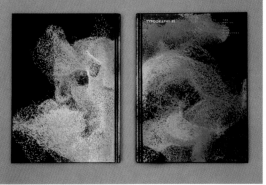

1
Chobani Probiotic
Packaging Design
and Advertising

2
Chobani Rebrand

3
Chobani Rebrand

4
*Type Directors Club
Annual*

Jason Ramirez @jasonramirez
jasonramirez.design

1

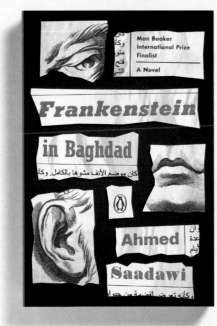

Jason is an award-winning designer and art director with Viking and Penguin Books in New York. Previously he worked with St. Martin's Press and Rodrigo Corral Design.

His work has earned recognition and honors from Communication Arts and Print magazines, the Type Directors Club, AIGA Eye on Design, the AIGA 50 Books I 50 Covers competition, and the New York Book Show. In addition, his projects have been published in several books related to graphic design and publishing. Jason is a graduate of Parsons School of Design and the University of Rochester.

2

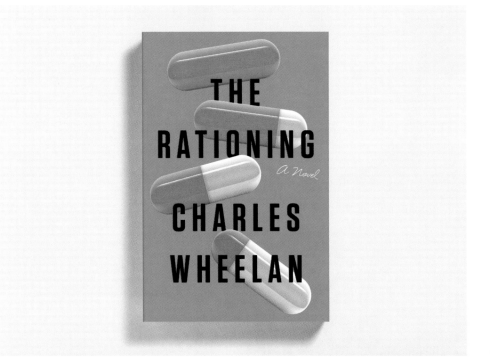

3

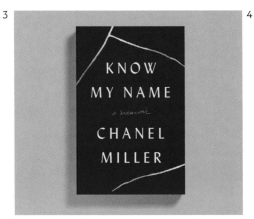

4

1.
Frankenstein in Baghdad
Publisher: Penguin Books

2.
The Rationing
Art Director: Ingsu Liu
Publisher: W. W. Norton

3.
Know My Name
Design: Jason Ramirez
and Nayon Cho
Publisher: Viking Books

4.
*Shutdown: How Covid Shook
the World's Economy*
Publisher: Viking Books

Jason Sfetko
@jasonsfetko
jasonsfetko.com

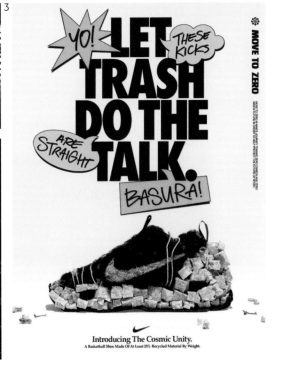

Jason Sfetko is an Art Director in the global brand design team at Nike in Portland, OR. He was previously the Deputy Art Director at The New York Times Magazine and studied design at Rochester Institute of Technology. In 2014 Jason was a member of the Design Team of the Year awarded by the Art Directors Club. He has also received an ASME National Magazine Award for design while at GQ and was named among the 25 Young Designers to Watch in 2012 by Complex.com.

His work has been recognized by various organizations including The Art Directors Club, The Type Directors Club, The Society of Publication Designers, D&AD, and Graphis, among others.

1
The New York Times Magazine
25 Songs That Tell Us Where Music Is Going
Design Director:
Gail Bichler
Lettering: Bráulio Amado

2
Nike Basketball
Kyrie 6
Quick To The Cut
Partner: The New Company

3
Nike Basketball
Cosmic Unity
Let Trash Do The Talk
Photographer: Ryan Unruh
Set Design: Matt Jones
Partner: Golden

4
Nike Basketball
GT Cut
Space Maker
Photographer:
Marcus Smith
Partners: Golden
and Chloe Scheffe

Juan Carlos Pagan
CarlosPagan.com
@JuanCarlosPagan

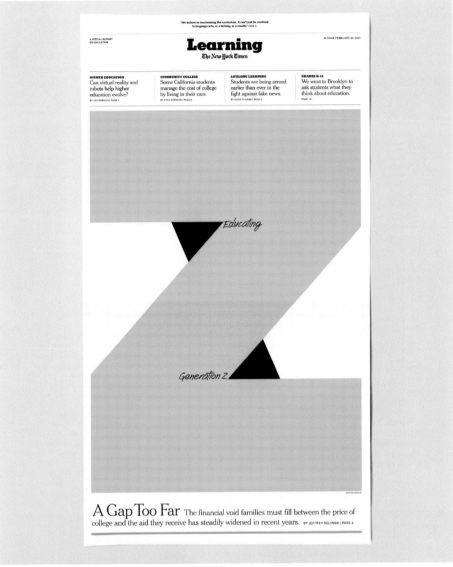

Juan Carlos Pagan is a multi-disciplinary artist, designer, creative director and typographer working in New York. He received his BFA from Parsons School of Design in 2006, and completed his postgraduate studies in typeface design at The Cooper Union in 2011. As a designer Juan has created iconic visual identities and campaigns for brands including Pinterest, Ciroc, Under Amour, as well as designed cover art for publications such as The New York Times, and Variety Magazine. Some of his client include Nike, The New York Times, Apple, Google, Disney, MTV, New York Lottery, Print Magazine, Google Creative Lab, Joan Creative, Jump Bikes, and ESPN Magazine.

Juan has been honored for his work by The Type Directors Club, Communication Arts, The ADC, The One Show, Graphis, Cannes Lions, Clios, FastCo, 4A's, and Print Magazine among others. In 2013 Juan received The prestigious Art Directors Club Young Gun Award, honoring vanguard creatives under the age of 30. That same year he was named the top of Adweek's Talent 100. He was subsequently nominated for Print Magazines New Visual Artist 20 Under 30. In 2018 Juan received the Type Directors Club Ascenders Award, which recognizes designers who are 35 years of age and under for their remarkable achievement in design and typography.

Juan previoulsy held Creative Director and Head of Design positions at MTV, DDB, Deutsch, and 72andSunny. In 2017 Juan co-founded Sunday Afternoon. A hybrid creative studio & artist management agency.

1
Educating Gen Z
as
section cover

2
Joan Creative
logo & identity

3
DesGin
poster campaign

4
Pinterest
logo & identity

5
Jump Bikes
poster campaign

Communication
Design

**Best in Show
Student Awards
Judges' Choices**

Concept: The San Francisco Symphony is a
108-year-old international cultural touchstone
with a deep legacy of rewriting the rules to
advance the orchestral arts. We were invited
to help define and express a new vision for
the future of classical music under Music
Director Esa-Pekka Salonen, the visionary
conductor and composer. As the Symphony
experiments, an ever-evolving visual system
brings to life the music itself. We used
responsive and variable font technology to
add unexpected contemporary behavior—
giving each typographic character the ability
to immediately change form in reaction to
sound and music.

Design
Yeun Kim, Sidney Lim,
Mackenzie Pringle,
Michael Taylor,
and Erik Vaage

Creative Direction
Ben Crick,
Louis Mikolay,
and Karin Soukup

Animation
Tomas Markevicius
and Eric Park

Content Strategist
Christine Takaichi

Digital Artist,
Multimedia
Neil Jackson

Type Foundry
Dinamo

Agency
COLLINS

Client
San Francisco
Symphony

Principal Type
Symphony in ABC

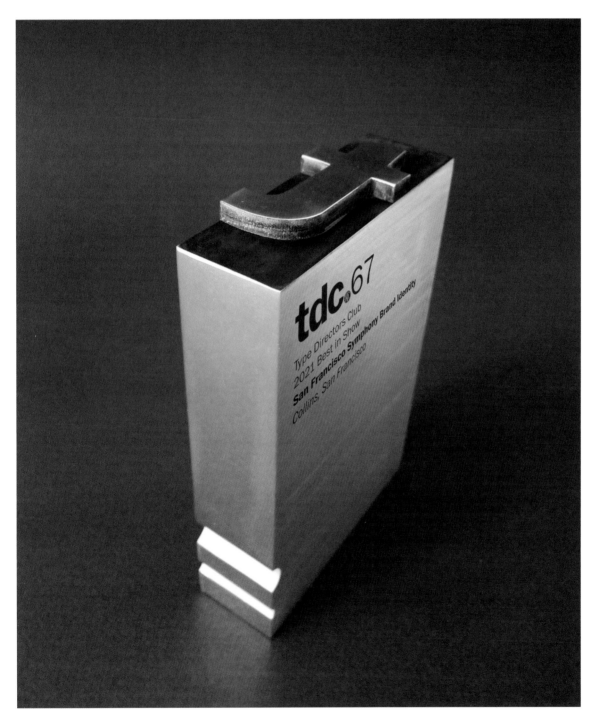

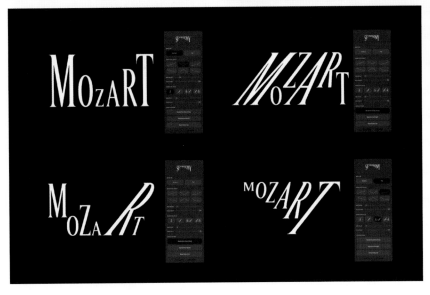

Concept: *This Is Not You* reflects on René Magritte's *The Treachery of Images.* It explores the beginnings of emojis and watches them become what they are today. Due to a lack of materials at home, experimentation drove the book's form and structural narrative—homing in on pages' asymmetrical interactions with one another while creating typographic texture through their low opacity. This was completed as an undergraduate thesis project.

Design and Writing
Troy Vasilakis
New York

Instructors
Sondra Graff and
Stephanie Tevonian

School
Fashion Institute of
Technology

Principal Type
Laica B, Mondwest,
Times New Roman,
and Vulf Mono

Dimensions
5.5 × 8.3 in.
(14 x 21.2 cm)

では、また。

FAME TO

:P

Emoji are arguably one of the greatest modern design systems. A complex system that many deem as a language as well with 4.12 billion people 'speaking' it.

Emoji are characters that we've grown to love and adore—facial expressions, common objects, places, types of weather, animals —and new ones are being continuously added. Unicode, or more specifically the Unicode Consortium, is the organization that oversees the addition and proposals of new emoji. They are responsible for their text-encoding language, Unicode.

Concept: Craigslist is so well known in the United States that most people are by now very familiar with its appearance. It was important to keep the original feeling and vibe of this classified advertising website while at the same time upgrading the brand. The new logo and brand are inspired by the ASCII codes drawing that Craigslist already has in its features. "<>" is a programming language symbol, and the shorthand logo version—"c<li>"—is based on how coding languages present lists as "<li>." Because Craigslist is an online source platform, the digital feeling is the new visual language.

Design
Shuchen Xu
Pasadena, California

Instructor
Rudy Manning

School
ArtCenter
College of Design

Principal Type
Courier,
Craigslist New,
and Helvetica
Regular

craigs<list>

Concept: Responding to the anxiety we faced during COVID-19 lockdown, this interactive and dynamic typographic artwork of breathing type is intended to remind the user to slow down. The artwork was coded in p5.js.

Design
Akshita Chandra°

Instructor
Dae In Chung

School
Maryland Institute
College of Art

Principal Type
Breathe, Elastic,
Fluff, Gossamer,
Lace,
Sharp Grotesk
Book 25,
and Silk

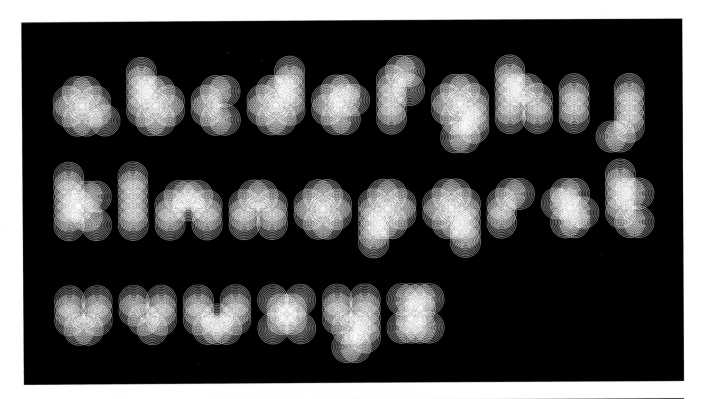

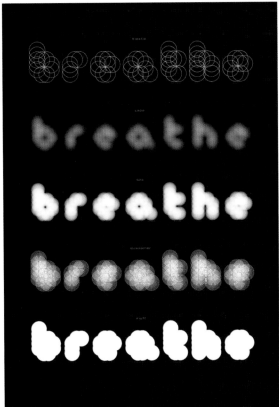

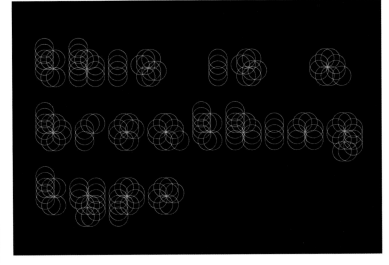

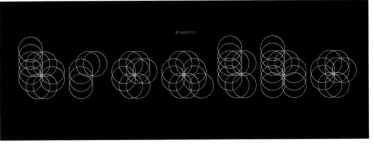

I love the way letters are pulled out from a cocoa seed or a palm tree leaf, the way it all looks kind of trival while still very fresh and sophisticated.
Marta Cerdà Alimbau

Hi, my name is Marta and I'm a designer at Marta Cerdà. My judge's choice is Saari. I love the way letters are pulled out from a cocoa seed or a palm tree leaf, the way it all looks kind of trivial while still very fresh and sophisticated. I think the result is unique and reflects perfectly the spirit of the brand which has both Finnish and Dominican Republic roots. Congratulations to Caio Evangelista and Renan Vizzotto on your Win!

When the client came to us with the brief, we knew an immersion would be needed.

Saari means "island" in Finnish, the language from the country the brand is originally from. However, the farm and factory are located in the Dominican Republic, so we had to find a connection between Finland and the Caribbean country.

The solution for the logotype came after a few days in the Caribbean when we turned our attention to the beautiful white spaces between the palm tree leaves in addition to the bold spots, which can be seen depicted in the brand's logotype.

Despite the evident use of visual clichés to represent both Finland and the Dominican Republic, the logotype resulted in a one-of-a-kind source of inspiration for graphic elements.

LOGOTYPES

Design
Renan Vizzotto
Parma, Italy

Writer
Caio Evangelista

Product Architect
Robert Ashorn

Client
Saari Chocolate

Principal Type
Halyard Micro
and Halyard Text

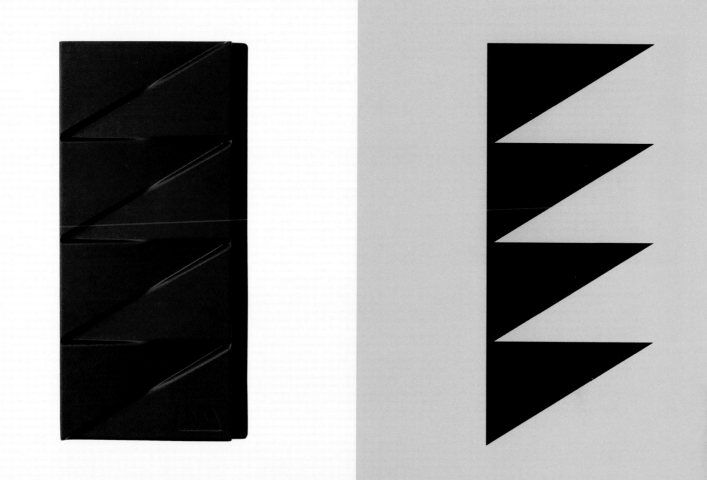

I voted for the book not only for its excellence in design but also for the importance of sending a message like Black Lives Matters to children and adults ...
Leandro Assis

I voted for the book not only for its excellence in design but also for the importance of sending a message like Black Lives Matters to children and adults in such an incredible, bold, positive and hopeful way!

The ability of design to expand messages is so powerful and I think Bobby did it very well by mixing important codes like typography, illustration and colors to give voice to the important messages that are in the book. A perfect match.

During 2020, so many of us grabbed a marker and a piece of cardboard to scrawl the words "Black Lives Matter" before heading to the streets in protest. The bigger, bolder, and louder the writing, the better. That same urgency is what inspired the graphic language for Have I Ever Told You Black Lives Matter. Each page is designed with a life-or-death need to be heard and understood.

We wanted to help canonize groundbreaking Black Americans, and at the same time introduce the power of design, so children, as well as adults, can be filled with optimism and joy and pride.

BOOKS
Have I Ever Told You
Black Lives Matter

Design
Bobby C. Martin, Jr. °
New York

Writer
Shani Mahiri King

Client
Tilbury House Publishers

Agency
Champions Design

Concept
This new children's book celebrates historic and contemporary Black role models who have shaped culture.

HAVE BLACK I EVER LIVES TOLD YOU MATTER

BY SHANI MAHIRI KING
ILLUSTRATED BY BOBBY C. MARTIN JR.

The reverse contrast in Anger especially stood out for me—its unusual proportions and inverted weight distribution caught my eye.
Melissa Deckert

When I initially read this project description, I had doubts that a golfing venue would manage to appeal to me (a person with zero interest in the sport) as much as it did. In fact, I found myself coming back to admire the work throughout the judging process.

The technical, monospaced typography perfectly represents gaming, while the graphic elevations bring a bold splash of color that breaks up the small details. The lighthearted ASCII illustrations weave seamlessly throughout the designs, adding fun easter eggs to discover. Finally, the photography goes above and beyond to bring out the spirit of the venue— from the oil-stained menu, to the golf ball martini and matchbook set ablaze. There is a controlled sense of chaos and humor in the images that represents everything I think of when family, games, food and cocktails mix together.

Overall, I loved this entry! It was approachable, unexpected, and has inadvertently converted me into a golf enthusiast. Congratulations to Grand Army for the outstanding work and win!"

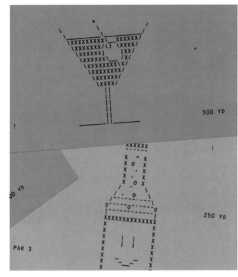

The Cup is an entertainment venue where family and friends gather to eat, drink, and compete. Topgolf Swing Suite bays host a range of virtual games, so the original brief was to create a brand identity that worked for serious golfers and non-golfers alike.

We developed a solution that overlapped the patina of classic scorecard typography, the technical language of ASCII computer art, and the progressive tone of a golf establishment founded in 2020. A system of logos, illustrations, copywriting, photography, and paintings was developed to create a whole new reality for The Cup. They were applied to signage, a menu system, web design, social assets, and print collateral.

IDENTITY/BRANDING
The Cup Brand Identity

Design
Michael Auer,
Raquel Scoggin,
and Michael Stone
New York

Creative Team
San Churnakoses,
Sterling Diaz, and
Caroline Main

Creative Direction
Michael Stone

Chief Creative Officer
Joey Ellis

Illustration
Ben Gallegos

Phtography
Michael Stone

Client
The Cup

Agency
GrandArmy

Principal Type
GT America Thin and
OCR-B

Dimensions
Various

IT'S EVERYBODY'S GAME

⊠

INFO:

THE CUP WELCOMES PLAYERS OF ALL AGES AND SKILL LEVELS TO COME TOGETHER FOR SPORT, FOOD, AND COMPETITION. TRY YOUR HAND IN ONE OF OUR TOPGOLF SWING SUITE GAMING BAYS, FEATURING BIG SCREENS, MULTI SPORT GAMES, AND LOUNGE SEATING. KICK BACK WITH GOOD FOOD AND DRINK AND CELEBRATE VICTORY. COME SEE WHY IT'S EVERYBODY'S GAME AT THE CUP.

AAAALLLLLL
YYEEEEAAARR
RRRROOOUNND

THE CUP

GAMES:

01 TOPCONTENDER   05 QB CHALLENGE
02 TOPPRESSURE   06 BASEBALL
03 TOPCHALLENGE   07 HOCKEY SHOTS

POWERED BY:

I absolutely loved this cover because it represented all the important parts of the story in a clever and unique way.
Joyce Ho

My judge's choice was The All Seeing Eye, which was a wonderful cover for *The New York Times Magazine*. I absolutely loved this cover because it represented all the important parts of the story in a clever and unique way. The software company, data processing, and the idea of surveillance, were distilled down to one, powerful image. It had a mysterious quality to it, which I felt in an instant. Congratulations to the team at *The New York Times Magazine* for their win.

Palantir, a software company that specializes in data integration and helps governments, law-enforcement agencies and other clients decipher vast amounts of information. At first, the cover looks like a collection of complex data in the shape of an eye, but soon the headline emerges, alluding to the process of sorting data.

EDITORIAL
The All-Seeing Eye:
Palantir

Design
Matt Curtis
New York

Art Direction
Ben Grandgenett

Chief Design Officer
Gail Bichler°

Typography
Nikita Iziev

Publication
The New York Times Magazine

Principal Type
GT Pressura Mono

Dimensions
8.9 x 10.9 in.
(22.7 x 27.6 cm)

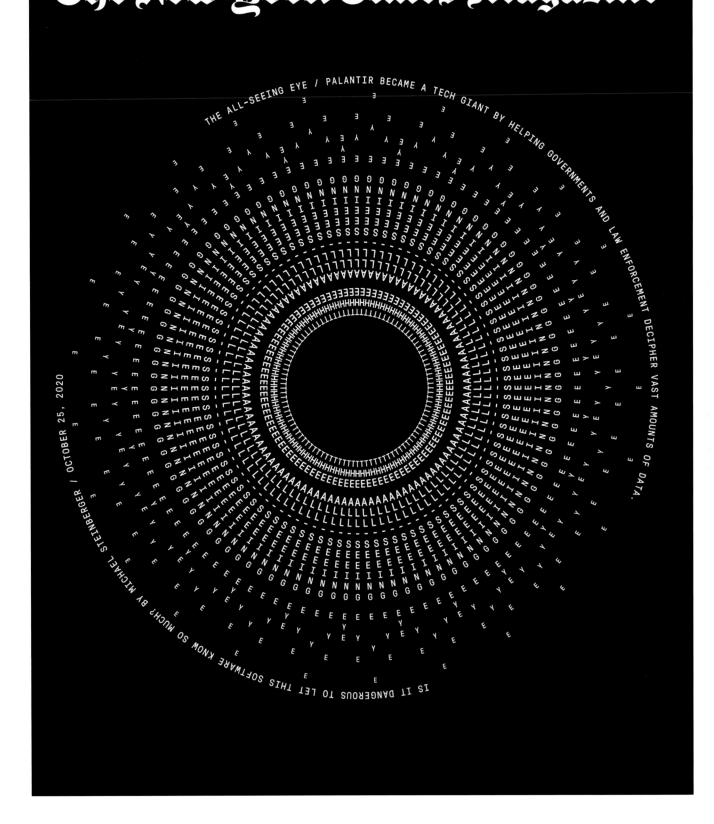

THE ALL-SEEING EYE / PALANTIR BECAME A TECH GIANT BY HELPING GOVERNMENTS AND LAW ENFORCEMENT DECIPHER VAST AMOUNTS OF DATA.

IS IT DANGEROUS TO LET THIS SOFTWARE KNOW SO MUCH? BY MICHAEL STEINBERGER / OCTOBER 25, 2020

HBO's *Perry Mason* show was great. But the reason I watched every week was to see the main title treatment again and again.
Leland Maschmeyer

HBO's *Perry Mason* show was great. But the reason I watched every week was to see the main title treatment again and again. I couldn't get enough. Not only splendid in its craft, it perfectly fit the genre, setting, and tone of the story allowing the viewer to be immediately transported from their couch into the grimy L.A. streets of this exquisitely rendered crime noir. I could not imagine a smarter opening title or a better selection for my judges pick.

The Perry Mason main title treatment was meant to bridge the relentlessly grim world of L.A. during the Great Depression and the world of today.

MOVIE TITLES/FEATURE
FILM/OPENING TITLES
Perry Mason

Creative Direction
Michael Riley°
Los Angeles

Producer
Bob Swensen

Digital Artist/Multimedia
Penelope Nederlander

Studio
Shine

Client
HBO

Principal Type
Future and Sauvage

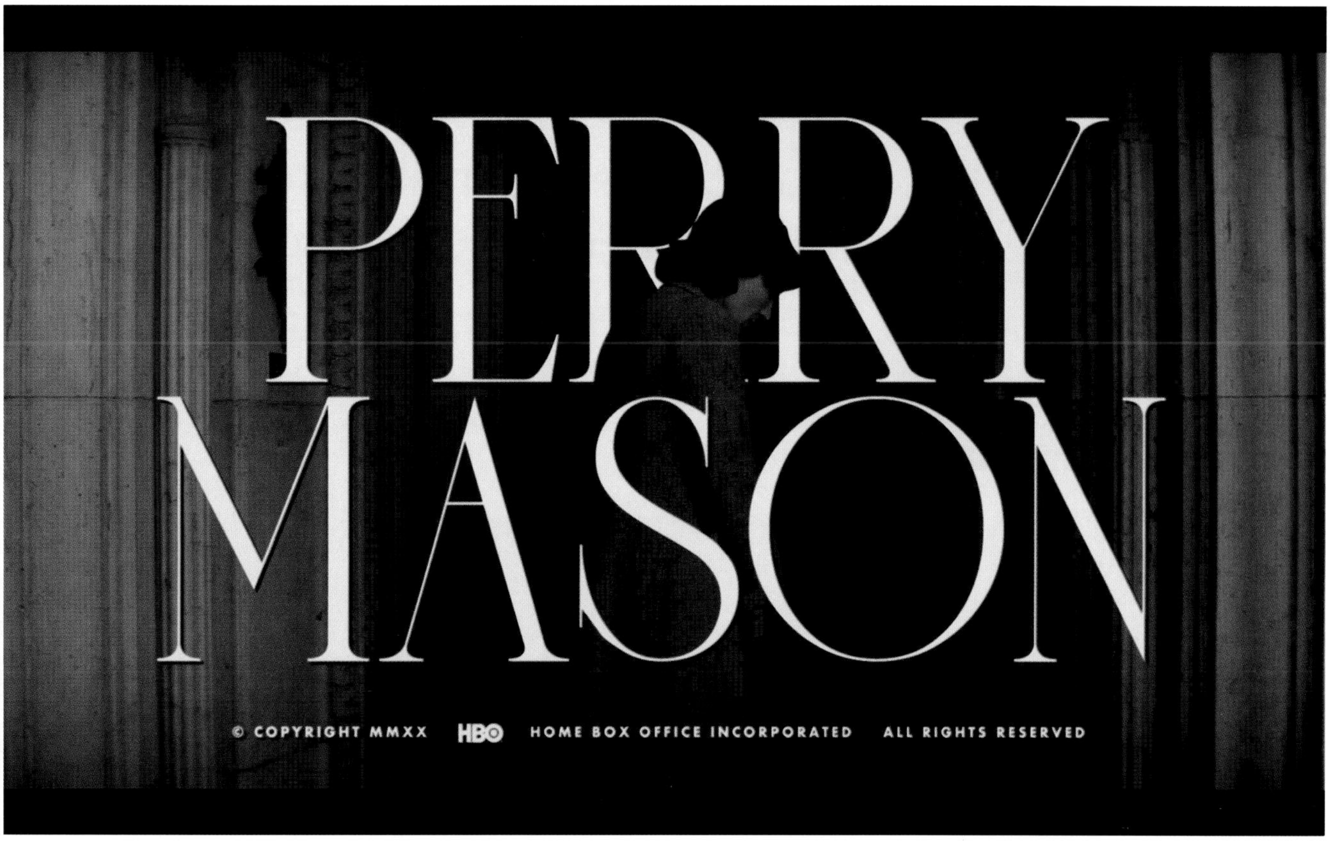
PERRY MASON
© COPYRIGHT MMXX HBO HOME BOX OFFICE INCORPORATED ALL RIGHTS RESERVED

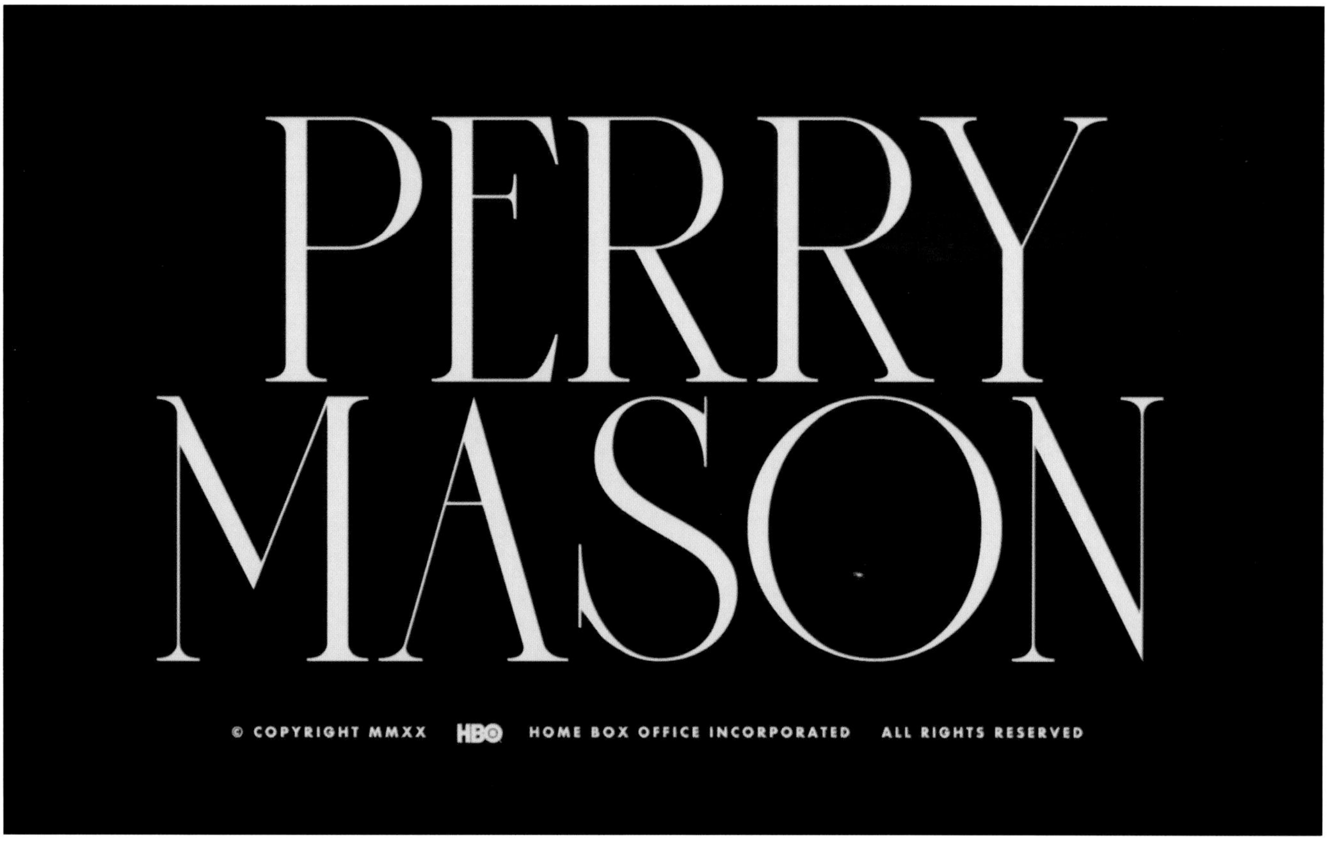
PERRY MASON
© COPYRIGHT MMXX HBO HOME BOX OFFICE INCORPORATED ALL RIGHTS RESERVED

...the branding campaign for Madre marries seemingly disparate elements to create a unique and meticulously crafted tribute to Neapolitan culture and its cuisine.
Jason Ramirez

Pizza and typography — two of my favorite things, the delightful branding campaign for Madre included.

I was immediately drawn to this project in part by the clever and expressive typography of the Madre logo in which each letterform of the pizzeria name is rendered to evoke the stretchy, pliable nature of pizza dough — an effect that is smartly enhanced with embossed lettering on its business cards. But the branding for Madre is not just about its dough. An alluring devotion to the Mother Mary, Neapolitan culture, and an eighteenth century Italian board game is deftly reflected in the whimsical pairing of playful typography and iconic illustration that is seamlessly applied across the dining experience.

Fresh, fun, and elegant, the branding campaign for Madre marries seemingly disparate elements to create a unique and meticulously-crafted tribute to Neapolitan culture and its cuisine. Congratulations to the creative team at Voice Design for their awe-inspiring and award-winning work.

Madre (Italian for Mother) is an Australian pizzeria that pays total devotion to all things Mother: Mother Mary, Mother Dough and Mother Ocean.

The logo is an expression of the stretchy, malleable nature of pizza dough and the graceful fluidity of the ocean, referencing the imported Mediterranean seawater used in the pizza dough.

Honouring the pizza makers Neapolitan culture, personal superstition with numbers and the eighteenth century board game Tombola, a range of meaningful numbers were incorporated into the branding and dining experience. These included:
No. 08: Mother Mary
No 09: Offspring (Pizza box)
No 22: The Madman
(Ettore Bertonati, Pizza Maker)
No 12: Soldiers (Staff)
No 46: Money (Bill plate)
No 82: The Laden Table (Menu)
No 14: The Drunk (Drinks menu).

IDENTITY/BRANDING
Madre

Design
Kieran Wallis
Adelaide,
South Australia

Typography
Keith Morris
and Kieran Wallis

Creative Direction
Scott Carslake°
and Anthony De Leo

URL
voicedesign.net

Design Firm
Voice®

Client
Madre

Principal Type
Founders Grotesk
and Savate

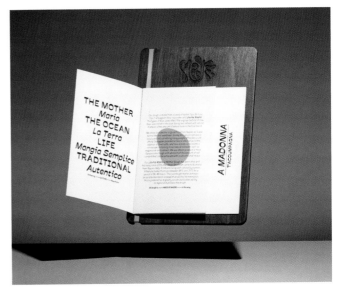

I love the modern take on the traditional blackletter typography combined with the unexpected color palettes and layouts.
Jason Sfetko

I selected this project as my judge's choice because I love the modern take on the traditional blackletter typography combined with the unexpected color palettes and layouts. Congratulations to the art department at *The New York Times Magazine* for the exceptional work and win!

Our Culture Issue this year included a series of profiles and essays on a diverse selection of topics that influence today's culture. These range from a profile on Puerto Rican reggaetón artist, Bad Bunny, to an essay and portfolio about the preservation of Black culture for future generations. By using blackletter typography with a colorful and unexpected palette, the design is a modern take on tradition, showing that today's culture is shifting and that there are new voices giving it new meanings.

EDITORIALS
The Culture Issue

Design
Claudia Rubin
New York

Art Direction
Ben Grandgenett

Creative Direction
Gail Bichler°

Director of Photography
Kathy Ryan

Deputy Director of Photography
Jessica Dimson

Photo Editor
David Carthas

Publication
The New York Times Magazine

Principal Type
Amador Regular and Good Sans Bold

Dimensions
18.9 x 10.9 in.
(22.7 x 27.6 cm)

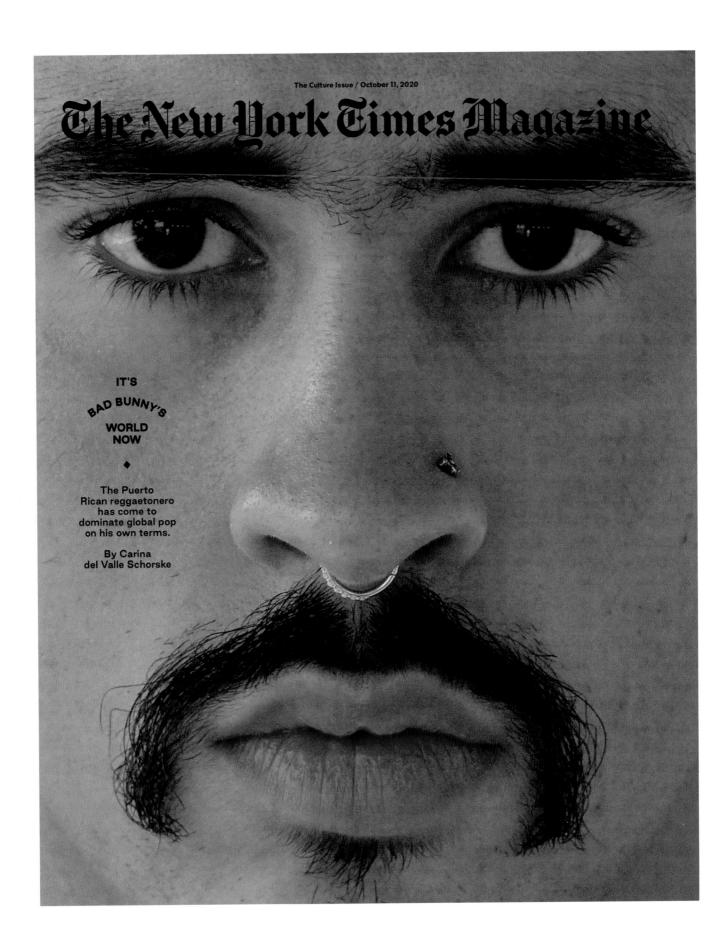

The Culture Issue / October 11, 2020

The New York Times Magazine

IT'S

BAD BUNNY'S

WORLD
NOW

◆

The Puerto
Rican reggaetonero
has come to
dominate global pop
on his own terms.

By Carina
del Valle Schorske

TDC 67
Communication
Design Winners

Concept: This is a playful tour through the accomplishments, resilience, and creativity of our customers—Against All Odds.

Agency
Mailchimp Brand &
Marketing Design

Design
James Abercrombie,
Chase Curry,
Meg Lindsay,
Chris Sandlin,
and Luke Webster

Art Direction
Ross Zietz

Copy
Austin Ray

Animation
Linda McNeil

Production
Troy Harris and
Jaclyn Stiller

Creative Direction
Christian Widlic

Senior Director
Katie Potochney

Communication Team
Chris McGee and
Christina Scavone

Principal Type
Means

Concept: This was a campaign for the 23rd
edition of the Barcelona Poesia festival.

Studio
Marta Cerdà
Alimbau°
Barcelona

Client
Ajuntament
de Barcelona

Concept: This is an advertisement for Japan's largest digital satellite broadcasting service provider. We used the main copy "TV makes home fun" in this ad that shows a snippet of a family enjoying TV. The typography, created by Yasaburo Kuwayama, is called Kodomo Shotai ("Children Font" in English). To try to express the fun the family is having while watching TV, we used a font inspired by kids that is both bold and playful.

Agency
Mailchimp Brand &
Marketing Design

Design
James Abercrombie,
Chase Curry, Chris
Sandlin, Meg Lindsay,
and Luke Webster

Art Direction
Ross Zietz

Copy
Austin Ray

Animation
Linda McNeil

Production
Troy Harris and
Jaclyn Stiller

Creative Direction
Christian Widlic

Senior Director
Katie Potocheny

Communication Team
Chris McGee and
Christina Scavone

Principal Type
Means

Concept: In *Almond*, a teenaged boy named Yunjae connects with humanity despite living with alexithymia, a medical condition caused by small amygdalae (sometimes referred to as "the almonds" for their shape) that manifests as difficulty feeling emotions such as fear or anger. Youthful handlettering is tucked into almond shapes on the cover, delicately balanced to reflect Yunjae's precariously navigated adolescence.

Art Direction
Stephen Brayda

URLs
stephenbrayda.com
harpercollins.com

Publisher
HarperCollins
Publishers
New York

Client
HarperVia
HarperCollins
Publishers

Principal Type
Handlettering

Dimensions
5.6 × 8.5 in.
(14.3 x 21.5 cm)

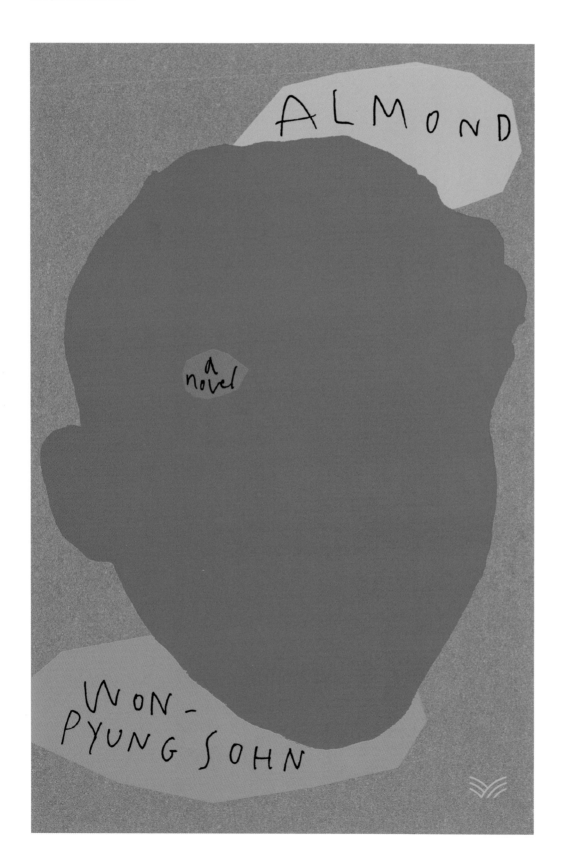

Concept: *The American Fiancée* is ambitious and daring: more than 700 pages chronicling 300 generations of one unforgettable family. Elaborate art by Kai McCall paired with big, bold, and unrestrained handlettering is the gateway to this wild adventure.

Art Direction
Stephen Brayda
New York

Illustrations
Kai McCall

URLs
stephenbrayda.com
harpercollins.com

Client
HarperVia/
HarperCollins
Publishers

Publisher
HarperCollins
Publishers

Principal Type
Handlettering

Dimensions
6.1 x 9.25 in.
(15.6 x 24.5 cm)

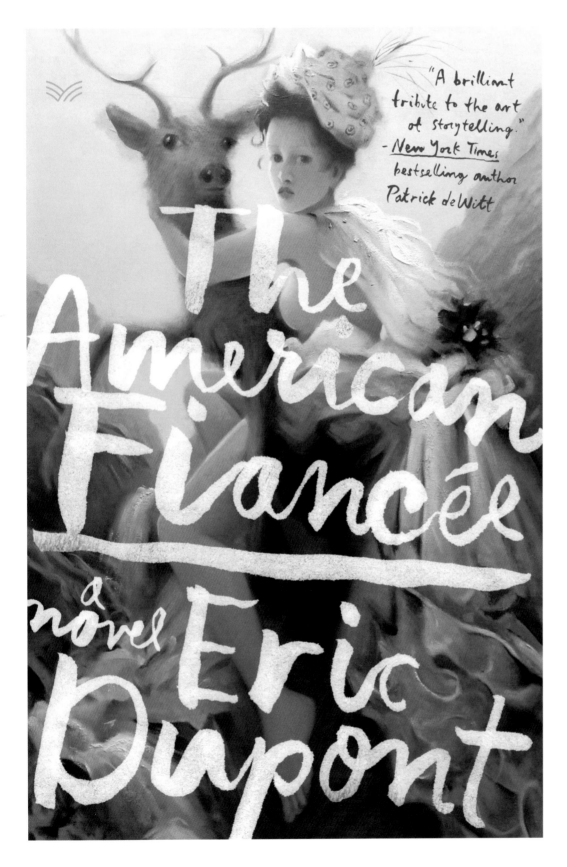

Concept: This autobiography assigns the author's Kanji name to the spin of all three books to show the inseparability of the set.

Creative Direction
Yu-Wen Hsu
Taipei

Studio
Wang Zhi-Hong
Studio

Client
Faces Publications

Principal Type
GT Super Display
Trial

Dimensions
5.3 x 7.9 in.
(13.7 x 20.1 cm)

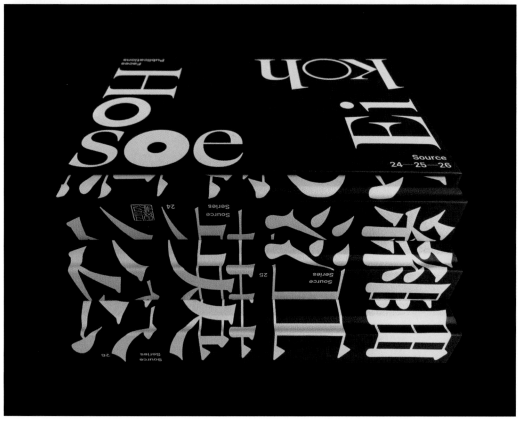

Concept: *Fukt Magazine's* 19th issue, *"Storylines,"* on the art of narration in drawing, unfolds its typography of the cover through zigzag folds into unexpected new meanings. The cover changes shape, reveals hidden messages, and invites the reader in an engaging way to dive into the issue, the contributing artists, and their wonderful artwork and stories.

Creative Direction
Ariane Spanier
Berlin

Design Firm
Ariane Spanier

Client
Fukt Magazine

Principal Type
Adobe Garamond
Pro, Alliance No. 1,
and Grand Slang

Dimensions
6.7 × 9 in.
(17 x 23 cm)

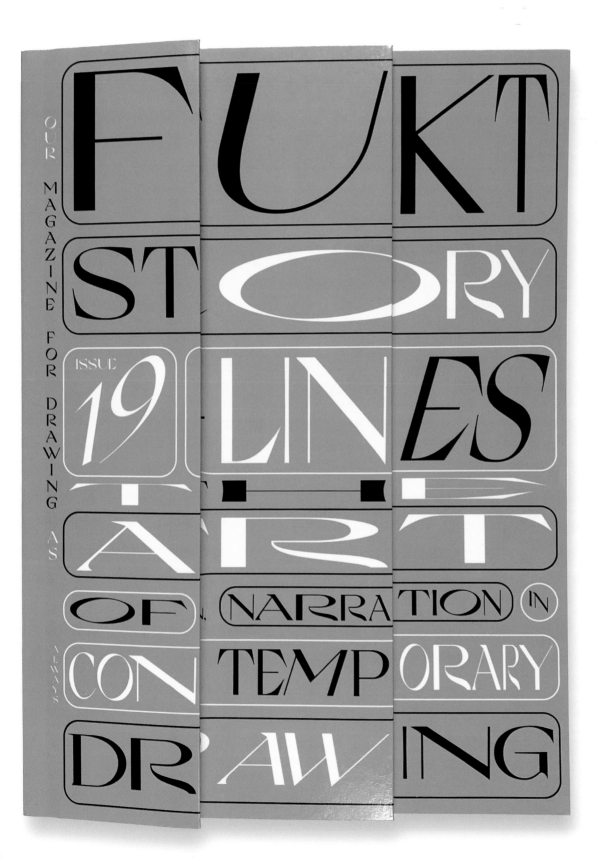

Concept: This is a design for a new Dutch edition for Jack Kerouac's classic book *On the Road*, referencing Beat-style lettering.

Design
Henk van het
Nederend
Amsterdam

Agency
Moker Ontwerp

Client
De Bezige Bij

Principal Type
Disturbed Script and
hand-drawn

Dimensions
5.4 x 8.5 in.
(13.6 x 21.5 cm)

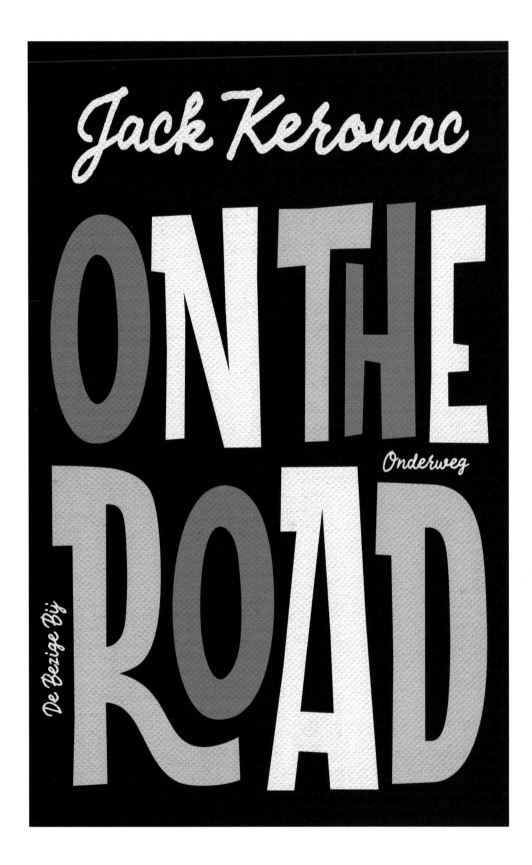

Concept Book jacket design for *Ingredients*.

Art Direction
Christopher Lin
New York

Design
Kaitlin Kall

Publisher
Penguin Random
House

INGREDIENTS

THE STRANGE CHEMISTRY OF WHAT WE PUT IN US AND ON US

GEORGE ZAIDAN

Concept: This new children's book celebrates historic and contemporary Black role models who have shaped culture.

Design
Bobby C. Martin, Jr. °
New York

Writer
Shani Mahiri King

URL
championsdesign.
com

Client
Tilbury House
Publishers

Agency
Champions Design

Principal Type
Halyard Micro
and custom

Dimensions
7 × 9.5 in.
(17.8 x 24.1 cm)

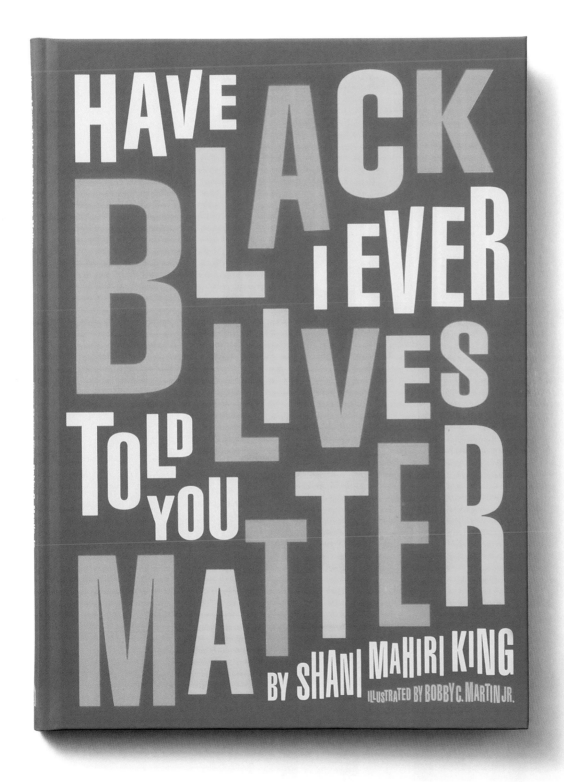

Concept: This new children's book celebrates historic and contemporary Black role models who have shaped culture.

Design
Bobby C. Martin, Jr. °
New York

Writer
Shani Mahiri King

URL
championsdesign.
com

Client
Tilbury House
Publishers

Agency
Champions Design

Principal Type
Halyard Micro
and custom

Dimensions
7 × 9.5 in.
(17.8 x 24.1 cm)

Concept: Theorbist J. M. M. Duran is publishing a solo album accompanied by an essay of the philosopher Ramón Andrés.

Design
Marta Cerdà
Alimbau°
Barcelona

Client
Josep Maria Martí
Duran

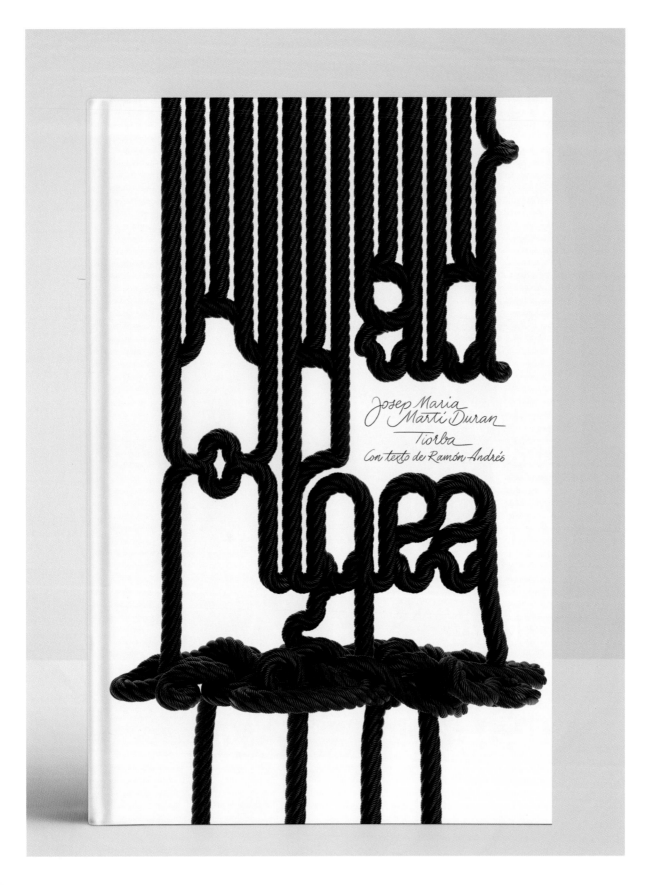

Concept: This is a colorful and flexible graphic project for the Agatha Christie books, serving the captive audience as well as new readers.

Design
Túlio Cerquize
São Paulo

Client
HarperCollins Brasil

Principal Type
Handlettering

Dimensions
5.3 x 8.1 in.
(13.5 x 20.8 cm)

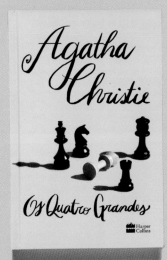

Concept: This is a cover design for a Women's
Classics series featuring four female writers and
four female characters.

Art Direction
Utku Lomlu°
Istanbul

Design Studio
Lom Creative

Client
Can Publishing

Principal Type
Custom

Dimensions
4.9 × 7.7 in.
(12.5 x 19.5 cm)

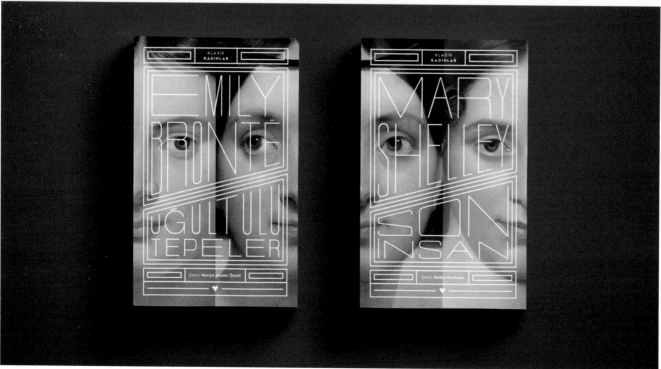

Concept: This RBook is about the RGruppe—America's cult Porsche car club. It's a coffee-table book of 580 pages filled with 840 brilliant images of awesome cars, candid visits of members' private garages, and beautiful Californian landscapes. The book is divided into five chapters, separated by huge, striking numbers. In between, there are double pages with quotations or titles in this large and bold typography. This characteristic typographical handling underlines the rough attitude of this club and gives the book a raw character. The choice of gray cardboard as the cover material reinforces this workshop character.

Creative Direction
Davide Durante,
Helen Hauert,
and Barbara Stehle
Stuttgart

Client
Frank Kayser

Design Firm
collect

Principal Type
LL Akkurat Mono,
Berthold Akzidenz
Grotesk, and Buzz

Dimensions
10 x 13 in
(26 x 32 cm)

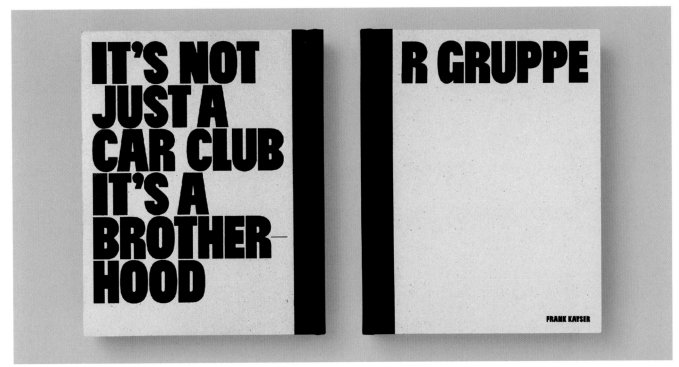

Concept: The Circulation Tank 2 (Umlauftank 2 1967–1974) is a protected landmark in Berlin built by German architect Ludwig Leo. The iconic building is a laboratory—a testing ground for flow experiments, modes of architectural expression, and now, since its restoration, a study in how to deal with recent monuments. The book design represents the architecture's spirit. It aims at communicating the social relevance of heritage protection to a broader public.

Art Direction
Siyu Mao
Berlin

Client
Wüstenrot
Foundation

Principal Type
Favorit
and Suisse Works

Dimensions
8.4 x 10.6 in.
(21.4 x 27 cm)

Concept: Underline Studio designed *Revision and Resistance*, a book that celebrates mistikôsiwak, by Kent Monkman.

Design
Michael Lorimer
Toronto

Creative Direction
Claire Dawson and
Fidel Peña

Product Manager
Lucas Abtey

Editor
Sara Angel

Client
Art Canada Institute

Studio
Underline Studio

Principal Type
Glossy Display
and Garamond
Premier Pro

Dimensions
9.4 x 11.75 in.
(24 x 30 cm)

Concept: An explorative study in language and semiotics, *Conjunglyph* celebrates the evolution of language, its ability to connect us, and the role of typography in visual communication. Combining the word "conjunction" and "glyph," *Conjunglyph* is an experiment to create nine new symbols as glyphs representing conjunctions that can be identified verbally and applied in writing. Our approach takes inspiration from the history of writing, tracing back to the origins of the ampersand (&), which was born from the conjoined letters of "et," the Latin translation of the word "and." It unearths the possibilities of new symbol creations from our existing conjunctions.

Design
Eva Mega Astria,
Pierre Ang,
Sasqia Pristia, and
Bram Patria Yoshugi
Jakarta

Art Direction
Ritter Willy Putra

Creative Direction
Eric Widjaja

Writers
Gana Adi
and Sasqia Pristia

Production Company
The Binary
Bandung, Indonesia

Design Firm
Thinking Room

Principal Type
TR Grotesk

Dimensions
6.25 × 7.5 in.
(16 x 19 cm)

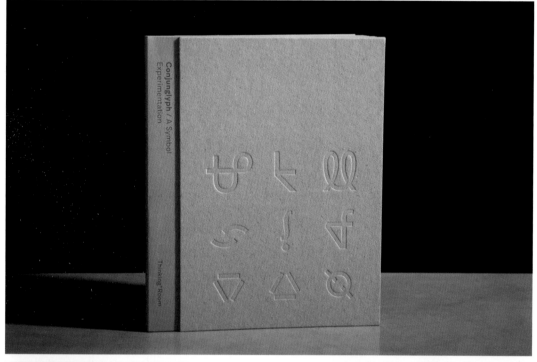

Concept: In this enormous human society, we are raised in a tiny box from generation to generation. But it is time for us to face ourselves, to break the territory set by others, and to identify with ourselves through collecting stories.

Design
Yi-Tzu Chan,
Szu-YU Chen,
Tzu-Ning Hsu,
Ting-Wei Liao,
Ji-Cheng Luo,
and Kuo-Ming Tsou
Taichung

Professors
Chien-Wen Chen
and Wei-Jen Huang

School
Ling Tung University

Principal Type
Handwriting

Dimensions
15.7 × 8.1 in.
(40 x 20.8 cm)

Concept: This is a journey through the delights of peninsular gastronomy and a celebration of Dalí's *Les Diners de Gala*.

Art Direction
Xavier Banús and
Armando Fidalgo
Barcelona

Photography
Carles Allende,
Alba Giné,
Xurxo Lobato,
and Sergi Provencio

Editor
Esther Gallart

Publisher
Editorial Planeta

Design Firm
Compañía

Client
Accenture

Principal Type
Graphik, Grifo,
and Love

Dimensions
10.2 x 13.4 in.
(25.8 x 34 cm)

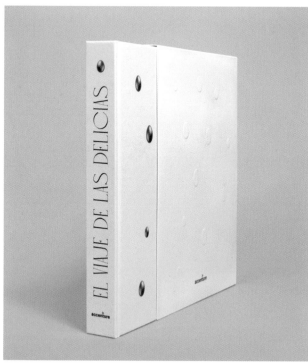

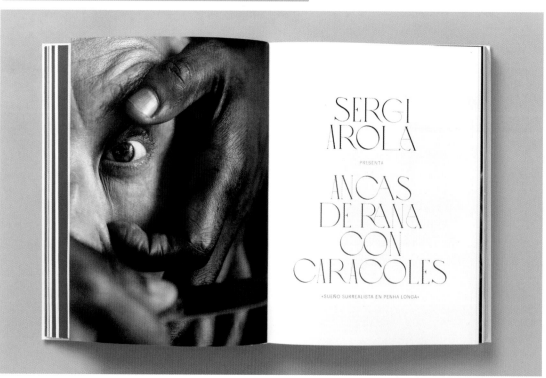

Concept: In December 2017, photographer William Mebane documented a Trump rally in Pensacola, Florida. Both moved by and fearful of what he'd seen and heard, Mebane withheld the content for almost three years. This 64-page tabloid—designed to work as a photo book and a collection of posters—documents the event through images, quotes, and a short story by the filmmaker Tim Sutton.

Creative Direction
Kevin Brainard and
Cybele Grandjean

Photography
William Mebane

Studio
Area of Practice

Client
William Mebane

Principal Type
Prophet

Dimensions
11.4 x 15 in.
(28.9 x 38 cm)

Concept: Philipp Fürhofer's book reflects his artistic practice—a blend of modern materials and dancing elements.

Art and Creative Direction
Daniel Robitaille
Montréal

Design Firm
Paprika

Client
Thierry-Maxime
Loriot

Concept: The School of Visual Arts *Viewbook* tells a visual story of what can be achieved and what life is like for art students in New York City.

Direction
Brian E. Smith
New York

Art Direction
Mark Maltais

Creative Direction
Gail Anderson°

Design Studio
Visual Arts Press, Ltd.

Client
School of Visual Arts,
New York°

Principal Type
Antipol, BB Book,
Bend, Beastly,
Enterline, Filosofia,
Haptik, Harbour,
Lil Thug, Neue Plak,
Playa, Scotch Modern,
and Zoo

Dimensions
8.5 x 11 in.
(21.6 x 27.9 cm)

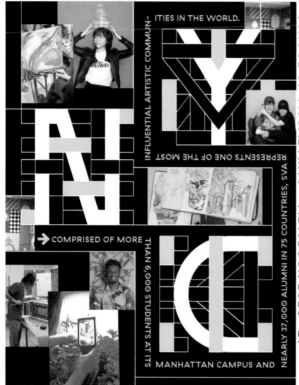
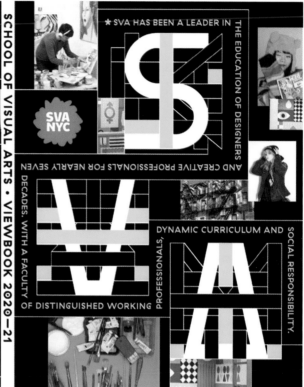

Concept: In 2020, I had the opportunity to study at a school in Rhode Island. During an online gathering before classes began, one of the current students suggested that new students introduce themselves and provide their preferred pronouns. Since I was born and raised in Korea, a non-English-speaking country, I was not able to understand exactly what preferred pronouns were, but I soon caught on. It was an inspirational moment for me. In many circumstances, one tends to be deprived of defining themselves and who they are. Others often create imaginary boxes for you to fit in before even fully getting to know you. As you are the master of your own life and destiny, you should be the only one who defines yourself. i.Am was created based on these ideas. The goal of i.Am is to support one's right to self-expression, liberty, and uniqueness.

Design
Halim Lee
Seoul

Instagram
@alim.db

URL
leehalim.com

Principal Type
Helvetica and i.Am

Dimensions
4.1 x 6 in.
(10.5 x 15.4 cm)

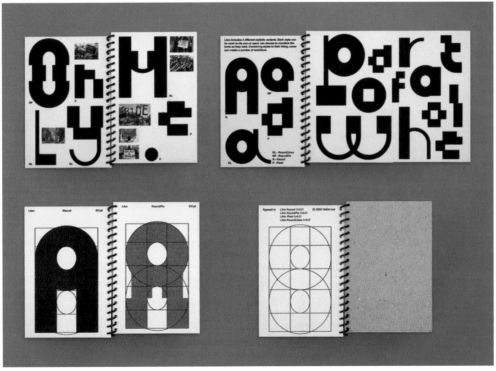

Concept: For this book about advocating and caring for a mentally ill child, I wanted to show the concept of fixing something from a place of love. The idea of a mother repairing a child's ripped clothing inspired the creative approach. The cover was designed, printed, cut in half, and then carefully sewn back together and photographed for the final effect.

Design
Catherine Casalino°
New York

Production Editor
Ana Bichanich

Studio
Casalino Design

Client
University of
Minnesota Press

URL
upress.umn.edu

Principal Type
Operetta

Dimensions
5.5 × 8.25 in.
(14 x 21 cm)

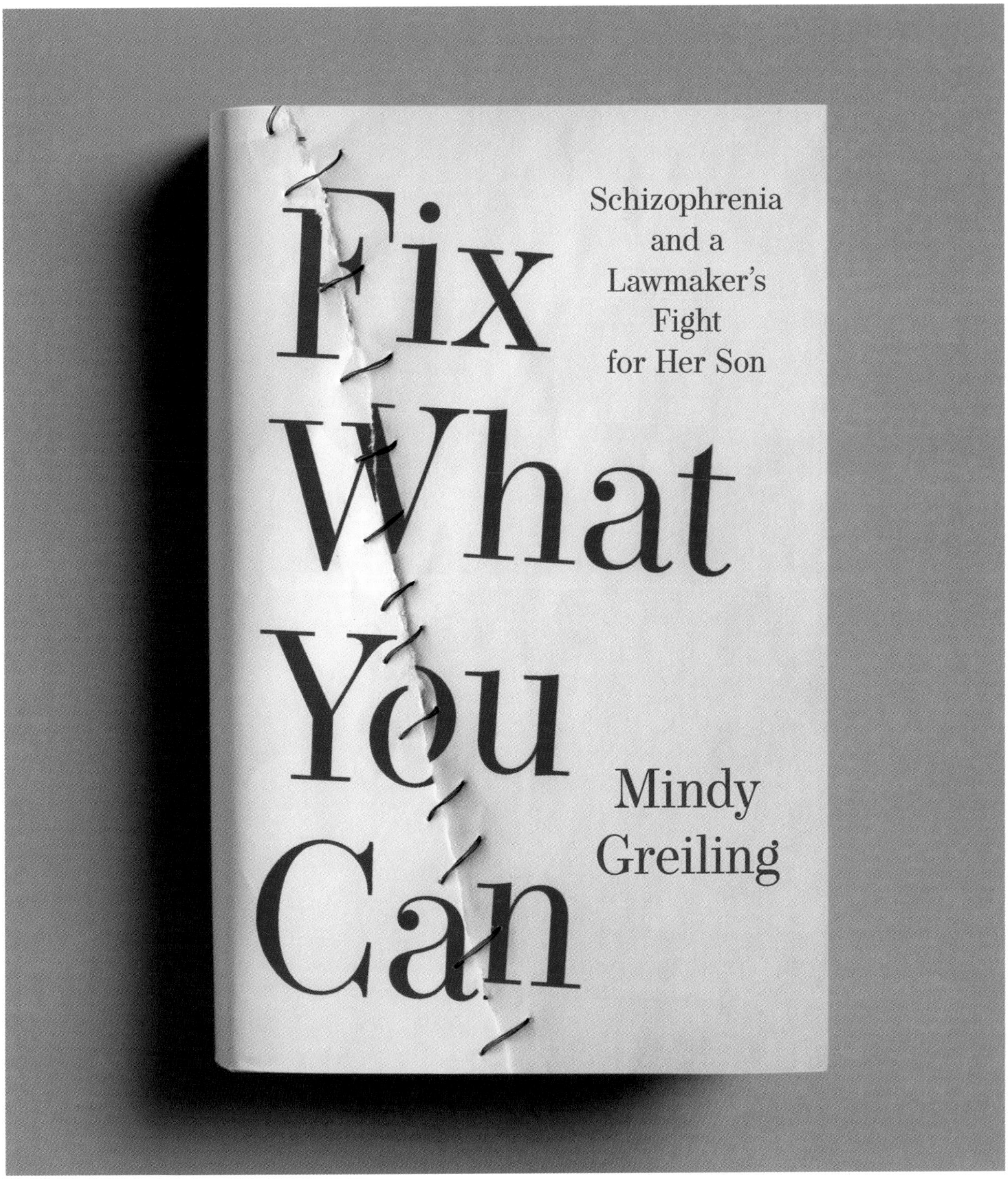

Concept: This publication seeks to give a visual testimony of the massive protests that took place in Peru after the putsch led by Manuel Merino on November 9, 2020. KWY gathered the work of more than 200 photographers to give an account of how this political crisis was lived in several cities across the country. Some essays contextualize these events on the verge of celebrating the bicentennial of Peru's independence. The format, binding, color, and typography were chosen after reviewing Latino American political manifestos from the 1970s. This publication was distributed for free in the streets where the protests took place.

Art Direction
Vera Lucía Jiménez
Araujo
Lima

Producer
Liliana Takashima

Editors
Musuk Nolte and
Fernando Fujimoto

Writer
Sandra Rodriguez

Client
KWY Editorial

Design Firm
Vera Lucia Jiménez
Araujo

Agencies
KWY Ediciones and
Vera Lucia Jiménez
Araujo

Principal Type
Caslon Extra Condensed
and Neue Helvetica

Dimensions
8.3 x 11.7 in
(21 x 29.7 cm)

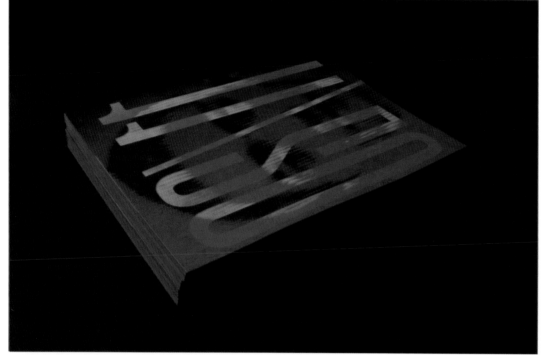

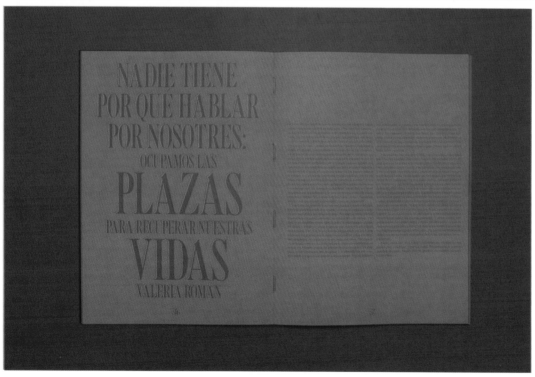

Concept: In order to maintain the character of a documentation, this catalog deals with both the context and the creative process of the installation *Eastern Munich*. Based on the art installation Sáiles, the catalog has been given the same aspect ratio as the Wittelsbacher Platz projections (16:9). A projection works with light; this catalog uses white lines on transparent paper and enables transitions that otherwise only animations can use. The choice of paper had to match both in terms of color and feel, yet still be able to handle the heavy contrast of the black ink. It is more a book for a coffee table than a shelf. Unfold it!

Art Direction
Matthias Hohmann
Stuttgart

Writers
Dr. Karin Hutflötz,
Prof. Michael Reder,
Lia Sáile,
Helmut Six,
and Dr. Martina
Taubenberger

Photography
Lisa Domin,
Adriana Lemus,
Michael Reder,
and Lia Sáile

Client
whitebox e.V.
(for Lia Sáile)

Studio
Matthias Hohmann

Principal Type
GT America Mono,
Relevant, and
SangBleu Kingdom

Dimensions
6.7 x 13.4 in.
(17 x 34 cm)

Concept: Inspired by the physical and spiritual principles of the Chinese arts, such as calligraphy and martial arts, this book is about the process of writing. Repetition, mindfulness, concentration, practice, and perseverance play a major role and thereby form the basis for handmade type design. Without providing technical knowledge, it is reminiscent of old type specimen books and offers insights into the creative process of lettering. Using letters and typography as some kind of external reference point, the sequence of the pages is finely tuned so that you feel as though you are moving through an exhibition inside a book.

Design
Merle Michaelis
Kiel, Germany

School
Muthesius
Kunsthochschule

Principal Type
Aktiv Grotesk

Dimensions
8 x 10.5 in.
(20.3 x 26.7 cm)

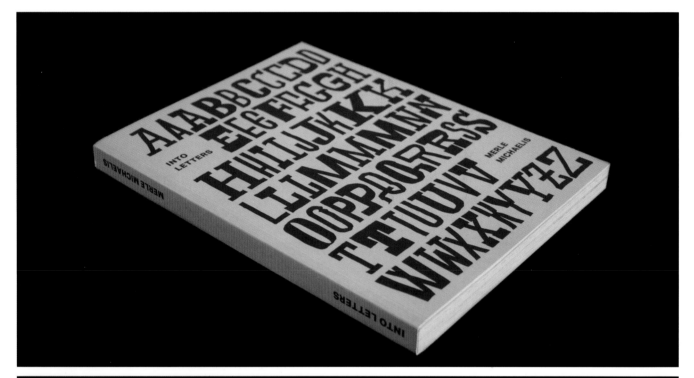

Concept: This book was published to accompany *Duro Olowu: Seeing Chicago*.

Design
Tim Curley,
Renata Graw, and
Crystal Zapata
Chicago

Art Direction
Renata Graw

Creative Team
Lorenzo Conte,
Tyler Laminack,
Sheila Majumdar,
Bonnie Rosenberg,
Claire Ruud, and
Jack Schneider

Editor
Naomi Beckwith

URL
thenormalstudio.com

Client
Museum of
Contemporary Art
Chicago

Studio
Normal Studio

Principal Type
Self Modern,
Serapion,
Suisse Int'l, and
Suisse Int'l Mono

Dimensions
5.5 × 7.5 in.
(14 x 19.7 cm)

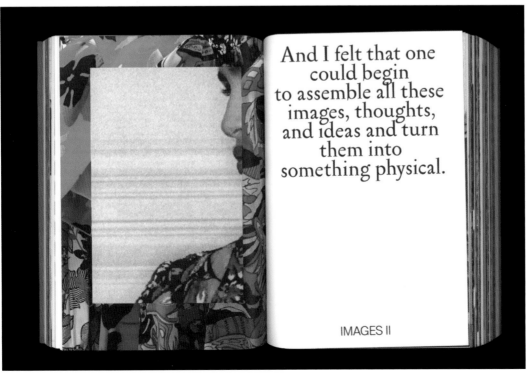

Concept: The catalog for the international group exhibition *Real Feelings* at HeK (House of Electronic Arts Basel) explores the rapidly changing relationship between technology and emotion. The works of the 20 artists inquire and show how technology today represents, manipulates, and changes our emotions. The client requested a contemporary design aimed at artists, creative coders, and people interested in the arts. We played throughout the design with dualities (cold/warm, technology/emotion, large/small) and used an eccentric font and a unique layout. The cover is made up of a transparent film that hides the face's emotion: Upon removing the film, the tears are revealed.

Design
Simon Hauser
and David Schwarz
Basel

Studio
Hauser, Schwarz

Client
House of Electronic Arts
Basel

Principal Type
Beatrice and
Beatrice Display

Dimensions
6.5 × 9.4 in.
(16.5 x 24 cm)

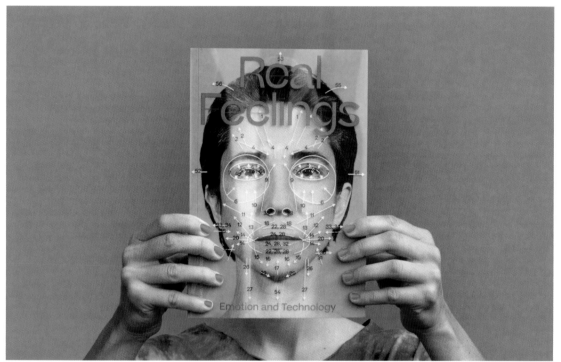

Concept: The futurist Joël Luc Cachelin is addressing the occasion of the 20th anniversary of the Forum Kultur und Ökonomie and takes a look into the year 2040 by collecting social developments and thinking ahead regarding its impact on cultural funding. The book object, Kultur 2040, was designed to be handy so that it could be given to the audience at the event. Ten manual interventions in the form of the publication—for example, torn-off pages or coffee stains—make every copy an original and illustrate the content. The elegant effect of the design contrasts with the brutal interventions.

Design
Amanda Züst
Basel

Art Direction
Anna Furrer

Creative Direction
Sascha Tittmann

URLs
druckereilutz.ch
kulturundoekonomie.ch
merianverlag.ch
sequenz.net
wissensfabrik.ch

Editor
Forum Kultur
und Ökonomie

Author
Joël Luc Cachelin

Publisher
Christoph Merian
Verlag

Printing
Druckerei Lutz

Processing/Manual
Interventions
Bildungsstätte
Sommeri

Design Studio
Büro Sequenz

Principal Type
SangBleu Empire,
SangBleu Kingdom,
and SangBleu
Versailles

Dimensions
3.9 × 6.6 in.
(10 × 16.8 cm)

Concept: This book design project is the record of a Japanese-style stone arch bridge on the Bulaohe River in Suyangshan Town, Pizhou, Jiangsu province. The bridge was damaged in Japan's aggression against China, and as the village residents moved away, it was forgotten and neglected. In considering the historical value of the bridge, I hope the record will awake the protection of the bridge. I would like to express the broken bridge in my heart with a visual image.

Creative Direction
Yuan Liu
Shanghai

URL
cargocollective.com/
yuan

Client
Pizhou Cultural
Office

Principal Type
Romie Font and
Source Han Serif

Dimensions
8.3 x 11.7 in.
(21 x 29.7 cm)

Concept: A uniquely shaped mirror in each college is shown on the cover with special craftsmanship.

Design
Zhu Chao,
Pan Yuchen,
and Zhao Yuelin
Beijing

Art Direction
Zhu Chao

URL
mintbrand.cn

Design Firm
Mint Brand Design

Client
BIFT

Principal Type
Haas Grot Disp
and Hanyi

Dimensions
11.4 x 7.8 x 4.3 in.
(30 x 19.8 x 10.9 cm)

Concept: W. Gordon Smith was an art critic, author, dramatist, photographer, and filmmaker known for his iconic BBC Scotland program. He and his wife, Jay Smith, spent a lifetime indulging their passion for the arts, culminating in an incredible collection. For the 2021 memorial exhibition, I designed and edited a book charting the collection, including the selection of archival material and exhibition reviews, to chronicle the unique relationship between artists and collectors. Inspired by Smith's record keeping, A–L/M–Z became a 400-page modern art reference book, with index-cut pages as well as a screen-printed and label-embossed cover.

Design and Editor
Sigrid Schmeisser
Maastricht,
the Netherlands

Writer
Siobhan McLaughlin

Copyediting
and Proofing
Helen Bleck

Printing
Karl Grammlich
GmbH

Bookbinding
Josef Spinner
Grossbuchbinderei

Creative Team
Helen Bleck

Client
Jay Gordonsmith
Estate

Principal Type
Founders Grotesk
Mono

Dimensions
7.2 x 9.25 in.
(18.4 x 3.5 cm)

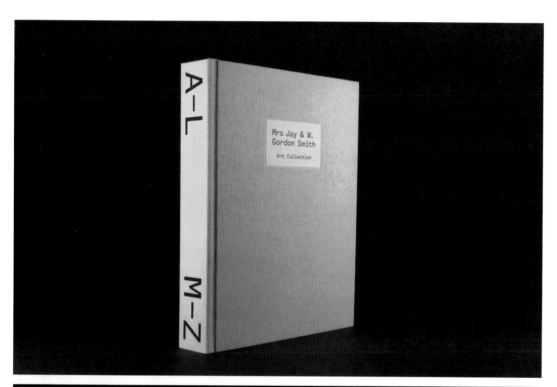

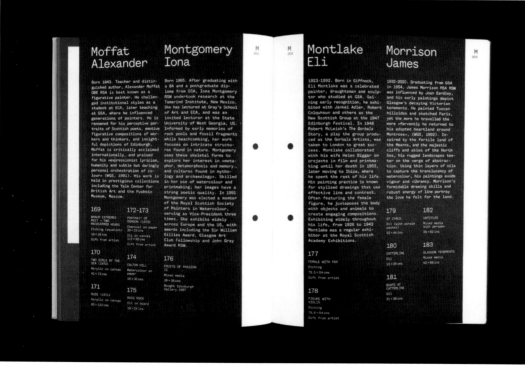

Concept: *Grief and Grievance* embodies protest and Black grief in the face of racism.

Design
Brian Johnson
and Silas Munro
Inglewood, California

Design Firm
Polymode

Clients
Phaidon and The
New Museum

Principal Type
Guardian Egyptian
and XYZ Egyptienne

Dimensions
11.4 x 9.8 in.
(29 x 24.9 cm)

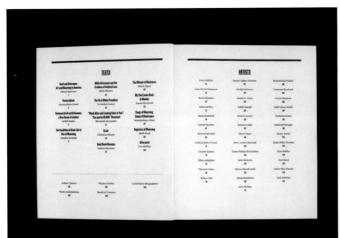

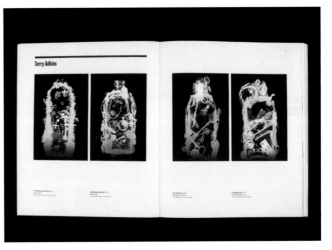

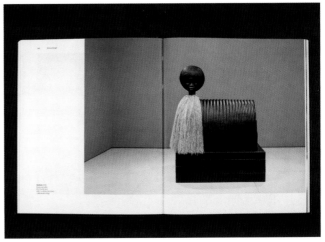

Concept: *Black Futures* is the long-awaited book by Kimberly Drew and Jenna Wortham that combines original artwork, essays, roundtable discussions, one-on-one interviews, poetry, and other forms of expression to pay tribute to the myriad modes of communication that have been championed by Black creatives, from the height of the AIDS crisis to the speculative future. The design is a compendium organized with multiple ways of accessing the variety of entries. From indices to physical hyperlinks, the book flows in a nonlinear yet interconnected fashion.

Design
Taylor Wood and
Rouba Yammine
Brooklyn, New York

Creative Direction
Jon Key°
and Wael Morcos°

URL
morcoskey.com

Instagram
@morcoskey

Client
Penguin Random
House

Design Studio
Morcos Key

Principal Type
Base Mono Narrow,
Graphik, and Graphic
XX Condensed

Dimensions
7.4 x 9.1 in.
(18.7 x 23.2 cm)

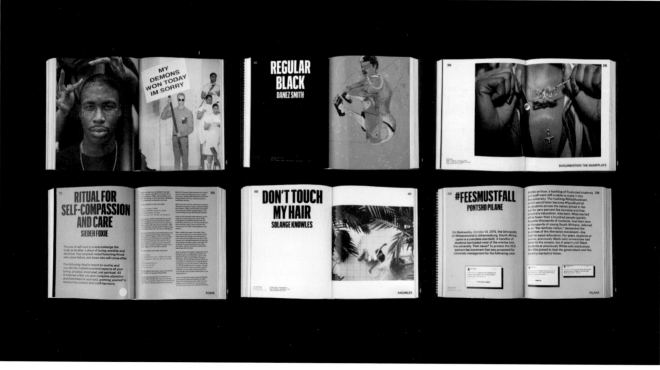

Concept: *Chinese Protest Recipes* is a project of resistance and a form of protest through Chinese food.

Design
Ronald Tau
Toronto

Studio
Meat Studio

Client
Personal with
@thegodofcookery

Principal Type
New Diane,
Right Grotesk
and Untitled Serif

Dimensions
4.3 x 6.7 in.
(11 x 17 cm)

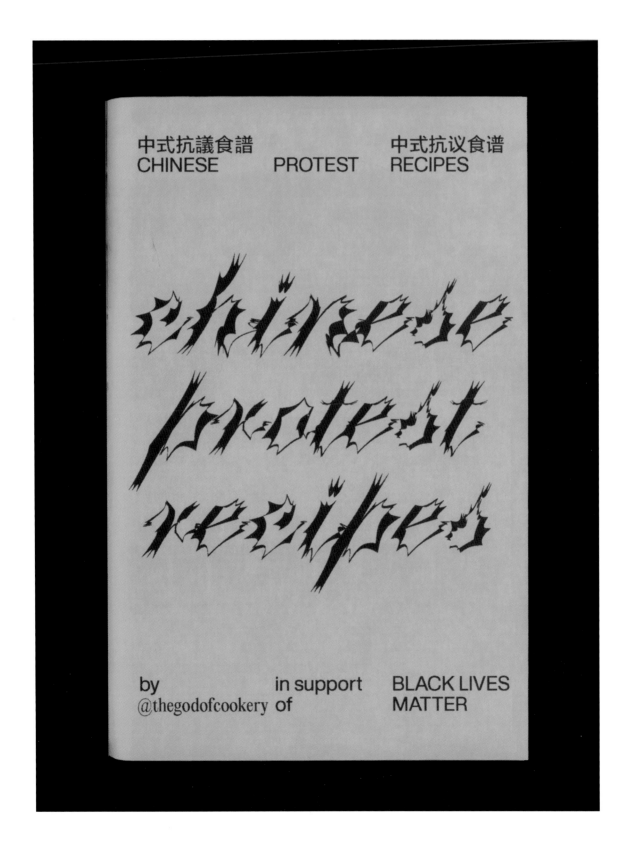

Concept: For the past two years, our team has leaned into the idea of sensemaking, striving to help others understand their world. But how do we find that same meaning ourselves? *Sensemaking 2020* is an expression of our team's collective vision and an acknowledgment of our experiences of a historically challenging year. Its eclectic and emotional mix of content, brought together in a visual and enduring format, reflects the diversity and vibrancy of our global community, and the themes that emerged—gratitude, creativity, and resilience—were simple yet profound. This book reflects us. It reflects what matters to us.

Design
Inyeong Cho,
Anna Sera Garcia,
Zak Klauck,
Megan Lynch,
Ingrid Ma,
Kellen Renstrom,
Anna Young,
and David Yun

Writer
Abbye Churchill

Producer
Esther Rosenberg

Content Strategists
Benjamin Dorvel and
Cliff Kuang

Direction
Rob Giampietro,
Chris Morabito,
Bobby Nath,
Christine Olson,
and Hector Ouilhet

Design Firm
Google

Agency
Wax Studios

Principal Type
Romie Regular,
Google Sans, and
Google Sans Text

Dimensions
8.4 x 10.9 in.
(21.3 x 27.5 cm)

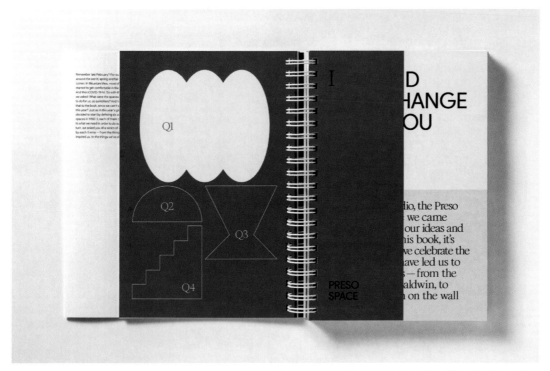

Concept: Our team initially set out to create a publication to document our current moment, working from home, as a cohort of designers. This publication is exactly that—a moment and a reflection of where we were in April 2020. Featuring imagery and recommended reading submissions from designers across our team, this community-led publication attempts to capture both the beautiful and the banal of what it often is to be working from home. It is a capsule for our team that is raw, curious, messy, romantic, introspective, rough, and actively seeking places of understanding, beauty, inspiration, and creativity.

Design
Anna Sera Garcia
and Megan Lynch
Mountain View

Direction
Chris Morabito

Design Firm
Google

Principal Type
Continua,
Google Sans, and
Google Sans Text

Dimensions
6.5 × 8.6 in.
(16.5 x 22 cm)

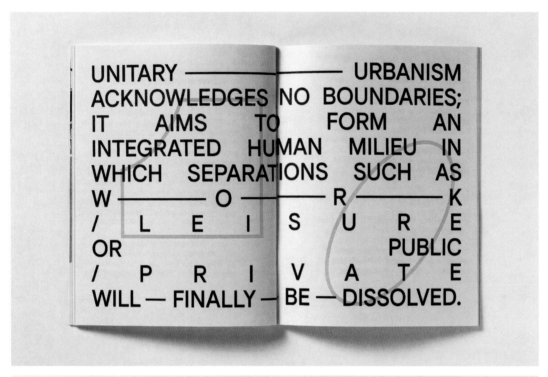

99

Concept: This is a selection of stories by D. H. Lawrence that has only female characters.

Technical Producer
Lilia Goes

Client
Carambaia

Studio
Tereza Bettinardi°
São Paulo

Principal Type
Abril Text,
Druk,
and Value Serif

Dimensions
4.5 × 6.2 in.
(11.5 x 16 cm)

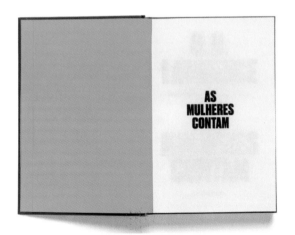

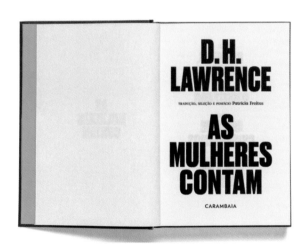

Concept: This is a handy, highly illustrated how-to guide packed with everything needed to produce professional lettering.

Design
Bondé Angeline
and Ken Barber
Yorklyn, Delaware

Art Direction
Andy Cruz

Writer
Ken Barber

Photography
Carlos Alejandro

Illustrations
Ken Barber

Media Company
Ten Speed Press

Typography
Bondé Angeline

Editor
Julie Bennett

Content Strategist
Barry Katz Sr.

Creative Team
Serena Sigona

Type Foundry
House Industries

Principal Type
Benguiat Montage,
Eames Century
Modern, Neutraface,
Pitch, and
handlettering

Dimensions
8.5 x 11 in.
(22 x 28 cm)

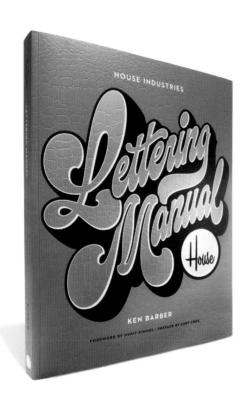

Grid Calendar 2021 "swims." The geometric Chinese Grid Hei and English Lattice Letter typefaces form the base design, which is printed and produced on Papersense washable paper. Every mark on the calendar is thus free to dive and breathe. Papersense is an innovative paper with bright and fashionable color that has been certified by the Forest Stewardship Council (FSC). The product is made of pure wood pulp and fiber pulp and is low-carbon and environmentally friendly. The calendar is based on fonts that we developed and designed.

Design and
Art Direction
Yi Tong
Hangzhou, China

Photography
Xiaolong Li

Supporting Firm
Double E
Photography

Design Firm
Quinsay

Principal Type
Grid Hei
and Lattice Letter

Dimensions
3.4 x 3.4 in.
(8.6 × 8.6 cm)

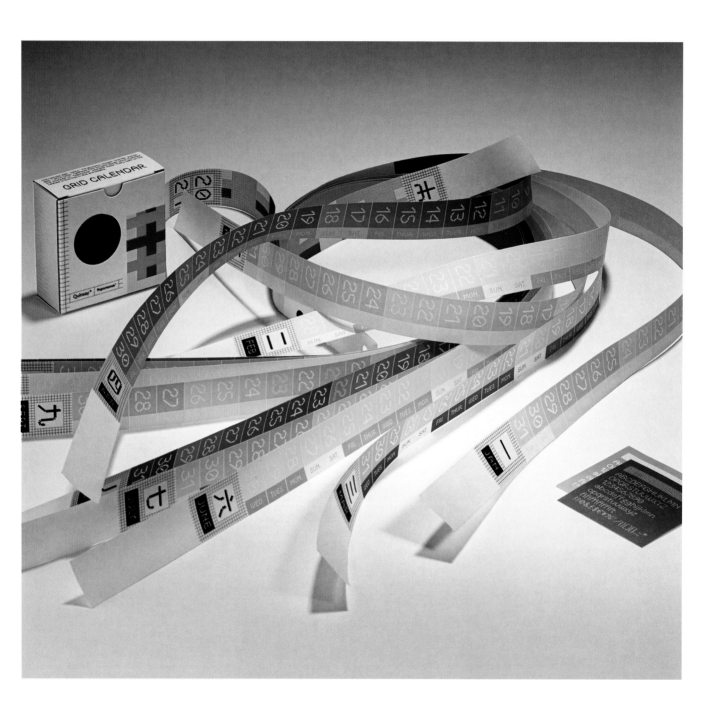

Concept: This calendar was inspired by the original form of Hindu-Arabic numerals.

Design
Shuyao Bian

Art Drection
Chen Xing

Product Manager
Xiang Li

Design Firm
STONES Design Lab.
Beijing

Principal Type
Custom

Dimensions
23 x 21 in.
(58 × 54 cm)

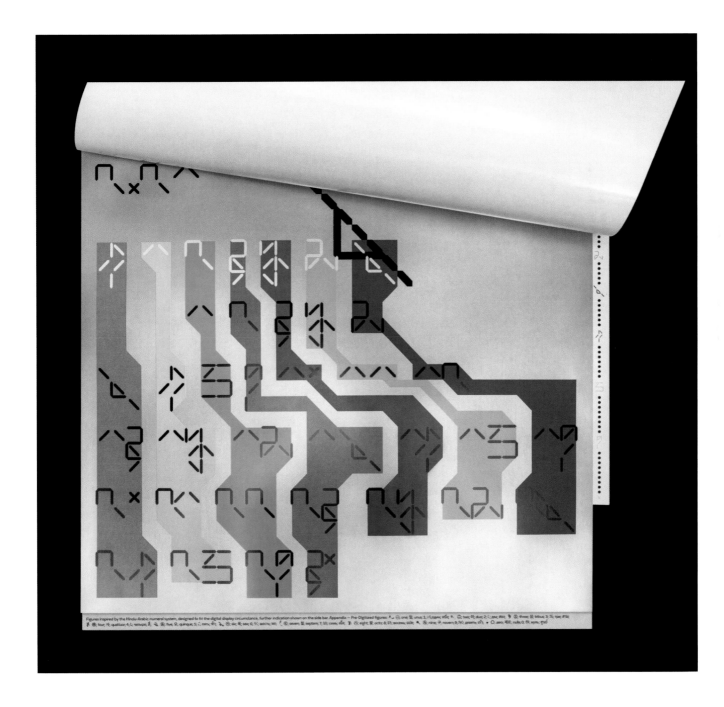

Concept: This catalog features transparent tracing paper that hides part of the text, to illustrate censorship.

Design
Varvara
Goncharova
and
Alexandra Korsakova
Moscow

Art Direction
Irina Kosheleva

Client
International
Memorial

Studio
Tuman Studio

Principal Type
CoFo Robert, Institut,
and custom

Dimensions
6.7 × 9.6 in.
(17 x 24.5 cm)

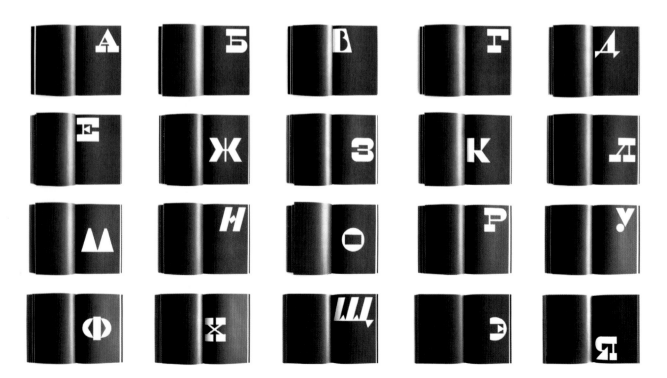

Concept: *Bird Machine* is a limited-edition print publication commissioned by Oiselle, a running company founded by women, for women. This inaugural issue celebrates the joy of body movement and explores how it is forever linked to what it produces: personal growth and collective power. It includes original writings from runners Lauren Fleshman, Kara Goucher, and Alison Mariella Désir—alongside a closer look at Oiselle's fall 2020 Flystyle.

Design
Regina Baerwalde
Seattle

Art Direction
Regina Baerwalde
and Steven Watson

Principal Type
Various

Writers
Sally Bergesen,
Alison Mariella Désir,
Lauren Fleshman,
and Kara Goucher,

Photography
Amber Fouts and
Ryan Warner

Client
Oiselle

Studio
Turnstyle

Principal Type
Bodoni 72, Druk,
Druk Wide,
and Gotham

Dimensions
12 x 17.5 in.
(30.5 x 44.5 cm)

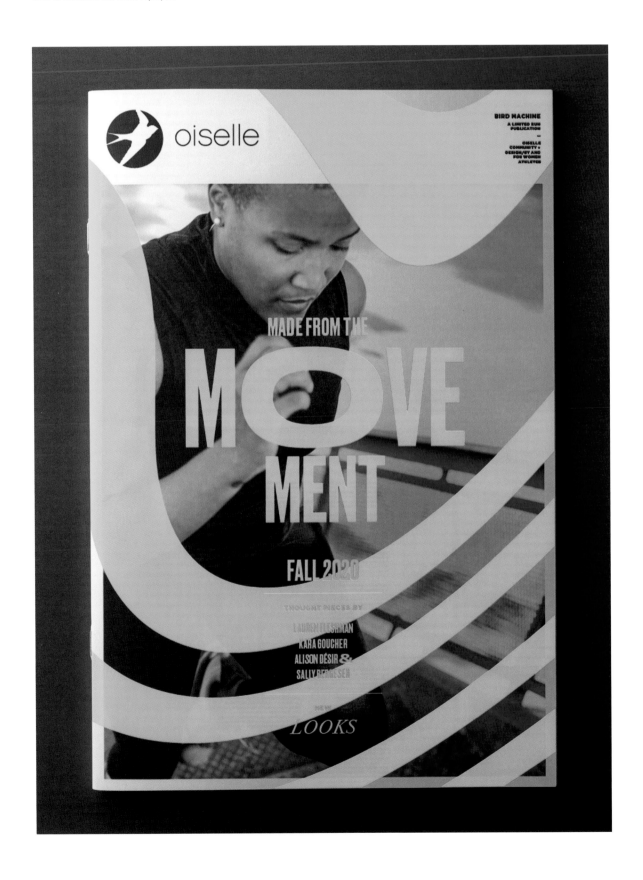

Concept: This design for the music poetry album is based on the connection of times through the poetry of typefaces.

Design
Ksenia
Kotlyarovskaya
Moscow

Art Direction
Irina Kosheleva
and Andrey Trukhan

Agency Producer
Konstantin Tolstikov

Studio
Tuman Studio

Principal Type
Apoc and
Nostra

Concept: This is a brand identity and website design for the digital publication that celebrates Jewish life and culture.

Design
Shigeto Akiyama,
Elyanna Blaser-Gould°,
Austin Maurer,
and Laura McNeill
New York

Producer
Ryan Smith

Creative Direction
Luke Hayman°

Client
Tablet

Design Firm
Pentagram Design
New York

Principal Type
LL Bradford,
ITC Cushing,
and
Gräbenbach

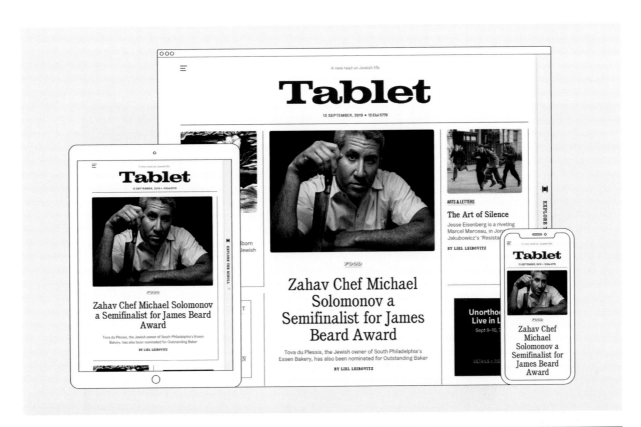

Concept: This website is for the concert IRRGARTEN (English "MAZE") by composer Yiran Zhao. The website refers to a maze, designed with multiple corridors leading to its center and finally uncovering all the previously hidden information that could be read only when hovering with the cursor. When you reach the end of the website maze, the site inverts the scroll direction. When you arrive at the supposed beginning, the scroll direction gets inverted again, and you find yourself in an endless loop. The website tries to trick users' sense of direction, causing them to unintentionally get lost for their own pleasure..

Design
Valentin Alisch,
Niklas Berlec,
and Tobias Hönow
Stuttgart

Studio
Alisch Berlec Hönow

Client
Musik der
Jahrhunderte
Stuttgart e.V.

Principal Type
Avara

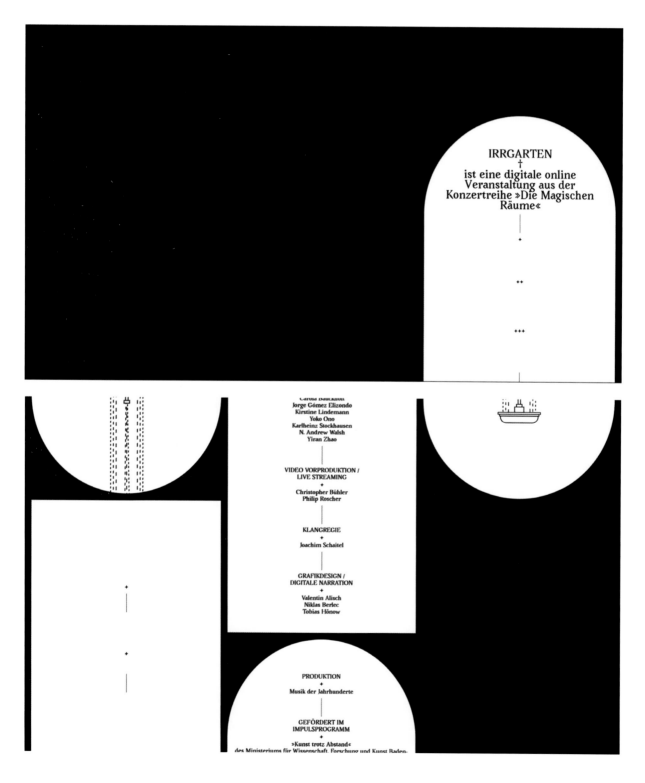

Concept: The aim was to apply kinetic typography and a visual identity to create a dynamic architecture website. The visual identity drives the composition and layout of the Sona Studio website, adding excitement and cohesion to each page. The interface intends to utilize the dynamic characteristics of the Sona logo, resulting in smooth transitions for the architectural project to be experienced in an inspirational way. The Sona identity essentially uses white space between its letters to emphasize the idea of framing space. This space, or room, can expand and contract. In essence, it demonstrates the studio's mission to provide flexibility and creativity to its clients.

Digital Artist,
Multimedia
Ralph Kenke
Cooks Hill, Australia

User Interface Design
Lachlan Golledge

URL
2-design.net

Studio
2 Design

Client
Sona Studio

Principal Type
Akzidenz
Grotesk and
Alte Haas
Grotesk

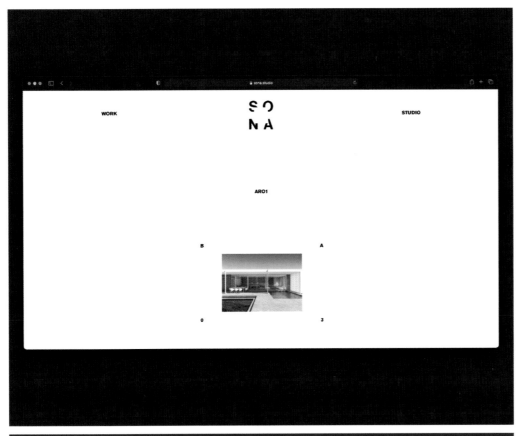

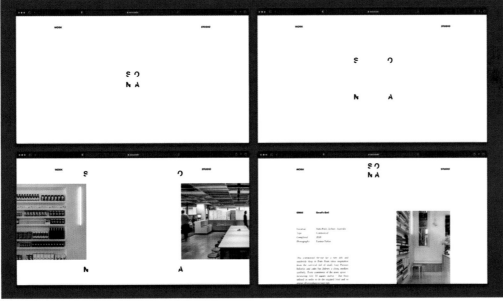

Concept: As founder Ev Williams said after the platform launched, "The ethos behind Medium is one of openness and democracy— like the internet itself." Since its founding, Medium has pursued that mission, acting as a counterbalance to the downward spiral of online discourse. This evolution of Medium's website encourages deeper relationships between readers and writers—a place for ideas to be challenged and flourish. Typographic illustrations throughout the site aim to bring readers and writers into discourse. Language becomes a tool for Medium to engage in conversation and speak in service of the great minds on the web platform.

Design
George Lavender,
Andy Liang,
Sidney Lim,
and Diego Segura
New York

Writer
Tom Elia

Photography
Mari Juliano

Animation
Tomas Markevicius
and Eric Park

Content Strategists
Matt Kuzelka and
Allison Solomson

Creative Direction
Nick Ace

Chief Creative Officer
Brian Collins

Client
Medium

Agency
COLLINS

Principal Type
Söhne and
GT Super

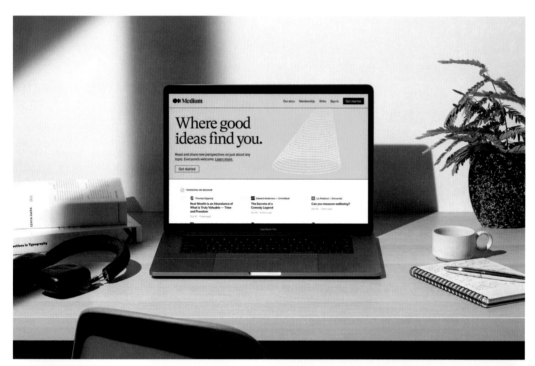

Concept: This is a playful tour through the accomplishments, resilience, and creativity of our customers—Against All Odds.

Design
James Abercrombie,
Chase Curry,
Meg Lindsay,
Chris Sandlin,
and Luke Webster

Art Direction
Ross Zietz

Writer
Austin Ray

Animation
Linda McNeil

Production
Troy Harris and
Jaclyn Stiller

Creative Team
Chris McGee and
Christina Scavone

Creative Direction
Christian Widlic

Chief Design Officer
Katie Potochney

Agency
Mailchimp

Concept: A watch face celebrates typography in three bespoke styles across four numeral systems.

Direction
Apple Design Team
Cupertino, California

Agency
Apple

Principal Type
New York,
San Francisco,
and ADT Tokyo

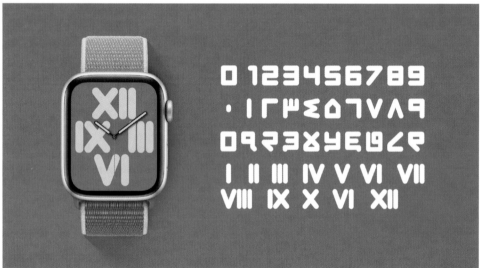

Concept: For our annual "How It Works" issue, we give our readers a concise visual primer on a variety of topics—one per broadsheet page. The challenge here was how to make a visually cohesive issue around an eclectic mix of topics. To do so, we created a compartmentalized design system using our proprietary typefaces. Each page has its own logo created by Francesco Muzzi. The cover type was designed and illustrated by Giacomo Gambineri.

Design
Najeebah Al-Ghadban
and Mia Meredith
New York

Design Direction
Deb Bishop

CreativeTeam
Jessica Tang
and Rory Walsh

Illustration (Cover)
Giacomo Gambineri

Photography (Cover)
Christopher Payne

Creative Direction
Gail Bichler°

Publication
The New York Times
for Kids

Principal Type
NYT Mag Sans

Dimensions
12 x 22 in.
(30.5 × 55.9 cm)

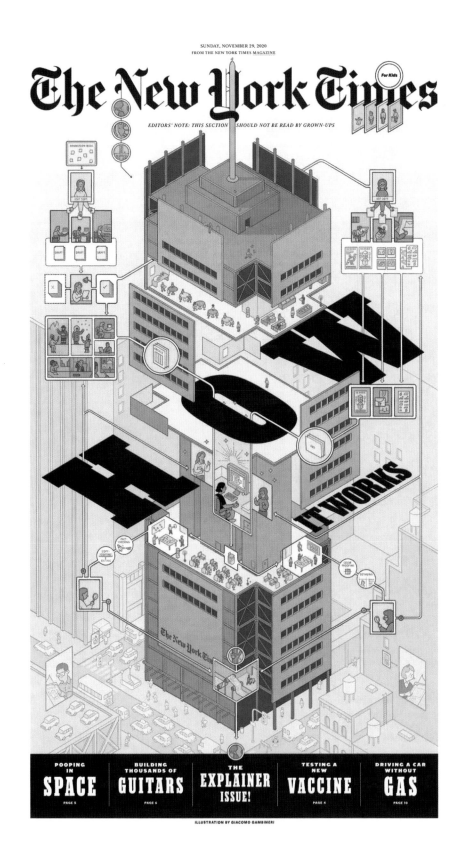

Concept For this special fiction excerpt, we worked with artist Martha Rich to create a variety of typefaces, some cut from paper and some hand-drawn, to illustrate the dark humor and jazz-like quality of James McBride's story.

Design and
Design Direction
Deb Bishop
New York

Illustration
Martha Rich

Creative Direction
Gail Bichler°

Publication
*The New York Times
Magazine Labs*

Principal Type
Handlettered

Dimensions
12 x 22 in.
(30.5 × 55.9 cm)

Concept: Theodore R. Johnson's powerful essay outlines the history of the Black voting bloc in the United States that, for decades, has mostly voted in favor of candidates who best represent a continued fight for their rights. To represent this diverse but ultimately unified voice, we commissioned letterpress artist Amos Kennedy Jr. to create a poster asking and answering one of the main questions put forward in the piece.

Design
Caleb Bennett
New York

Art Direction
Ben Grandgenett

Creative Direction
Gail Bichler°

Typography
Kennedy Prints

Publication
The New York Times Magazine

Principal Type
Assorted WoodType

Dimensions
17.9 x 10.9 in.
(45.4 x 27.6 cm)

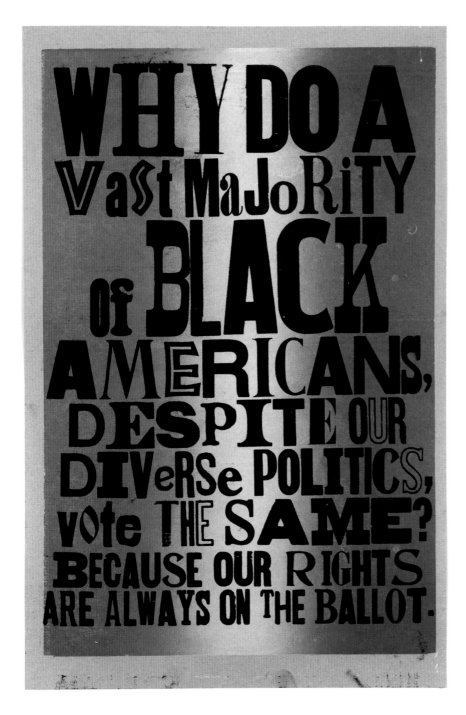

BY THEODORE R. JOHNSON   THE MONOLITH   POSTERS BY KENNEDY PRINTS

Concept: For our special all-fiction issue inspired by Boccaccio's The Decameron, we worked with the artist Sophy Hollington to create a variety of hand-carved linocut typographic elements and illustrations. For the cover, Hollington used a selection of imagery from various stories in the collection combined with hand-drawn typography and a customized masthead to create this beautiful piece packed with meaning. These densely composed pairings of type and image also served as a visual nod to 14th-century illuminated manuscripts.

Design
Rachel Willey
New York

Art Direction
Ben Grandgenett

Creative Direction
Gail Bichler°

Illustrations
Sophy Hollington

Publication
The New York Times Magazine

Principal Type
Handlettering

Dimensions
8.9 x 10.9 in.
(22.7 x 27.6 cm)

Concept: *Uno Due* Vol. 3 captures the vibrance of football through typography and layout moves inspired by the sport.

Creative Direction and Design
Andrea A. Trabucco-Campos and Lorenzo Fanton
Brooklyn, New York

Editor
Matteo Cossu

Client
Uno Due

Principal Type
LL Bradford and Unica77

Dimensions
6.7 × 9.4 in.
(17 x 24 cm)

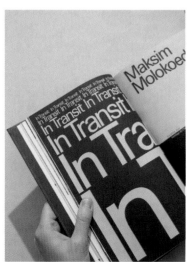

Concept: "Well Done" means good work has been done in the kitchen and the guests are satisfied. Creative, simple cooking and a relaxed approach to the ingredients are the main focus of this magazine. Cooking can and should be fun, which is underlined by the calligraphic, playful use of typography. The handwritten style translates the craft of cooking into graphic design. Taste can enchant and surprise—that's what it's all about.

Art and
Creative Direction
Gerhard
Kirchschläger
Wels, Austria

Illustration
Annie Jen

Photography
Karin Stöttinger

Client
Karin Stöttinger—
Geschmacksmomente

Principal Type
Ogg

Dimensions
8.3 x 12 in.
(21 x 30.5 cm)

Concept: This cover is about Black Hollywood speaking out about underrepresentation and discrimination within the Hollywood system. The cover was inspired by the protest posters from the 1960s civil rights movement. The type is silkscreened onto a board to make it feel authentically like a protest poster.

Creative Direction
Raul Aguila
Los Angeles

Illustration
Annie Jen

Publication
Variety

Principal Type
Graphik Super
and Graphik XXX
Condensed

Dimensions
10.25 x 13.25 in.
(26 x 33.7 cm)

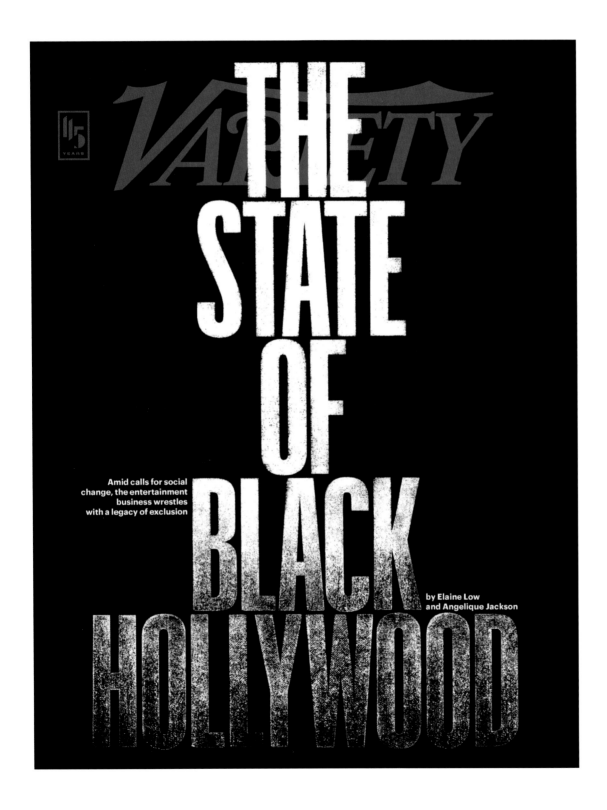

Concept: This is the opener for the "Power of Young Hollywood" (P.O.Y.H.) special issue. P.O.Y.H. showcases the most powerful young talent in Hollywood once a year. The design system includes geometric color-blocking composition integrated with the NB Akademie Pro typeface. The design is bold and graphic, with an organic modern composition for a playful aesthetic.

Art Direction
Haley Kluge
Los Angeles

Creative Direction
Raul Aguila

Publication
Variety

Principal Type
NB Akademie Bold
and
IBM Plex Serif Text

Dimensions
10.25 x 13.25 in.
(26 x 33.7 cm)

Even with the entertainment industry stifled under quarantine, the talent and enthusiasm of youth has a way of breaking loose. So far this year, Megan Thee Stallion scored her first No. 1 hit with the raucous "Savage." Maluma continued to establish himself as the standard-bearer for Latin music. And Shira Haas lit up the internet — and received her first Emmy nod — for "Unorthodox."

These stars — along with other young performers and innovators changing the game — would normally be attending our annual Power of Young Hollywood party. But this year, *Variety* has partnered with Facebook to produce a one-hour program benefiting Rock the Vote. Tune in to Facebook on Aug. 6 at 6 p.m. PT to see our honorees answer fan questions, deliver musical performances and more. Safely socially distanced, they'll be bridging the gap with their talent.

Concept: This is the feature opener for *Variety's* profile on David Fincher and the making of his film Mank. We commissioned a charcoal portrait by artist Dylan Andrews. The portrait contrasts with the bold typographic design for the opener. The typeface is the Sohne Collection from Klim Type Foundry.

Creative Direction
Raul Aguila
Los Angeles

Publication
Variety

Principal Type
Söhne Breit Extrafett,
Söhne Breit Fett, and
Söhne Schmal Buch

Dimensions
20.5 x 13.25 in.
(52.1 x 33.7 cm)

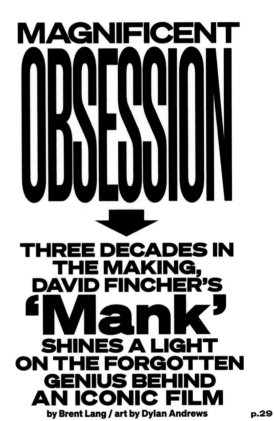

MAGNIFICENT
OBSESSION

THREE DECADES IN
THE MAKING,
DAVID FINCHER'S
'Mank'
SHINES A LIGHT
ON THE FORGOTTEN
GENIUS BEHIND
AN ICONIC FILM
by Brent Lang / art by Dylan Andrews   p.29

Concept: This data visualization documents life during the COVID-19 pandemic lockdown.

Design
Giorgia Lupi
New York

Producer
Phillip Cox

Client
The New York Times

Design Firm
Pentagram Design
New York

Dimensions
11.6 x 16.75 in.
(29.5 x 42.5 cm)

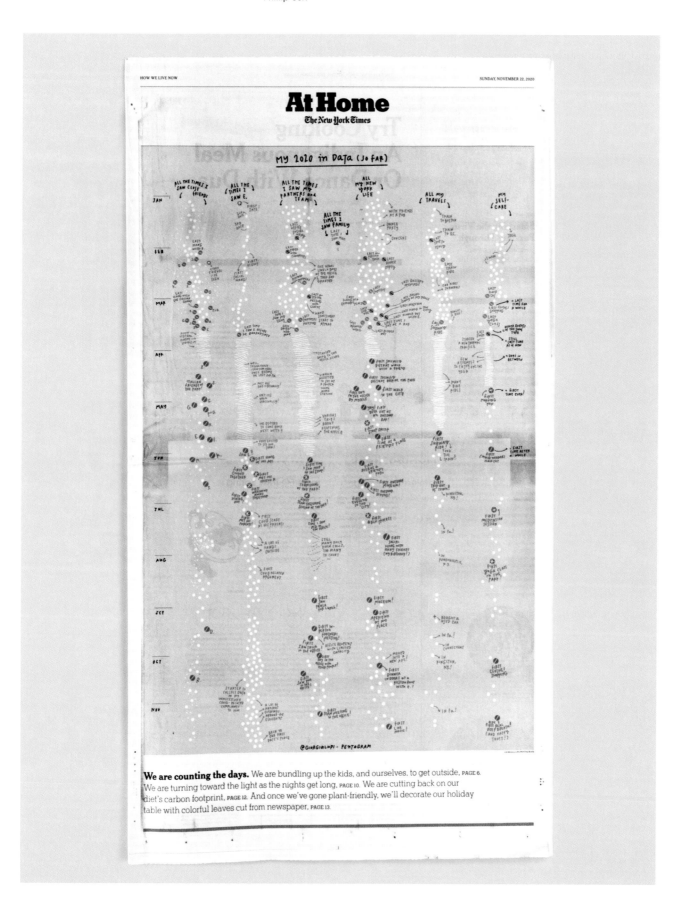

Concept: For the annual exhibition program, individual sheets make up an unbound booklet, leading to surprising typographic and pictorial combinations. Each exhibition is featured on a single sheet, with the title of the show on the front and the corresponding image on the back. The sheets can be recomposed individually as well as taken out as mini posters. In addition, the unbound booklet responds to the COVID-19 pandemic: The realization of an upcoming exhibition is still loose and uncertain, yet the museum is present, providing bold images to its audience.

Design Studio
TGG Hafen
Senn Stieger
St. Gallen,
Switzerland

Client
Kunstmuseum

Principal Type
ABC Whyte

Dimensions
5.8 × 8.3 in.
(14.8 x 21 cm)

Concept: The "I Am a Man" poster inspired this design about the civil rights advocacy company Color of Change.

Art Direction
Chelsea Schiff
New York

Creative Direction
Mike Schnaidt

Director of
Photography
Jeanne Graves

Associate Photo
Editor
Daisy Korpics

Photography
Dee Dwyer

Publication
Fast Company

Principal Type
A2 Beckett and
Centra

Dimensions
16 x 10.5 in.
(40.6 x 26.7 cm)

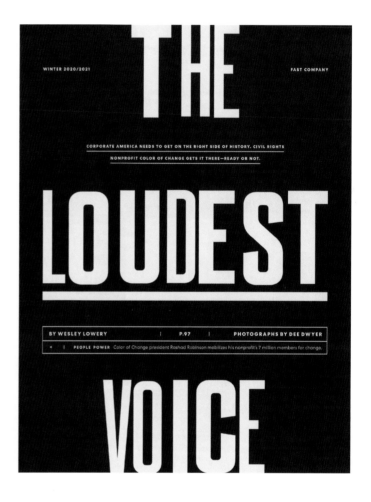

EDITORIAL: The Loudest Voice

Concept: The "I Am a Man" poster inspired this design about the civil rights advocacy company Color of Change.

Concept: This editorial is one part typographic solution, one part data visualization.

Art Direction
Chelsea Schiff
New York

Creative Direction
Mike Schnaidt

Publication
Fast Company

Principal Type
Voyage

Dimensions
10.5 x 16 in.
(26.7 x 40.6 cm)

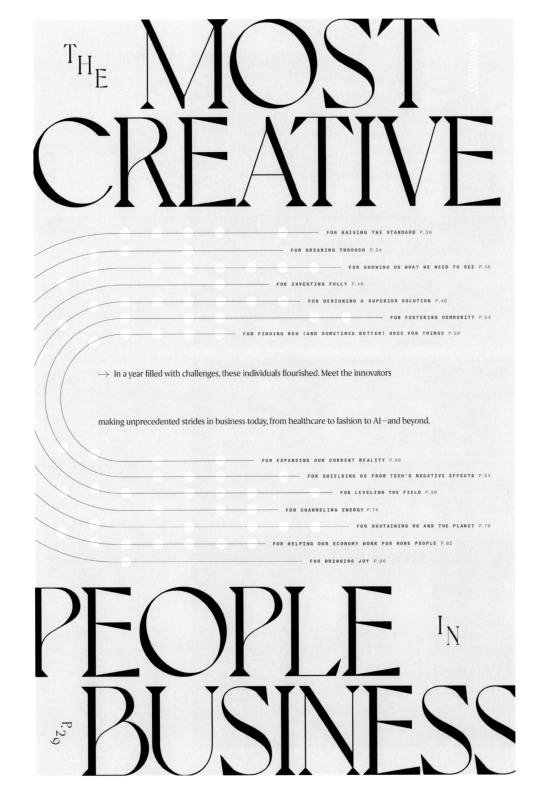

THE MOST
CREATIVE

FOR RAISING THE STANDARD P.30
FOR BREAKING THROUGH P.34
FOR SHOWING US WHAT WE NEED TO SEE P.38
FOR INVESTING FULLY P.46
FOR DESIGNING A SUPERIOR SOLUTION P.48
FOR FOSTERING COMMUNITY P.54
FOR FINDING NEW (AND SOMETIMES BETTER) USES FOR THINGS P.56

→ In a year filled with challenges, these individuals flourished. Meet the innovators

making unprecedented strides in business today, from healthcare to fashion to AI—and beyond.

FOR EXPANDING OUR CURRENT REALITY P.60
FOR SHIELDING US FROM TECH'S NEGATIVE EFFECTS P.64
FOR LEVELING THE FIELD P.68
FOR CHANNELING ENERGY P.74
FOR SUSTAINING US AND THE PLANET P.78
FOR HELPING OUR ECONOMY WORK FOR MORE PEOPLE P.82
FOR BRINGING JOY P.86

PEOPLE IN
BUSINESS

P.29

Concept: *RdV Black Book* is a magazine created to elevate the brand of a boutique American vineyard. Located in a relatively unknown wine-producing region, the vineyard needed a way to reach and persuade its audience, convey its luxury status, and mark itself as a serious contender in the wine world. Through design, stories, and images, the publication distills the essence of RdV—polished yet down to earth, with a reverence for old-world tradition and an adventurous American spirit.

Creative Direction
Marco Javier
Washington, D.C.

Editor
Lauren Hassani

Client
RdV Vineyards

Studio
Ultra Studio

Principal Type
Aktiv Grotesk,
Le Monde Livre,
Orpheus Pro, and
Plaak 1 Sathonay

Dimensions
9.9 x 14 in.
(25 x 35.5 cm)

Art Direction
Johannes Spitzer

Creative Direction
Sascha Lobe

Client
Architectural
Association School
of Architecture,
London

Design Firm
Pentagram Design
Ltd.

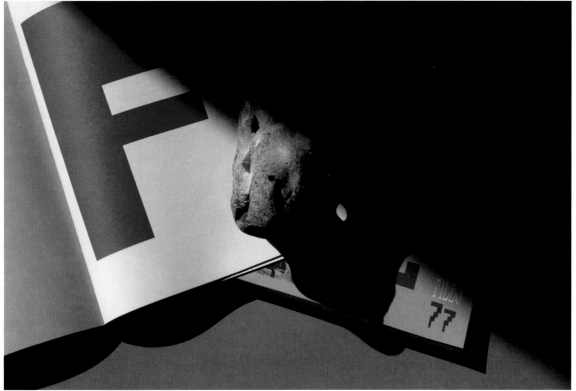

Kunsthaus Zürich Signage

Concept This is the wayfinding system for the Kunstmuseum Zürich.

Art Direction
Marvin Boik
and Oliver Wörle

Creative Direction
Sascha Lobe

Design Firms
L2M3 and
Pentagram London

Client
Kunsthaus Zürich

Principal Type
DIN Mittelschrift

Concept: Large white letters on the walls of this pool and wellness center in the heart of Salzburg'ßs old city pave the way to the sauna, therapy facilities, and pool. The 3D letters are arranged in their own rhythmical wave patterns, as if gently in motion, referencing not just the water itself but also the building's architectural showpiece: the stunning wave-shaped roof that extends over the pool and offers magnificent views out over the undulating rooftops of the skyline.

Chief Creative Officers
Carolin Himmel and Andreas Uebele°
Stuttgart

Studio
büro uebele visuelle kommunikation

Client
Stadt Salzbur
Immobilien GmbH

Principal Type
GT America

Concept: This is about the duality of finding new energy and motivation while accepting the status quo..

Studio
Appear Offline

URL
appear-offline.com

Principal Type
Arial and
EB Garamond

Dimensions
19.7 x 27.6 in.
(50 × 70 cm)

"THE ART OF DOING NOTHING"
WHAT TO DO WHEN THERE'S NOTHING TO DO?
MARCH — 2020

Concept: Braille Dingbats, where braille meets emoticons, is an emoticon addition to the Braille alphabet in a nine-dot grid. People who are using the Braille language are forced to use the 26-letter alphabet to describe their emotions. This insight became a starting point for setting up an experimental addition to the existing Braille alphabet, based on our emoticons, converted into a "dot" language that characterizes Braille. Braille Dingbats tries to build a bridge to visual language for the visually impaired. It's designed as a typographical experiment, with 22 of the most common emoticons translated into this "new" Braille grid.

Design
Walda Verbaenen
Holsbeek, Belgium

URL
walda.be

Principal Type
Braille alphabet with
nine-dot addition;
overview alphabet
and emoticons: Braille
Dingbats and PT Sans

Dimensions
19.7 x 27.6 in
(50 × 70 cm)

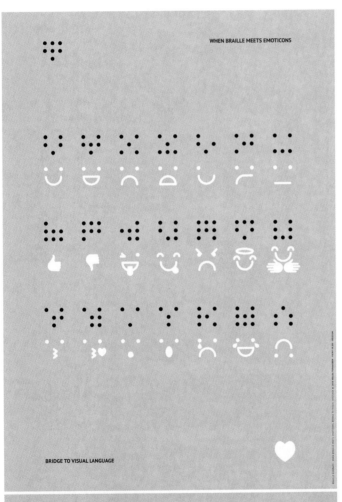

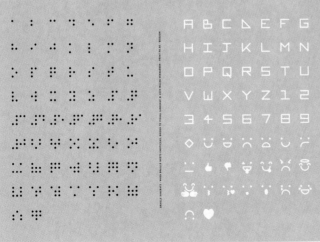

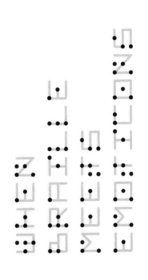

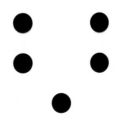

Concept: This "uncreative" and "unoriginal" publication reflects on technology's growing control on daily life, which has been further emphasized through the stay-at-home response to the COVID-19 pandemic. Through use of a series of poems, it aims to explore the nexus of privacy and the vulnerability of information. The poems were written by remixing user reviews, news headlines, and terms and conditions of digital conference platforms such as Zoom—all while keeping in mind the concepts of appropriation, processing, reconstruction, recycling, and intentional plagiarism.

Design
Rommina Dolorier
London

Principal Type
Lausanne Concept

Concept: This is a paradox that answers the question "What's wrong with the world?" as part of the Protest! Exhibition.

Design
Abraham Lule°
New York

Principal Type
Halogen Bold

Dimensions
42 x 30 in.
(106.7 × 76.2 cm)

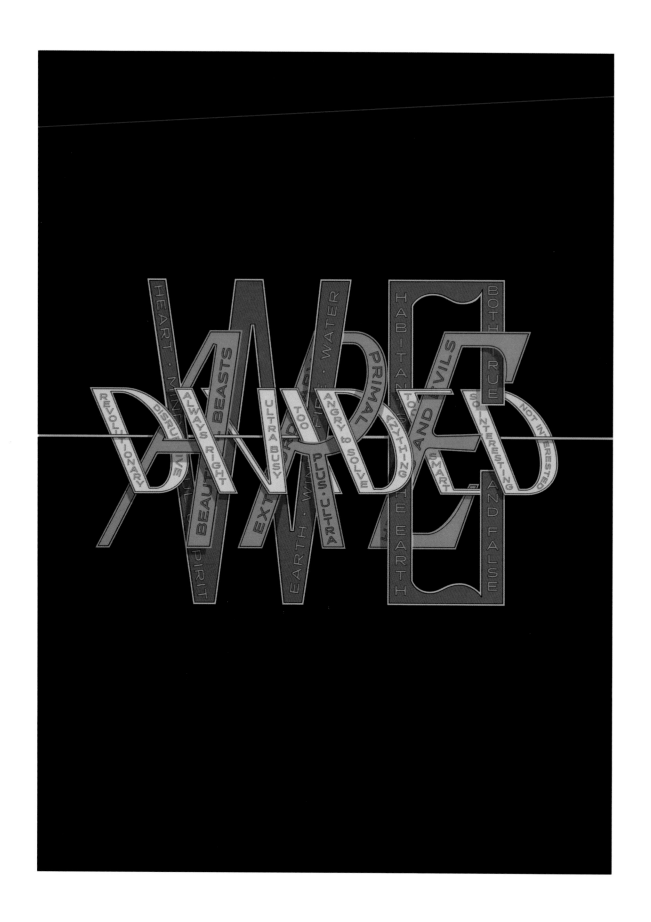

Concept: This experimental project was aimed at consumerism. Instead of positioning myself in the subjective perspective to criticize modern consumerism like everyone else, I chose to visualize months' worth of my purchase receipts and organically combine them with my purchase experience as a Chinese person living in the United States, in order to present how consumerism in this country has impacted me.

Design
Ruichao Chen
Brooklyn, New York

Instructor
Maria Gracia
Echeverria

School
Pratt Institute

Principal Type
Dhama Gothic,
Monument
Extended, and
Source Han Sans
Bold

Concept This letter drawing project incorporates programming and choreographic notation.

Design
Goeun Park
Seoul
Wei-Hao Wang
Taipei

Principal Type
Body Type (custom)

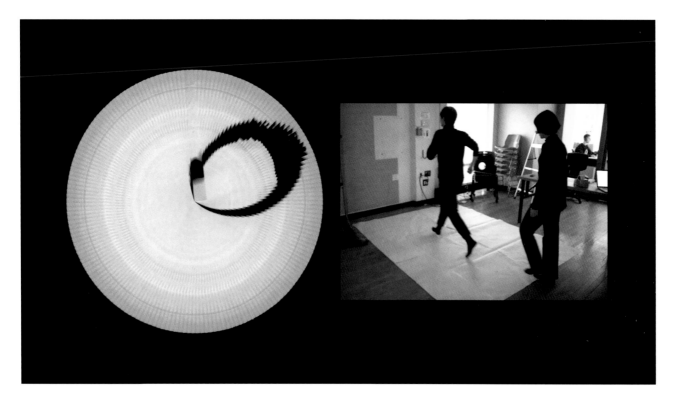

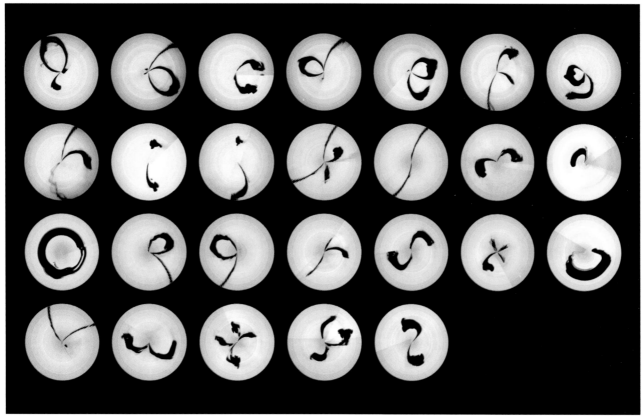

Concept: The Ampersand Series explores different ampersand shapes by playing with optical dimensions over hand-drawn forms.

Design
Bianca Dumitrascu
Bucharest

Concept: We created Hopersand as a symbol of solidarity during the COVID-19 pandemic.

Art Direction
Yana Ee
Singapore

Creative Direction
Jun Teo

Studio
Büro UFHO

Principal Type
Custom

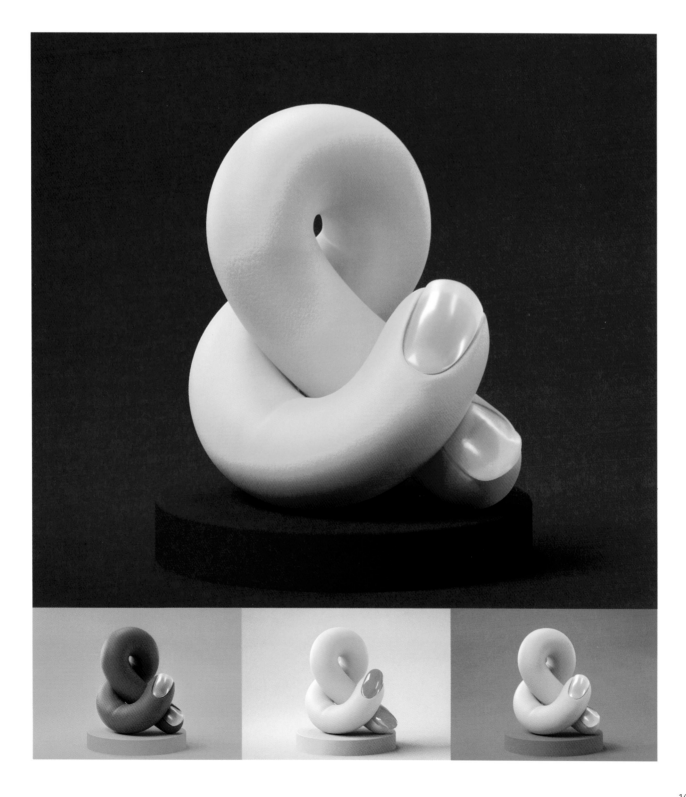

Concept: Resilience Type aims to be versatile and adaptable into different forms and treatments.

Art Direction
Yana Ee
Singapore

Creative Direction
Jun Teo

Studio
Büro UFHO

Principal Type
Custom

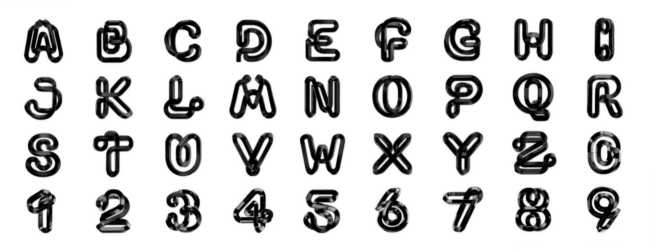

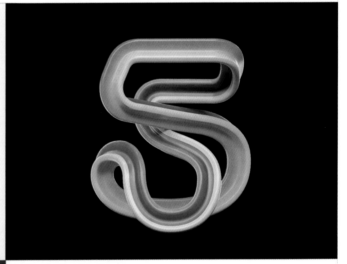

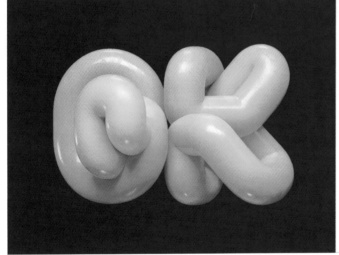

Concept: Full of ligatures and curly lines, these little typography monsters are my "Type Beast," despite their beauty.

Design
kissmiklos
(Miklós Kiss)
Budapest

URL
kissmiklos.com

Principal Type
Custom

Concept: This visual identity interprets the UIUC's 2020 MFA curriculum as a primary shape-based design system.

Creative Direction
JP Ramirez
Crockett, California

Programmer
Bryant Smith

User Interface
Design
Andrew Reaume

Studio
JP Ramirez Studio

Client
University of Illinois
School of Art + Design

Principal Type
GT Eesti and Custom
display face

Dimensions
Various

Concept: Tank Arts Festival is one of the biggest art festivals in China.

Design
Yihe Wang
Shanghai

Art Direction
Roger Lo

Creative Direction
Dorothy Wang°

Agency
x1000 Company

Client
Tank Shanghai

Principal Type
DIN Pro,
Noto Sans,
and custom

Concept: XTAD company is a visual design service provider.

Design
Yanqing Sun

Art Direction
Guosheng Lin

Editor
Tingting Wang

Client
XTAD (象渡)

Agency
K-INGO (开眼壹果)

Principal Type
Source Han Sans
(Adobe)

Dimensions
11.7 × 8.3 in.
(29.7 × 21 cm)

Concept: With the theme of Post-Information Era, this Chinese character designing event includes a forum and an exhibition. Not only do Chinese characters represent the traditions, but they also bear the future of the Chinese culture. With the advent of the post-information era, Chinese characters are facing a new innovation of visual expression. The identity design of this activity echoes such an attempt. It highlights the role of Chinese characters in a multilingual environment. On the other hand, it emphasizes the characteristics of information superposition and programming in the post-information era.

Design
Tian Bo
Guangzhou

Studio
TEN BUTTONS

Client
Ihsoat Creative Lab

Principal Type
HYQiHei and
Neue Machina

Dimensions
Various

Concept: A set of 3D fonts was designed based on a closed circle. Applying transparent material on the letters allows it to reflect and shine into neon color, which brings youthfulness and playfulness into the design. The four letters of "GAFA" represent "Guangzhou Academy of Fine Arts." The letters were paired in twos and layered together to create an illusion that interfered and merged.

Design
Tian Bo
Guangzhou

Studio
TEN BUTTONS

Client
Guangzhou Academy
of Fine Arts

Principal Type
Neue Machina
and custom

Concept: The identity uses a unit system as an optical sequence, and the Future Format pairs create a unique language.

Design
Jack Hands,
Dimitris Koliadimas,
and George Sartzis
Thessaloniki, Greece

Photography
Stefanos Tsakiris

Creative Direction
Dimitris Koliadimas

Typographer
MuirMcNeil

URL
semiotikdesign.com

Instagram
@semiotik_Design

Design Agency
Semiotik Design
Agency

Client
Future Format

Principal Type
FourPoint
type system

Concept: How is attention generated? Be bold, colorful, and strong—the 2020 edition of the c/o pop Festival.

Design
Laurent Patz,
Pit Stenkhoff, and
Katerina Trakakis
Berlin

Design Studio
Neue Gestaltung
GmbH

Client
cologne on pop

Principal Type
Boogie School
Sans and Whyte

Concept: The logo is always used to extend the application in a multidimensional and dynamic way through the whole image.

Design
Zhenxing Shi
Beijing

Creative Direction
Guanru Li

Client
Jetlag Books

Branding Company
L3branding

Principal Type
Custom

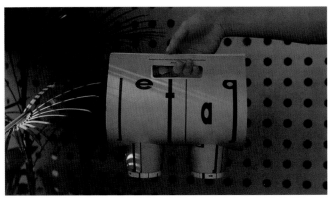

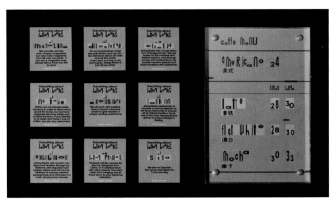

Concept: Inspired by American ephemera and beverage canning, Palmer uses expressive and illustrative typography.

Kevin Cantrell
Mantua, Utah

Typography
Kevin Cantrell and
Andrei Robu

Content Strategist
Erik Attkisson

Client
Palmer Beverage
Systems

Studio
Kevin Cantrell Studio

Principal Type
Amplitude,
Palmer Sans
(custom),
Palmer Script
(custom), and
Tabac Slab

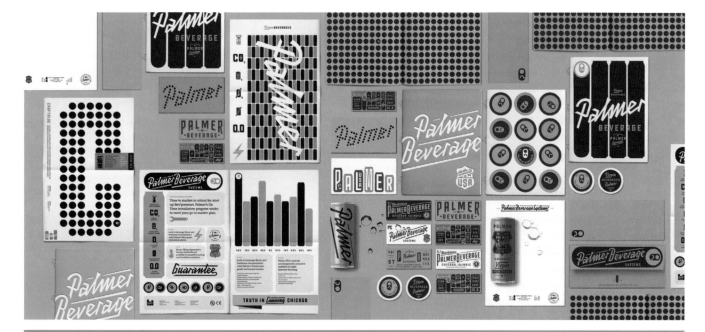

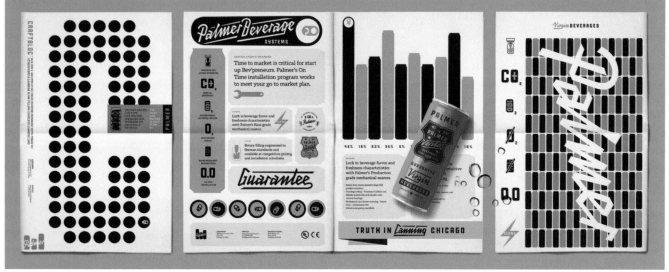

Concept: Intricate engravings and type blended with overlapping wave patterns suggest perpetual economic growth.

Creative Direction
Kevin Cantrell
Mantua, Utah

Client
Profi

Studio
Kevin Cantrell Studio

Principal Type
Farnham,
Flama, and
Profi Display
(custom)

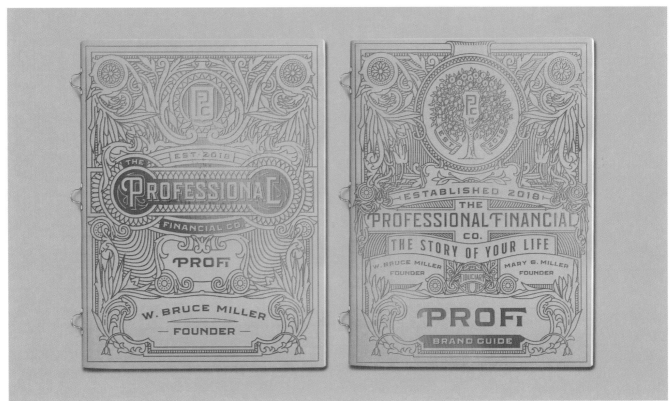

Concept: The Château Grande Hotel identity plays off the word "grande" and features bold crops of the logotype.

Design
Miguel Cano
Mantua, Utah

Creative Direction
Kevin Cantrell

Typography
Kevin Cantrell and
Andrei Robu

Content Strategist
Erik Attkisson

Client
The Château
Grande Hotel

Studio
Kevin Cantrell Studio

Principal Type
Château
Grande Display
(custom),
Chronicle Deck,
and Metric

Concept: The idea was to capture the cultural energy of the theater through expressive typography, color, and layering.

Design
Javier Arizu
and
Andrea A.
Trabucco-Campos
Brooklyn, New York

Design Firm
Pràctica

Studio
Andrea A.
Trabucco-Campos

Client
Irvington Theater

Principal Type
Irvington Modern
Gothic and
Pyte Legacy

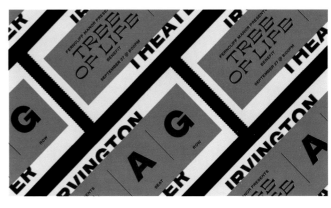

Concept: This is a visual identity for an exhibition and benefit at the Storefront for Art and Architecture in New York.

Design
Jonathan Katav and
John Sampson

Product Manager
Veronica Hoglund

Creative Direction
Natasha Jen

Client
Storefront for Art
and Architecture

Design Firm
Pentagram Design
New York

Principal Type
Balloon, Coign, and
Druk

Dimensions
Various

Concept: Utilitarian identity using one weight of Untitled Sans provides a neutral framework to showcase innovative work.

Creative Direction
and Design
Andrea A.
Trabucco-Campos
Brooklyn, New York

Driving Force
Adam S. Wahler

Production Director
Johnny Cruz

Web Developer
Chris Corby

Studio
Andrea A.
Trabucco-Campos

Photography
William Mullan

Client
A2A Studio

Principal Type
Untitled Sans

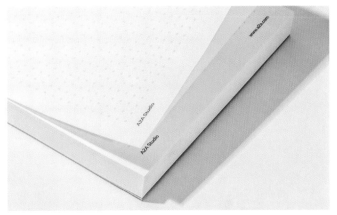

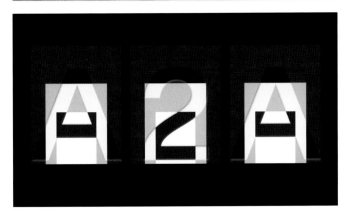

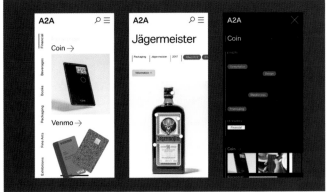

Concept: This is the brand identity framework, editorial design, and website for this journal of liberal opinion.

Design
Lindsay Ballant,
Jack Collins,
Leo Field,
Xinle Huang,
Steven Merenda,
and Siung Tjia
New York

Illustration
Daniel Stolle

Editing
Chris Lehmann

Editor-in-Chief
Win McCormack

Editorial Director
Emily Cooke

Creative Direction
Eddie Opara

Client
The New Republic

Design Firm
Pentagram Design
New York

Principal Type
Eksell Display, Fakt,
IKANSEEYOUALL,
Stadt, and Tiempos

Dimensions
8 x 10.5 in.
(20.3 x 26.7 cm)

Concept: Roger&Sons, next-generation carpenters, wanted a new identity to disrupt their traditional business.

Design
Huinee Lim
Singapore

Creative and Art
Direction
Yah-Leng Yu

Client
Roger&Sons

Design Firm
Foreign Policy
Design Group

Principal Type
GT America and gc16

Concept: This is a branding system referencing roofs of the different homes curated for the co-living brand Figment.

Design
Dandy Hartono,
Jiani Lu, and
Celsy Sabilla
Singapore

Creative Direction
Yah-Leng Yu

Design Firm
Foreign Policy
Design Group

Client
Figment

Principal Type
Mazius Display Regular
and Sharp Grotesk

Concept: Design Pasar is about bringing design, craft, and arts to the hood and sticking together as a community.

Design
Dandy Hartono
and Sylvester Tan
Singapore

Creative and
Art Direction
Yah-Leng Yu

DesignFirm
Foreign Policy
Design Group

Client
Design Pasar

Principal Type
Becker Gothics,
Egyptian Rounded,
and Gosha Sans

Concept: This distinctive brand identity and design system reflects a unique cinematic experience for a visionary film festival with a rich history.

Design
Stephan Bender,
Mareike Nollert, and
Anja Schneider
Mannheim, Germany

Art Direction
Andrea Herrmann

Creative Direction
Stephan Bender and
Simon Daubermann°

Client
International
Film Festival
Mannheim-
Heidelberg

Design Firm
DAUBERMANN GmbH

Principal Type
Swiss Int'l Mono
and
Titling Gothic

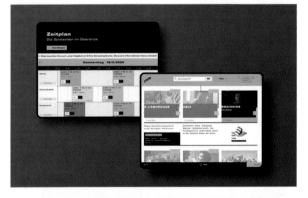

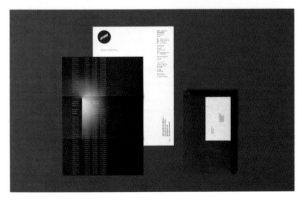

Concept: Based on "Diversity breeds," a dynamic visual identity was created by means of a bespoke program.

Design Studio
Studio Dumbar
Rotterdam

Client
Cumulus Park

Principal Type
Felix and Media Sans

Concept: D&AD's Imagine Everything festival identity celebrates the vast potential of creativity.

Design Studio
Studio Dumbar
Rotterdam

Client
D&AD

Principal Type
Marfa

Concept: Sweety Ripple is a new brand of tea drinks, and its main product is fresh fruit tea. In the visual design of brand, I expressed the core points of brand promotion, such as ripple, satisfaction, and fresh. There is no logo in the traditional sense in the visual design of Sweety Ripple. I combined information, expression Illustrations, and pictures in a wavy format, open and rich, which constitutes a unique brand visual memory point.

Art Direction
Siguang Wu

Studio
HDU23 Lab
Wuxi, China

Client
Sweety Ripple

Principal Type
Alibaba-
PuHuiTi Bold
and Univers LT
Std 65 Bold

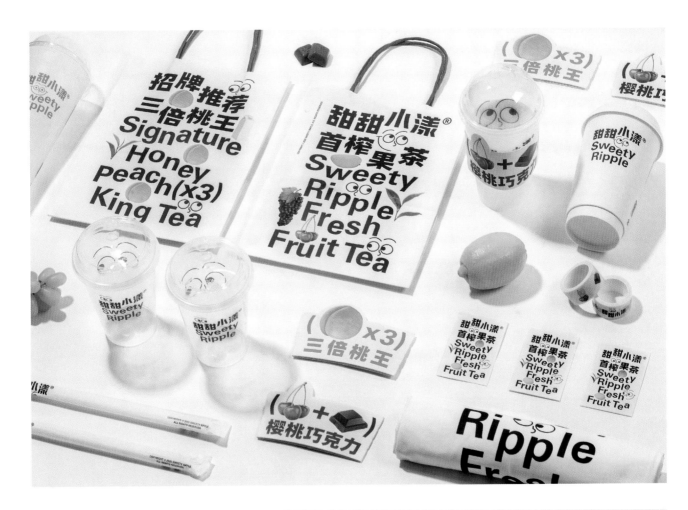

Concept: The fluorescent pink line brings out the stroke of a Chinese character "坐"(sit), new blood for the chair's next generation. The font is custom-made; the extending structure looks like the surface of the seat, creating the imagination of Sit Down Please. By presenting the characteristics of the physical exhibition in the leaflet, the low-cost but effective design gives visitors the space for their own creation.

Art Direction
Tunghung Tsai
New Taipei City

Creative Direction
Hsiuchun Hsu

Client
Taiwan Design
Research Institute

Design Firm
adj. everything

Principal Type
Helvetica and
Noto Sans CJK
TC

Concept: This visual identity for Cannibal, a content and media shop in New York City and Los Angeles, disrupts cultural narratives.

Design
Phil Gibson and
Joshua Lepley
New York

Sound Design
Seth Olinsky

Creative Direction
Joshua Lepley

Client
Cannibal

Design Studio
M M NT

Principal Type
Robert Bold

Concept: This is a visual universe for Mack & Pouya, a wedding photography brand.

Art Direction
and Illustration
Nubia Navarro
Bogotá

Digital Agency
Timothy Ricks

User Interface
Design
Timothy Ricks

Production Company
Pouya Nia

Client
Mack & Pouya
Photography

Studio
Nubia Navarro

Principal Type
Anybody
Variable and
Gulfs Display

172

Concept: Heidi Hackemer approached Studio HMVD as she was launching a new evolution of her strategy practice, Zwolf. Building on many years of industry-leading experience, she needed a brand that matched her wicked smart approach and packed a powerful visual punch. Zwolf translates to the number 12 in German (Heidi's lucky number), which was a point of inspiration for both the brand mark as well as the 12-column grid. The complexity of her work sparked the idea of "magic tensions," which informed visual aspects, including color, shape, and texture.

Creative Team
Heather-Mariah Dixon
and Abigail Kerns
Brooklyn, New York

Studio
Studio HMVD

Client
Zwolf Strategy

Principal Type
LL Bradford Regular, Druk Wide Medium, and Portrait Condensed Bold

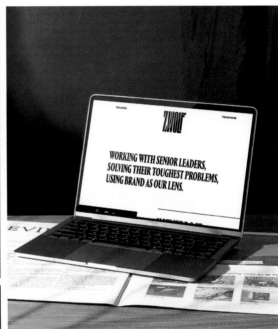

ZWOLF IS SOPHISTICATED & FERAL. WORKING IN THE WHITE HOUSEWITH A HALF-SHAVED HEAD. ORDERING TWO SHOTS OF MACALLAN 12. THERE'S A WILLINGNESS TO JUST FUCKING GO THERE— WITH A PURPOSE.

Concept: Founder Namu Park came to Studio HMVD to brand her sustainable fashion resale platform, The Sloth. We built a comprehensive identity over a two-week sprint, giving Namu the power to launch and grow. Merging the worlds of high fashion and slow fashion, nature and the machine, we paired luxe typography with a fresh color palette and structured lines with natural textures and settings. Our four-part logo system is flexible and modular, suiting the various applications in which The Sloth appears: packaging, app, website, and social.

Creative Team
Heather-Mariah Dixon
and Abigail Kerns
Brooklyn, New York

Studio
Studio HMVD

Client
The Sloth

Principal Type
GT Alpina,
Bianco Sans,
and
Oroban Masuria

Concept ACX's new visual identity embraces creative growth through play and the modular nature of its offerings.

Design
Matt Adams
and Alex Seth
Pasadena, California

Art Direction
Winnie Li

Writer
Solvej Schou

Editor
Mike Winder

Creative Team
Audrey Krauss

Creative Direction
Scott Taylor

Client
ArtCenter College
of Design

Principal Type
ACX-Mixed,
MGD Rotter,
and Neue Haas
Grotesk

Concept: LUUX is a Swiss company founded by two women, Valeria and Virginia (U = V in latin). "Lux" means "light."

Design
Miklós Kiss
Budapest

Client
LUUX SA

Principal Type
Brice and custom

Concept: Forever Young juxtaposes masterpieces of pop art with pop type to celebrate Museum Brandhorst's 10-year anniversary.

Design
Johanna Wenger
Stuttgart

Art Direction
Jonas Beuchert,
Nam Huynh, and
Tilman Schlevogt

Agency
PARAT.cc

Client
Museum Brandhorst

Principal Type
GT America
and custom

Concept: This is the brand identity for Sandbox Films, a science documentary film studio.

Design
Joe Haddad
and Lauren King
New York

Photography
Jack Nesbitt

Creative Direction
Lauren King

Client
Sandbox Films

Agency
GrandArmy

Concept: The typography was the protagonist chosen to celebrate diversity of the many Brazils we have.

Design
Alexandre Baltazar, Julia Custodio, and Daniel Escudeiro
Rio de Janeiro

Typography
Daniel Escudeiro, Carlos Mignot, and Rodrigo Saiani

Animation
Paulo Caetano

Production Company
Plau

In-House Agency
Marca e Comunicação Globo

Executive Creative Direction
Ricardo Bezerra

Chief Creative Officer
Fred Gelli

Design Firm
Tátil Design

Client
Canal Brasil

Principal Type
Canal Brasil VF and
Sharp Grotesk

Concept: This is a brand identity created by the movement of a wheat grain mill—a modern way of representing the baking tradition.

Design
Migue Martí
and Javi Tortosa
Valencia, Spain

Studio
democràcia estudiò

Client
Mòlt. Bakery

Principal Type
LA Nord

Concept: Designing a Better Chicago is an annual celebration that shines a light on the extraordinary impact of design on civic life. Together with theMART, NeoCon, DCASE, and the Design Museum of Chicago, we developed a thoroughly contemporary system that is deeply rooted in Chicago's history of design excellence. To develop the logo, we discovered inspiration in the overlooked—Chicago's municipal device. An iconic symbol that hides in plain sight throughout the city, it references the 19th-century engineering feat of reversing the flow of the Chicago River. The linear forms provide a pared-down yet meaningful foundation for the entire visual system.

Design
Dean Sweetnich
Chicago

Creative Direction
Will Miller

Clients
theMART
and NeoCon

Studio
Firebelly Design

Principal Type
Telegraf

Dimensions
Various

Crane has made paper for 250 years. Stephen Crane purchased the Liberty Paper Mill in Dalton, Massachusetts, establishing the business in 1770. Paul Revere chose Crane paper for the first currency of the American colonies, and Crane pioneered anticounterfeit measures with complex, embellished engravings. At the turn of the century, a push against the mechanization of humanity was taking place: The Art Nouveau movement was influencing Crane's paper products, and it inspired a new tactile experience within Crane's current evolution to revitalize their brand, reboot their digital presence, and develop a relevant voice.

Design
Jump Jirakaweekul,
Tomas Markevicius,
and Camille Sauvé
New York

Art Direction
Theo Livaudais

Creative Direction
Nick Ace

Writer
Tom Elia

Photography
Mari Juliano

Typography
Jacob Wise

Content Strategists
Shazeeda Bhola,
Gena Cuba, and
Elizabeth Talerman

Agencies
COLLINS and
The Nucleus Group

Client
Crane

Principal Type
Monarch
and Whtye

Concept: Robinhood, one of the fastest growing brokerages in history, believes everyone, not just the affluent, should have clear, accessible pathways to wealth creation—the creation of a better future. We were invited to help define the brand strategy and its expression for Robinhood to forge this future. Our insight? Don't just make finance "less difficult." Make finance more engaging and understandable, unlike anybody else. Imaginative illustrations and information graphics aim to evoke and instruct. Visual metaphors translate ETFs, fractional shares, and even the American dream into relatable concepts. An educational ethos is articulated across the product ecosystem.

Design
Daniel Haire,
L. A. Hall,
Yeun Kim, Elaine Lin,
Mackenzie Pringle,
and Erik Vaage

Creative Direction
Zane Bevan,
Ben Crick,
Karin Soukup, and
Robert Thompson

Illustrations
Matias Basla,
Liam Cobb,
Jaedoo Lee,
and Ilya Milstein

Animation
Victor Bivol
and Drew Nelson

Producer
Victoria Thomas

Content Strategists
Taamrat Amaize
and Anjelica Triola

Client
Robinhood

Agencies
COLLINS
and Robinhood

Principal Type
Capsule and Nib

To *invest* is to imagine a brighter future & in doing so, take the *first step* towards it.

Concept: Primary is a go-to children's line of high-quality staples parents can rely on and kids feel comfortable in. They make clothing categorized by "baby" and "kids" (not "boys" and "girls"). Freed from labels, kids live bolder, brighter lives. This springboard led to an evolution of the identity, drawing inspiration from the arc of light in a sunrise to radiate this vibrance. We developed The Primaries, a curious cast of typographic characters with playful energy. Our new tagline, "Live your true colors," articulates Primary's mission—encouraging every kid to be the most full-volume, full-colored versions of themselves.

Design
Jump Jirakaweekul
and
George Lavender

Creative Direction
Thomas Wilder

Animation
Tomas Markevicius
and Eric Park

Writer
Madeleine Carrucan

Content Strategist
Dashiell Alison

Agency
COLLINS

Client
Primary

Principal Type
GT Alpine

Concept: As founder Ev Williams said after the platform launched, "The ethos behind Medium is one of openness and democracy—like the internet itself." Since its founding, Medium has pursued that mission, acting as a counterbalance to the downward spiral of online discourse. This evolution of Medium's website encourages deeper relationships between readers and writers—a place for ideas to be challenged and flourish. Typographic illustrations throughout the site aim to bring readers and writers into discourse. Language becomes a tool for Medium to engage in conversation and speak in service of the great minds on the web platform.

Design
George Lavender,
Andy Liang,
Sidney Lim, and
Diego Segura

Creative Direction
Nick Ace

Writer
Tom Elia

Photography
Mari Juliano

Animation
Tomas Markevicius
and Eric Park

Content Strategists
Matt Kuzelka and
Allison Solomson

Agency
COLLINS

Client
Medium

Principal Type
Söhne and
GT Super

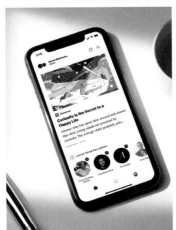

Concept: Kalevala Jewelry, a Finnish jewelry brand from 1937, wanted to reimagine their brand as part of a major strategy renewal. The challenge was to create a modern brand identity that respects the company's history and heritage while guiding the company to a new era. The new Kalevala brand plays with the contrast between a modern, simple look and the rich, mystical world of the Finnish national epic The Kalevala, compiled by Elias Lönnrot in the 19th century. The visual identity of the new Kalevala is built around the recognizable and confident logo—respecting the past, ready for the future.

Design
Jesper Bange,
Teo Georgiev,
and Kevin Hytönen
Helsinki

Photography
Paavo Lehtonen

Typography
Teo Tuominen

Content Strategists
Nils Kajander
and Martin Mohr

Agency Producers
Juulia Järvi
and Piia Suhonen

Creative Team
Marko Rantanen

Client
Kalevala Jewelry

Agency
BOND

Principal Type
Kalevala and
Studio Feixen
Sans Serif

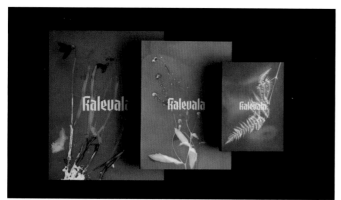

Concept: Yegor Gaidar Foundation's virtual academic project Gaid University looks to hold free, online expert tutorials across Russia regarding the contemporary economic and social science scene—hoping to be as accessible, publicly fruitful, and popular as possible. The system incorporates a dynamic set of shapes, collating a system that has two functions: to organize space on paper and to formulate interesting compositions through the use of rulers. The shapes themselves pay homage to the tables, diagrams, and graphics found within the university and economic setting, without the result being so restricting.

Creative Direction
Nastya Vishnyakova
and
Svyat Vishnyakov
New York

Client
Egor Gaidar
Foundation

Agency
Electric Red

Principal Type
Soyuz Grotesk

Creative Team
Droga5
Design Department
New York

Design Firm
Droga5

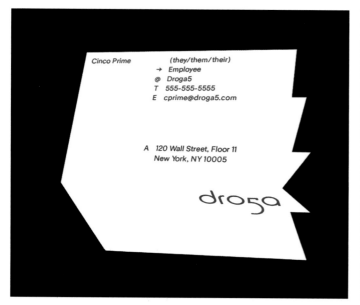

THIN
LIGHT
REGULAR
MEDIUM
BOLD

Drotesk No5

Sphinx of black and blue quartz, judge my vow.

abcdefghijklmnopqrstuvwxyz
ABCDEFGHIJKLMNOPQRSTUV
WXYZ ///// 0123456789

Concept: Ampey is a Beijing-based fashion brand committed to creating innovative footwear and accessories that evolve with the urban lifestyle. Through the use of an airy and imaginary typography system, along with a high-contrast color combination, we intended to bring out the freshness and simplicity of the brand.

Art Direction
Zifei Li
Shanghai

Creative Direction
Kekfeng Lee

Studio
KAUKAU

Client
Ampey

Principal Type
Circular

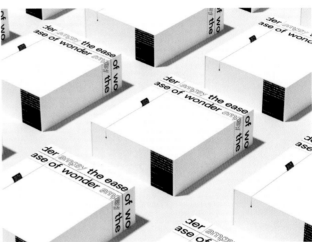

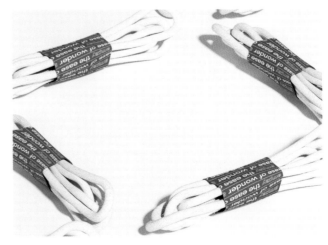

Concept: Whereas many chefs specialize in one cuisine, Food Society sees the world as their playground, uniting some of the world's best kitchens by exploring a wider array of flavors. The identity for the one-stop takeaway shop embodies the idea of community, using the shared "O" to represent the point where the different kitchens come together. As the focal point of the identity, the "O" is consistently used as a key visual gesture across the different applications and has the flexibility to open up, allowing the different cuisines to live within the main brand.

Design
Camille M. Sauvé
Oslo

Creative Direction
Svein Haakon Lia

Design Studio
Bleed

Client
Askeladden & Co.

Principal Type
Louize
and Moderat

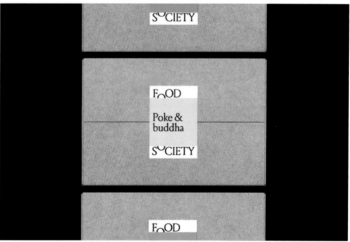

Concept: This consists of a visual identity and marketing materials for the global architectural design competition.

Design
Shantanu Sharma
Brooklyn, New York

Creative Direction
Hannah Meng

Executive
Creative Direction
Andy Chen and
Waqas Jawaid

URL
isometricstudio.
com/aiany-de-
sign-awards

Studio
Isometric Studio

Client
American Institute of
Architects, New York
Chapter

Principal Type
Bau and Plaak 1

Concept: The typography-only visual identity for the Igor Zabel Award 2020 uses distortion, motion, and interactivity.

Design
and Art Direction
Anja Delbello
and Aljaž Vesel
Ljubljana, Slovenia

Programmer
Žan Marolt

Client
Igor Zabel
Association

Design Firm
AA

Principal Type
Muster Grotesk

Dimensions
Various

Concept: The San Francisco Symphony is a 108-year-old international cultural touchstone with a deep legacy of rewriting the rules to advance the orchestral arts. We were invited to help define and express a new vision for the future of classical music under Music Director Esa-Pekka Salonen, the visionary conductor and composer. As the Symphony experiments, an ever-evolving logotype brings to life the music itself. We used responsive and variable font technology to add unexpected contemporary behavior—giving each typographic character the ability to immediately change form in reaction to sound and music.

Design
Sidney Lim,
Michael Taylor,
Yeun Kim,
Mackenzie Pringle,
and Erik Vaage

Creative Direction
Ben Crick,
Louis Mikolay,
and Karin Soukup

Animation
Tomas Markevicius
and Eric Park

Content Strategist
Christine Takaichi

Digital Artist/
Multimedia
Neil Jackson

Production Company
Dinamo

Agency
COLLINS

Client
San Francisco
Symphony

Principal Type
Symphony
in ABC

Concept: The identity uses a unit system as an optical sequence, and the Future Format pairs create a unique language.

Design
Jack Hands,
Dimitris Koliadimas,
and George Sartzis
Thessaloniki, Greece

Creative Direction
Dimitris Koliadimas

Photography
Stefanos Tsakiris

Typographer
MuirMcNeil

Design Agency
Semiotik Design
Agency

Client
Future Format

Principal Type
Four Point Type
System

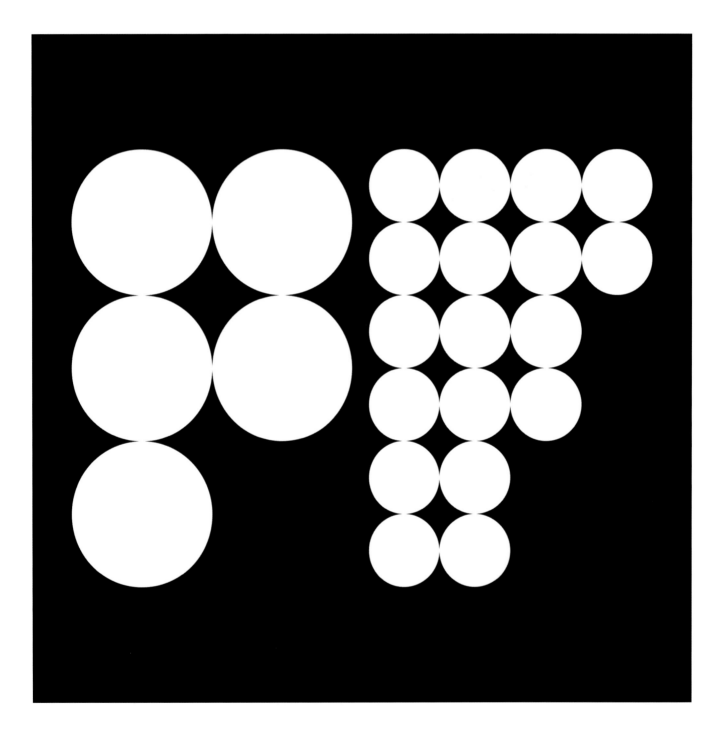

Concept: Telegraph Media Group's corporate logotype redesign takes inspiration from both the company history and visual heritage and from the city where it's based, London. With references coming from both a lettering created by Percy J. Delf Smith for the building at 55 Broadway and the London Tube signage, the new typeface has classical proportions with slight serifs coming from the iconic Telegraph diamond to create a visual link with the newspaper and work as part of the same family.

Art Direction
Dario Verrengia
New York

Creative Direction
Kuchar Swara

Executive Creative
Direction
Nicola Ryan

Typography
Christian Schwartz

Design Firm
Commercial Type

Client
Telegraph
Media Group

Principal Type
TMG Serif

TELEGRAPH MEDIA GROUP

Chris Evans
Editor
The Daily Telegraph

TELEGRAPH MEDIA GROUP

chrisevans@telegraph.co.uk
+44 (0)20 6931 1738
+44 (0)7708 275 436

111 Buckingham Palace Road
London, SW1 0DT

Concept: This is the brand identity framework for the journal of liberal opinion.

Design
Jack Collins,
Leo Field,
Xinle Huang, and
Steven Merenda
New York

Creative Direction
Eddie Opara

Producer
Dana Reginiano

Design Firm
Pentagram Design
New York

Client
The New Republic

Principal Type
Fakt,
IKANSEEYOUALL,
and Tiempos

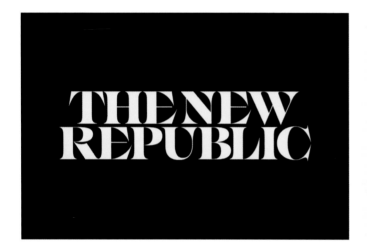

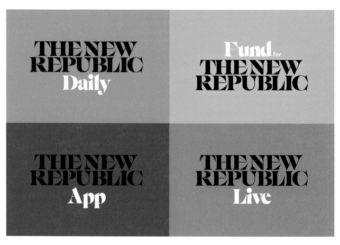

Concept: The new identity for SIPF captures the festival's dynamic spirit of bringing people together.

Design
Dandy Hartono
Singapore

Creative and Art
Direction
Yah-Leng Yu

Agency
Foreign Policy
Design Group

Client
Singapore
International
Photography Festival

Principal Type
Stabil Grotesk

Concept Bossette is a beauty brand for Millennials and Gen Z girls.

Design
Miklós Kiss
Budapest

Client
Bossette

Principal Type
Custom

Concept: Crane has made paper for 250 years. Stephen Crane purchased the Liberty Paper Mill in Dalton, Massachusetts, establishing the business in 1770. Paul Revere chose Crane paper for the first currency of the American colonies, and Crane pioneered anticounterfeit measures with complex, embellished engravings. At the turn of the century, a push against the mechanization of humanity was taking place: The Art Nouveau movement was influencing Crane's paper products, and it inspired a new logotype. It aims to harmonize with the engravings seen throughout the visual identity and strike a balance between a centuries-old heritage and a sharp, clear future.

Design
Jump Jirakaweekul and Camille Sauvé
New York

Creative Direction
Nick Ace

Typography
Jacob Wise

Animation
Tomas Markevicius

Client
Crane

Agency
COLLINS

Principal Type
Monarch and Whtye

Concept: Movement fuses with the typography used to portray it, creating a dynamic system.

Design
Migue Martí
Valencia, Spain

Animation
Juli Martinez

Client
Societat Sardina Toné
Franché

Principal Type
Akzidenz
Grotesk BQ
Super
MaisFontes

Concept: Caobu Public Library required a logotype that could communicate the essence of a library as well as the name of the town, Caobu. The logo is the Chinese word "書" ("book") in positive space. The word "曹" (Caobu village's initial in Chinese) is hidden in the negative space.

Design
Zhaoluo He,
Jingyi Huang,
and Chunyu Liang
Zhongshan City,
China

Creative Direction
Zhuopeng Ou

Client
Caobu Public Library

Design Firm
Centre Design

Principal Type
Akzidenz
Grotesk,
Noto Serif,
and custom

曹步图书馆
CAOBU PUBLIC LIBRARY

Concept: The typography was the protagonist chosen to celebrate diversity of the many Brazils we have.

Design
Alexandre Baltazar,
Julia Custodio, and
Daniel Escudeiro
Rio de Janeiro

Typography
Daniel Escudeiro,
Carlos Mignot,
and Rodrigo Saiani

Animation
Paulo Caetano

Production Company
Plau Rio de Janeiro

In-House Agency
Marca e
Comunicação Globo

Executive
Creative Direction
Ricardo Bezerra

Chief Creative Officer
Fred Gelli

Design Firm
Tátil Design

Client
Canal Brasil

Principal Type
Canal Brasil VF
and
Sharp Grotesk

Concept: This is a series of covers for the bimonthly booklets for Sesc 24 de Maio courses and workshops.

Art Direction
Tereza Bettinardi°
São Paulo

Studio
Tereza Bettinardi

Client
Sesc 24 de Maio

Principal Type
Atlas Grotesk and
Atlas TypeWriter

Dimensions
4.9 × 7.8 in.
(12.5 x 20 cm)

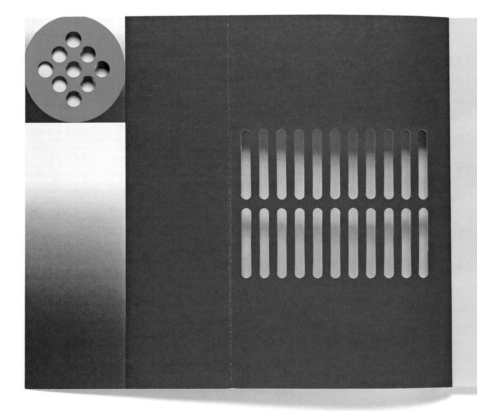

O Sesc oferece cursos em diversas áreas do conhecimento, com o objetivo de aproximar o público do universo das artes e humanidades através de ações orientadas por educadores e especialistas.

Nos meses de janeiro e fevereiro, o Sesc 24 de Maio apresenta um conjunto de vivências, aulas abertas e demonstrações, proporcionando ao público um primeiro contato com essas práticas, além de cursos e bate-papos que ampliam os temas apresentados.

sumário

Concept: This is the first type treatment uniquely designed to help physicians identify and diagnose rare forms of epilepsy. Crafted in a partnership between typography designs and medical experts, the type treatment leverages a serif that resembles medical literature and animates with blurs, shakes, droops, and jerks to reflect the important nuances of specific seizure types. Diagnosing Epilepsy Type was made for Epidiolex® (cannabidiol) and was available to physicians inside a virtual booth that saw 200 unique visitors within just the first few days of launch.

Agency
The Bloc
New York

Client
Greenwich

Principal Type
Apoc(alypse)

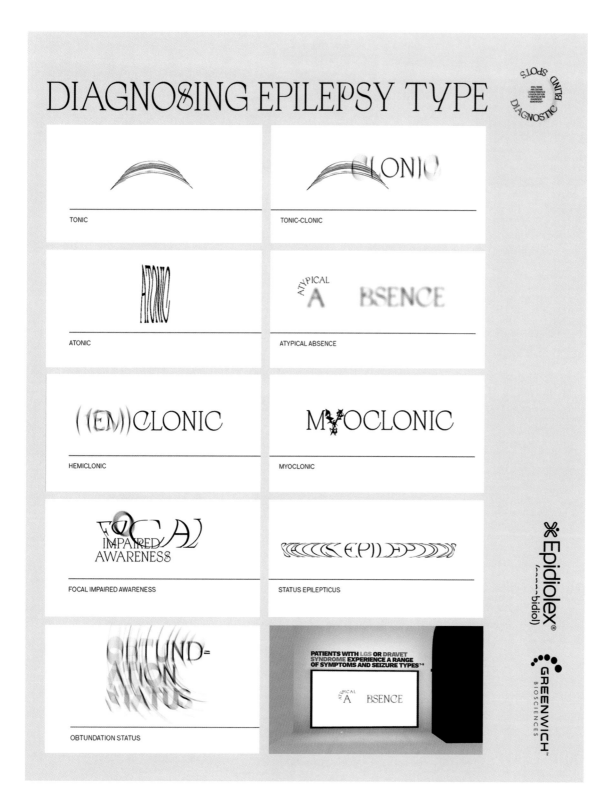

Concept: This custom laser-etched guitar award features Qualtrics key brand pillars.

Typography
Kevin Cantrell
Mantua, Utah

Studio
Kevin Cantrell Studio

Client
Qualtrics

Concept: Five animated type specimens featuring "magnetic" movement showcase Magnet, a new typeface by Frere-Jones Type.

Design
Yotam Hadar
Brooklyn, New York

Animation
Jonathan Katav

Client
Frere-Jones Type

Principal Type
Magnet

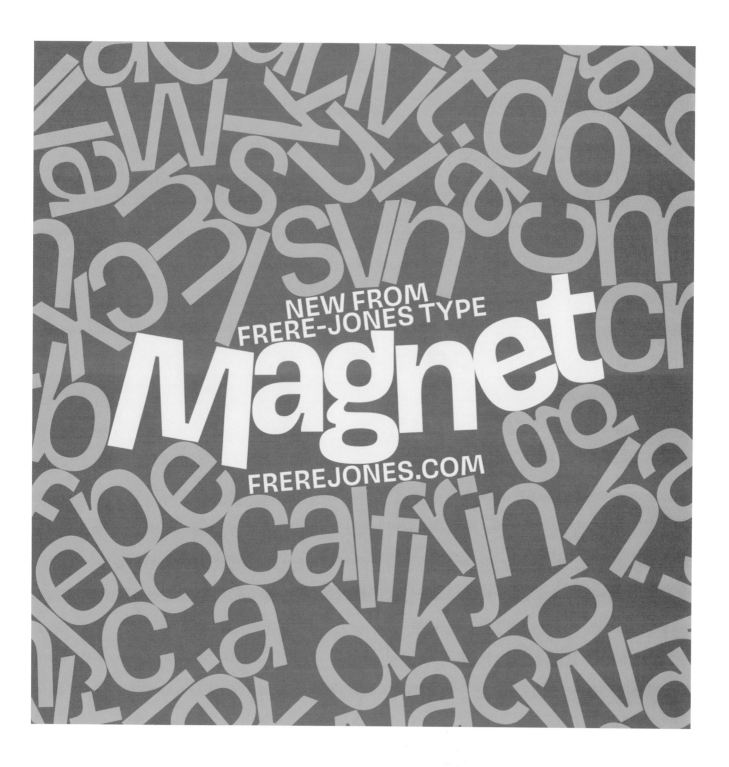

Concept: A series of vibrant postage stamps commemorate the 75th anniversary of the United Nations.

Creative Direction
Matt Willey

Design Firm
Pentagram Design
New York

Client
United Nations
Postal
Administration

Principal Type
Custom

Dimensions
2 x 1.4 in.
(5 x 3.5 cm)

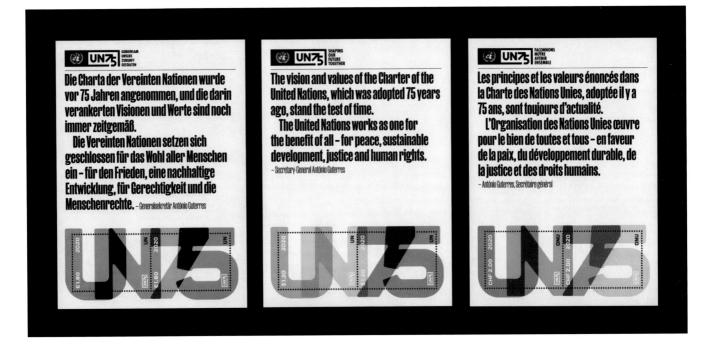

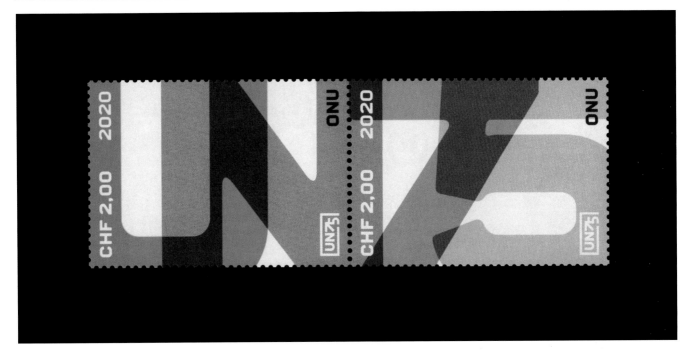

Concept: Queersicht is an LGBTI film festival that takes place annually in Bern. The program consists of short and feature movies, documentaries, and side events, such as conferences and parties. For the new communication products (poster, booklet, flyer), we combined different colors to represent the diverse mix of the community. The additional application of silver reflects the glamorous touch of the festival. Just as in the movies, the letters on the communication products that form the word "QUEER" provide insight into a life story.

Design
Sam Divers,
Nadia de Donno,
Philipp Lüthi,
Andrea Noti, and
Giannina Ronchetti
Bern, Switzerland

Design Firm
Heyday Konzeption
und Gestaltung
GmbH

Client
Queersicht
LGBTI-Filmfestival

Principal Type
Favorit

Dimensions
Various

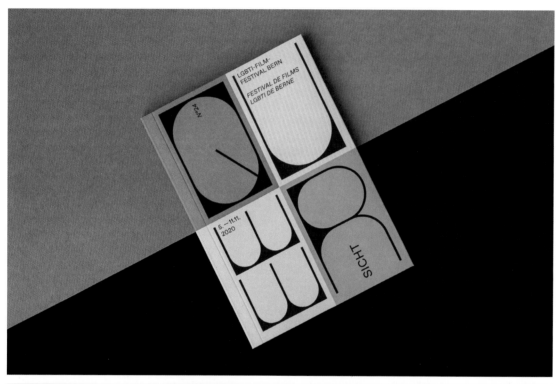

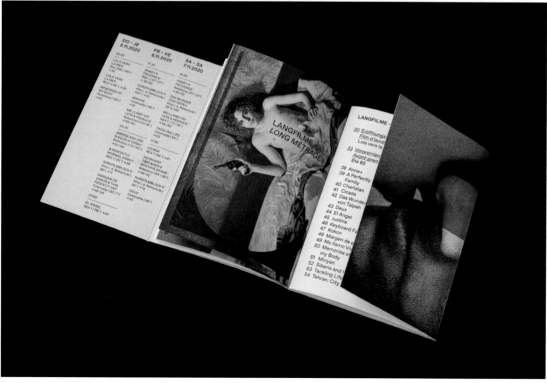

Concept: This ongoing project translates the text of E. E. Cummings into moving compositions.

Design
Fionn Breen
Brooklyn, New York

Principal Type
Maria

Concept: This experimental campaign was designed to remind people to consider other people's perspectives online.

Art Direction
Masahiro Naruse°
New York

Principal Type
Unknown

Concept: The theme of the 2021 Advertising and Design Club of Canada Awards was "Unquarantine Your Creative," celebrating all the best creative work done from home in 2020. The design elements reflect the idea that despite lockdowns, our creativity couldn't be contained. Our logo illustrates this with a typographic release from "Unquarantine" to "Creative." Purposeful keylines provide a nod to a year of confinement, and our color palette communicates that even in dark times, gold-winning work shines through.

Design
Jeff Watkins
Toronto

Art Direction
Jenny Luong
and Andrea Por

Creative Direction
Zak Mroueh

Writers
Nick Asik
and Christina Roche

Production
Sarah Dayus,
Houng Ngui,
and Ola Stodulska

Editing
Ashlee Mitchell and
Jessie Posthumous

Production Company
Zulubot

Agency
Zulu Alpha Kilo

Client
Advertising
and Design Club
of Canada

Principal Type
Circular Std

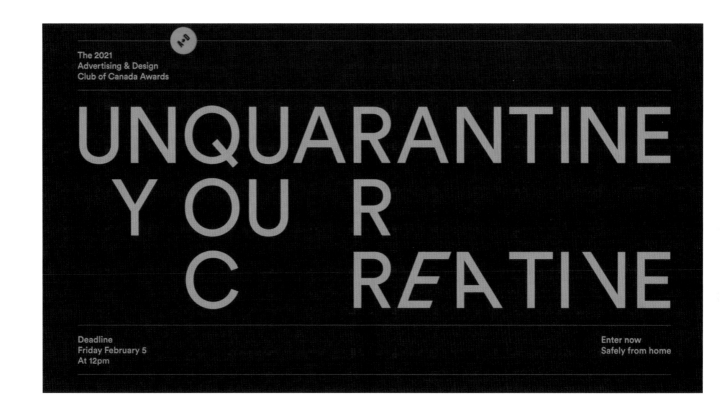

211

Concept: This is the logo animation for Sandbox Films, a science-driven documentary film studio.v

Creative Direction
Lauren King
New York

Animation
Ian Crane
and Mai Saito

Client
Sandbox Films

Agency
GrandArmy

Principal Type
Custom

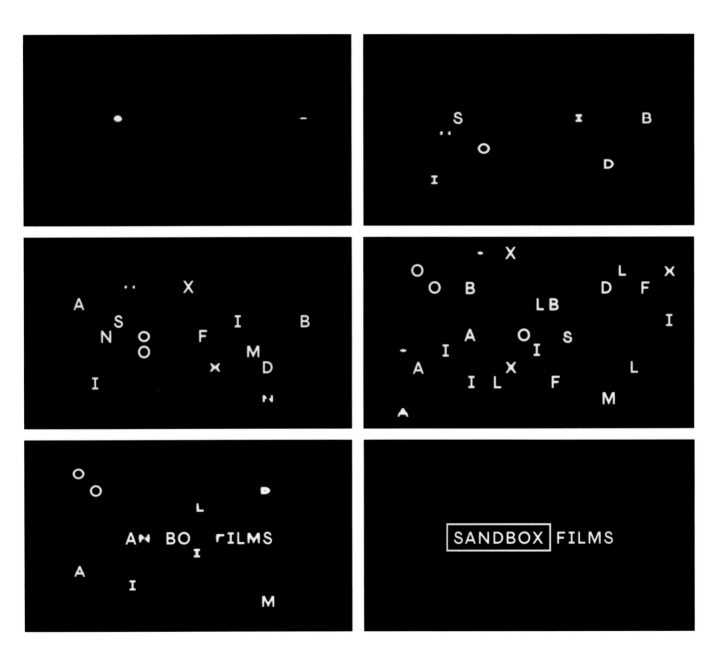

Concept: The outline of the figure in the poster is a mirror image of "2020" in digital form.

Design
Dong Haoyue,
Wu Shuang,
and Yan Zhihang
Beijing

Art Direction
Zhu Chao

Design
Wu Shuang,
Dong Haoyue,
and Yan Zhihang

Digital Artist/
Multimedia
Zhao Lin

Design Firm
Mint Brand Design

Client
BIFT

Principal Type
Haas Grot Disp
and Hanyi

The SNL cast comes home to 30 Rock in a new opening title sequence for the show's return in fall 2020.

Design
Laura Berglund,
Jase Hueser,
and Matt Varner
New York

Illustration
Daniel Zender

Producer
Zoe Chrissos

Direction
Emily Oberman

Design Firm
Pentagram Design
New York

Client
Saturday Night Live

Principal Type
The Saturday
Night Live logo
is a hand-
painted custom
cut of Druk. The
cast members'
names are all
handwritten in
custom script.

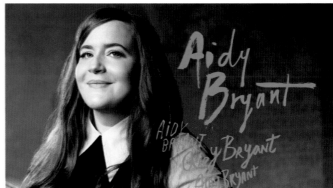

Concept: The theme of the 2021 Advertising and Design Club of Canada Awards was "Unquarantine Your Creative," celebrating all the best creative work done from home in 2020. The design elements reflect the idea that despite lockdowns, our creativity couldn't be contained. Our logo illustrates this with a typographic release from "Unquarantine" to "Creative." Purposeful keylines provide a nod to a year of confinement, and our color palette communicates that even in dark times, gold-winning work shines through.

Design
Jeff Watkins
Toronto

Art Direction
Jenny Luong
and Andrea Por

Creative Direction
Zak Mroueh

Writers
Nick Asik
and Christina Roche

Production
Sarah Dayus,
Houng Ngui,
and Ola Stodulska

Editing
Ashlee Mitchell and
Jessie Posthumous

Production Company
Zulubot

Agency
Zulu Alpha Kilo

Client
Advertising
and Design Club
of Canada

Principal Type
Circular Std

Concept: This is repackaging for Beneduce Vineyards in New Jersey through typographic compositions for the modern wine drinker.

Design
Abraham Lule°
New York

Photography
Francisco De Deus

Creative Direction
Corey Lewis

Studio
Work by Lule

Client
Beneduce Vineyards

Principal Type
BigSmalls and
Cardigan Regular,
Bold, and Semi-Bold

Dimensions
3.1 x 7.5 in.
(7.9 x 10 cm)

Concept: Dark Matter Coffee's select rebrand takes a dip into sci-fi psychedelia, where symbolism reigns supreme.

Design
Jim Zimmer
Louisville, Kentucky

Photography
Richard Gary

Illustration
Raul Urias

Creative Team
Adam Grimshaw

Creative Direction
Nathan Weaver

Executive
Creative Direction
Jessica Zimmer

Design Firm
Zimmer-Design

Client
Dark Matter Coffee

Principal Type
Draft Family,
Flashback Dropout,
and Heavitas

Dimensions
8.6 x 4.9 x 2.5 in.
(22 x 12.5 x 6.5 cm)

Concept: The design was inspired by Farmer's Almanac covers, with hand-drawn type and drawings of local flora.

Design and Illustration
Teddy Kurniawan
Napa, California

Art Direction
Antonio Rivera

Chief Creative Officer
David Schuemann

Design Firm
CF Napa Brand Design

Client
La Crosse Distilling Co.

Principal Type
Centennial, Cento, Interstate, Quimby, AT Sackers Heavy Roman, and custom

Dimensions
4.3 x 4.6 in.
(10.5 x 11.8 cm)

Concept: The design, featuring nostalgic hand-drawn type, is printed and embossed on metal, creating a tactile experience.

Design
and Art Direction
Antonio Rivera
Napa, California

Chief Creative Officer
David Schuemann

Design Firm
CF Napa Brand
Design

Client
Fordham Lee Distillery

Concept: Saari is a Dominican chocolate brand with a Finnish twist.

Design
Renan Vizzotto
Parma, Italy

Writer
Caio Evangelista

Product Architect
Robert Ashorn

Client
Saari Chocolate

Principal Type
Halyard Micro and
Halyard Text

Dimensions
2.4 x 5.3 x 0.25 in.
(6 x 13.5 × 0.7 cm)

Concept: Finery is sophistication in a can. For the discerning drinker, the brand mark is a fashion statement.

Design
Michael Nicholls
Auckland

Art Direction
Sam Allan

Creative Direction
Matt Grantham

Design Firm
Onfire Design

Client
The Fine People

Agency
Onfire Design

Principal Type
Domaine Display,
Neue Montréal,
and Novecento Wide

Dimensions
5.3 x 4.2 in.
(13.5 x 10.6 cm)

Concept: Clear aligners, an alternative to braces, are designed to move teeth into their proper position. Our goal was to create a kit for a delightful teeth-straightening journey. The packaging relies upon a delicate serif with a refreshing color palette. We chose a four-division structure to neatly display the sets of aligner bags and added a convenient removable box to store dental goodies such as whitening gel. A pop-of-orange carrying case rounds out the packaging. Soft and flexible silicone allows it to fit conveniently into a pants pocket and provides for easy cleaning and safe aligner storage.

Design
Jiwon Chong
San Francisco

Writer
Julia Stinebaugh

Direction
Meghan Jewitt

Chief
Marketing Officer
Amanda Salinas

URL
uniformteeth.com

In-House Agency
Uniform Teeth

Principal Type
Centra No. 2 Regular,
Messian Serif Italic,
and Messian Serif
Regular

Dimensions
Various

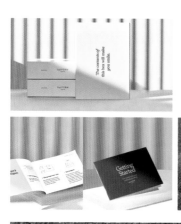

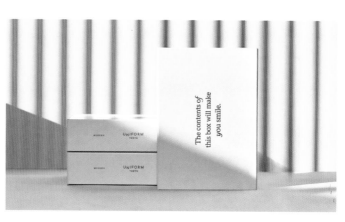

Concept: Bacio di Latte is the largest Italian handmade ice cream brand in Brazil. Bacio expresses sophistication, tradition, and authenticity in its DNA, and our challenge was to translate the experience lived in the brand's stores, with all its elements of sophistication, for the supermarkets. The development of the entire visual language was supported by elements of Art Deco Italiano, such as carved metalwork, ornaments, and other details of this artistic style.

Design
Bruno Faiotto,
Camilla Mattos,
and Pedro Mattos
São Paulo

Writers
Fernando Andreazi,
Fernanda Damas,
and Giovanna
Marques

Creative Direction
Fernando Andreazi
and Pedro Mattos

Client
Bacio di Latte

Studio
Rebu Consultoria
Ltd.

Principal Type
PF Din,
VJ Love Regular,
and ITC Slimbach Std

Dimensions
25.4 x 25.4 x 25.4 in.
(10 x 10 x 10 cm)

Concept: This is the packaging design for thematic gift boxes containing essential oils reminiscent of nature and well-being.

Art Direction
Daniel Robitaille
Montréal

Creative Direction
Daniel Robitaille

Design Firm
Paprika

Client
Naturiste

Principal Type
Kessler

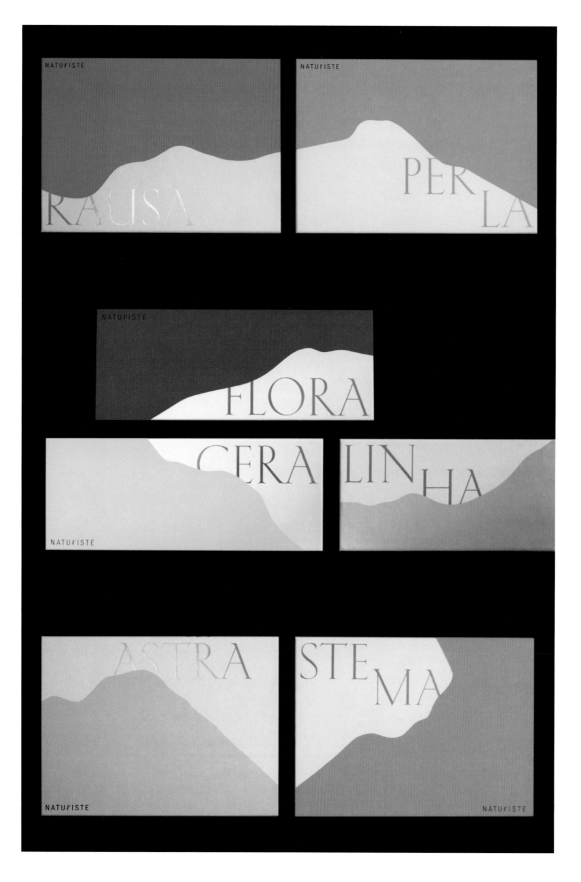

Concept: This citrus package has an animal motif associated with the name of citrus.

Design
Minako Endo
Tokyo

Art Direction
Koichi Sugiyama

Writer
Yuta Naruse

Producer
Taku Kitano

Client
Kadoya

Studio
MARU

さんガオーかん

しらイヌ

きよミミー

せみのーブー

クマなつ

からパンダりん

しゅんパオ

はっサル

せとガー

はるメェ

ニャーふる

ぼんタン

Concept: These are the posters and program for You Are Here, 2020 edition. Designed as a stroll show, You Are Here presents the various performances that were developed during the preceding one-week residency. The concept of the posters is to evoke ideas of strolling, paths, and movement using typography.

Art Direction
Marie-France Gaudet
and Eveline Lupien
Montréal

Studio
Supersystème

Client
LA SERRE—arts
vivants

Principal Type
Neue Haas Grotesk
Display

Dimensions
Poster:
24 x 36 in.
(61 x 91.4 cm);
Program:
7 × 8.5 in.
(17.8 x 21.6 cm)

Concept: Independent letters, independent cinema! This poster series, titled "Bağımsız Çarşamba" (Independent Wednesday), is designed for Kadir Has University Cinema Club. The project's intended purpose is based on motion typography for every selection of the movies. The grid system of kinetic letters provides a unique frame to look at every movie from another perspective. The event is a movie selection organized between January and February for seven weeks.

Design
Alp Eren Tekin
Istanbul

URLs
khas.edu.tr/en
behance.net/
alperentekin

Client
Kadir Has University
Cinema Club

Principal Type
Notable
and Roc Grotesk

Dimensions
19.7 x 27.6 in.
(50 × 70 cm)

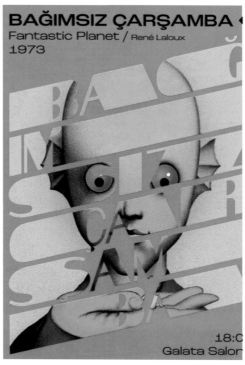

Concept: The 2019 Gwangju Design Biennale addresses social issues through the value and role of design within the theme of humanity. The exhibition highlights design for a sustainable society and human community. The typographically focused poster presents a quote by Chinese philosopher Lao Tzu: "Good is like water." The typeface of the quote in English is covered with drops of water, which act like a prism and distort the typeface. Thus, the quote can only be read clearly by taking a closer look. The 3D contours of the drops form the Chinese character for "good."

Design
Chaosheng Li°
Hangzhou, China

School
Zhejiang
Gongshang
University

Client
Gwangju Design
Biennale

Principal Type
Helvetica
Neue LT Std,
77 Bold Condensed,
and Source Han
Sans Bold

Dimensions
27.6 x 30.4 in.
(70 x 100 cm)

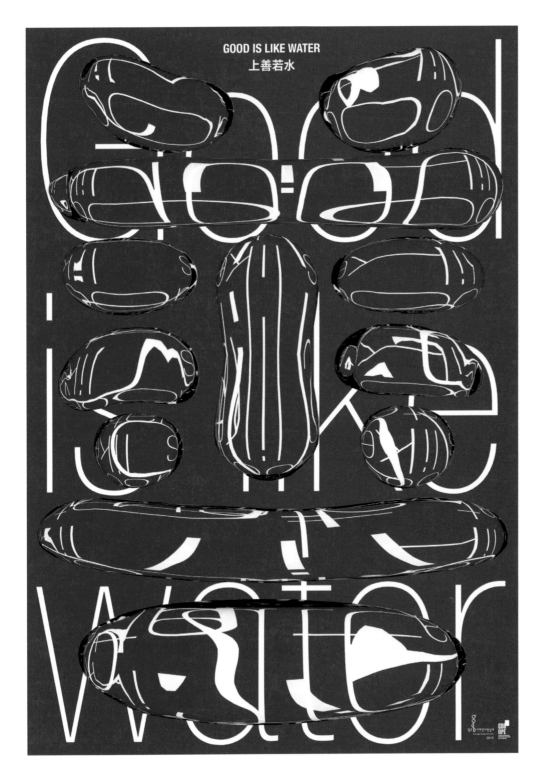

Concept: To emphasize the merger of Western mythology and Eastern tradition in an intercultural theater experiment, the poster design refers to the underlying origins: the codes of the Chinese Opera and the archaic themes of the German Nibelungen myth. A Chinese Opera dancer is integrated in a ring consisting of two formally different halves—one standing for the Nibelungen myth, the other one representing the Chinese Opera. The image composition is augmented by eye-catching bilingual typography following the reading direction of the ring. The type composition intrigues viewers to go on their own quest for information and inspiration.

Art and
Creative Direction
Simon Seidel
Berlin

Studio
betterbuero

Client
MINZ Internationale
Kulturprojekte

Principal Type
Base & Bloom,
Basis Grotesque,
and Ping Fang

Dimensions
33.1 x 46.8 in.
(84.1 x 118.9 cm)

Concept: This poster was designed by tape and handwritten information for my own exhibition with Tape Works.

Design
Niklaus Troxler°
Willisau, Switzerland

Studio
Niklaus Troxler
Design

Client
A–Z Presents

Principal Type
Hand-drawn
and hand taping

Dimensions
35.6 × 50.5 in.
(90.5 x 128 cm)

Concept: The purpose of this self-initiated poster of the Top 10 Books Read in 2019 was to promote reading.

Design
Fidel Peña
Toronto

Creative Direction
Claire Dawson
and Fidel Peña

Photography
Paul Weeks

Studio
Underline Studio

Principal Type
Sharp Grotesk Black
and
Neue Haas Grotesk

Dimensions
20 x 28 in.
(50 × 71 cm)

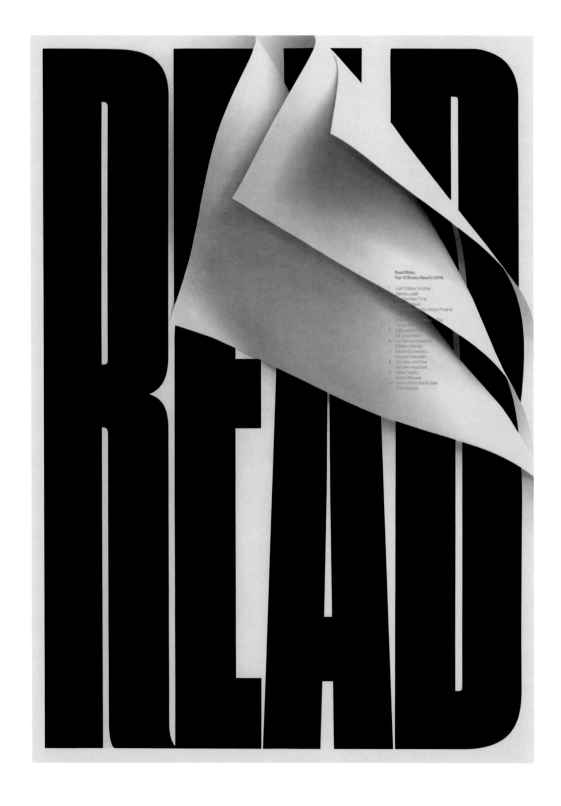

Concept: To celebrate the 100th anniversary of the Italian director Federico Fellini, the University of Missouri hosted the Fellini 1920–2020 Project and invited Fons Hickmann to contribute one piece of work. He designed the diptych Fellini 8½ in the Italian national colors. Both works mimic the expressive Fellini lettering and are also posters for Fellini's masterpiece, 8½.

Design
Fons Hickmann°
Berlin

Studio
Fons Hickmann M23

Client
University
of Missouri

Principal Type
Custom

Dimensions
33.1 x 46.8 in.
(84.1 x 118.9 cm)

Concept: The Museum of Art and Design Hamburg houses an impressive collection of posters from the past 200 years. The exhibition Das Plakat presented a selection of 400 posters by the renowned and unknown designs. For this exhibition, we designed a poster series and a catalog. At the center of our ideation process were the aesthetics of posters glued on top of one another, reminiscent of the ones we see in the public space. Fragments of the over-glued posters come through at the edges and give a hint of the richness of the history this impressive medium possesses.

Design
Fons Hickmann°
Berlin

Studio
Fons Hickmann M23

Client
Museum für
Kunst und Gewerbe
Hamburg

Principal Type
Gerstner-Programm
(Regular)

Dimensions
23.4 x 33 in.
(59.4 x 84.1 cm)

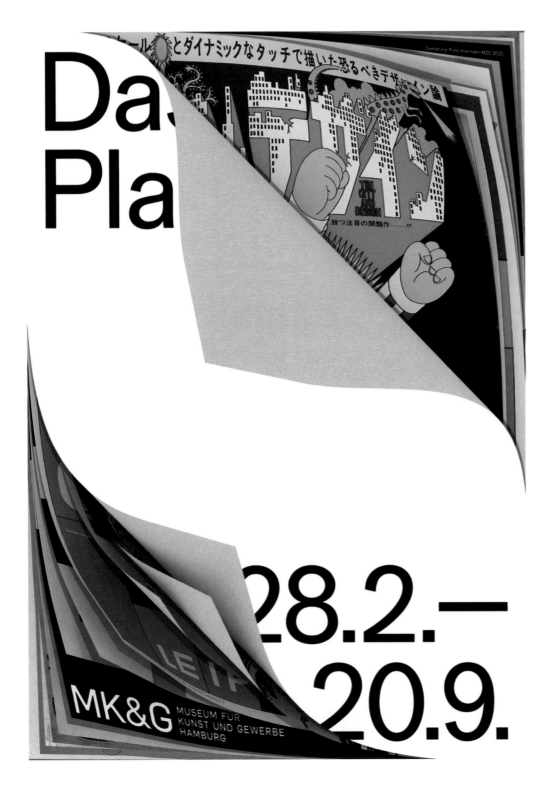

Concept: This is a letterpress-printed promotional poster for typographic-summerprogram.ch.

Typography
Dafi Kühne
Näfels, Switzerland

Design Studio
babyinktwice

Client
Typographic
Summer Program

Principal Type
Gill Sans Ultra Bold,
GT Super Display, and
Times New Roman
Bold

Dimensions
21.6 × 34.6 in.
(55 × 88 cm)

Three steps to a new
way   of   life:

I)
Go to www.typographic-summerprogram.ch

Apply for Session 1 (June 21–July 4, 2020)
or for Session 2 (July 26–August 8, 2020)

CULT

II)
Travel to Switzerland for two
weeks   to   study
typographic poster design and
letterpress printing with Dafi
Kühne and his team.

III)
From   now   on: be   a   follower.   Believe   in   type!

Concept: bēi xǐ jiāo jí (悲喜交集) is the emotion alternating between joy and grief. By adding the number of strokes in the Chinese characters and rearranging the reading order, my work conveys complex emotions.

Art Direction
Bing Chen
Hangzhou, China

Dimensions
27.5 x 39.3 in.
(70 x 100 cm)

悲喜
交集

JOY
&
GRIEF

Concept: This poster features two-color silkscreen (black and fluorescent yellow) on high-white paper, printed in an edition of 50.

Chief Creative Officer
Goetz Gramlich
Heidelberg

Design Firm
gggrafik

Client
karlstorbahnhof
heidelberg

Dimensions
27.6 x 39.4 in.
(70 x 100 cm)

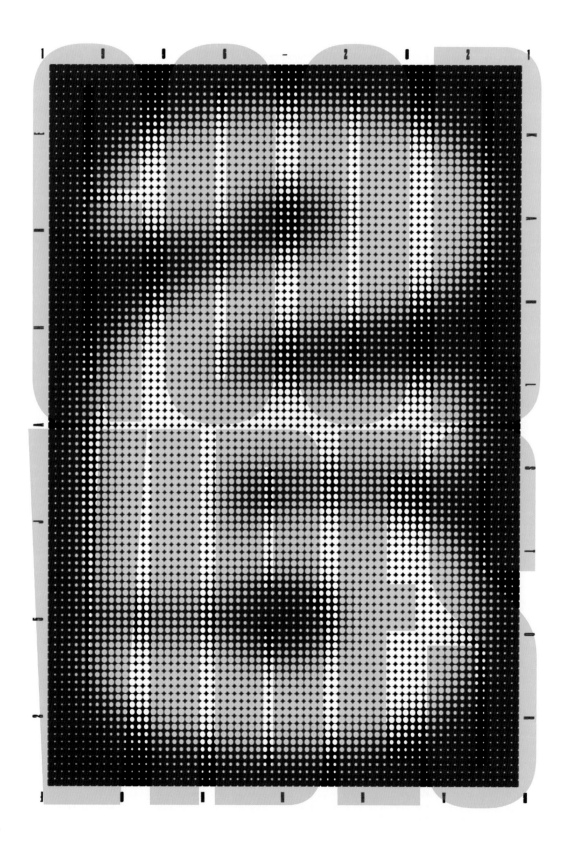

Concept: On the occasion of the 25th anniversary of Tipoteca Italiana, 20 international designers were invited to design a single page of a type specimen book that will be printed on the old letterpress printing machines of the museum. The poster shows Jianping He's design and adds additional content about the typeface and his designer Alessandro Butti.

Art Direction
Jianping He
Berlin

Design Firm
hesign

Client
Tipoteca Italiana
Fondazione

Principal Type
Veltro

Dimensions
33.1 x 46.8 in.
(84.1 x 118.8 cm)

Concept: This is a poster for Cinema Paradiso: Solo Exhibition of Li Bin Yuan at Pingshan Art Museum in Shenzhen, China.

Art Direction
Jianping He

Design Firm
hesign

Client
Pingshan
Art Museum

Principal Type
Helvetica Neue

Dimensions
33.1 x 46.8 in.
(84 x 118.8 cm)

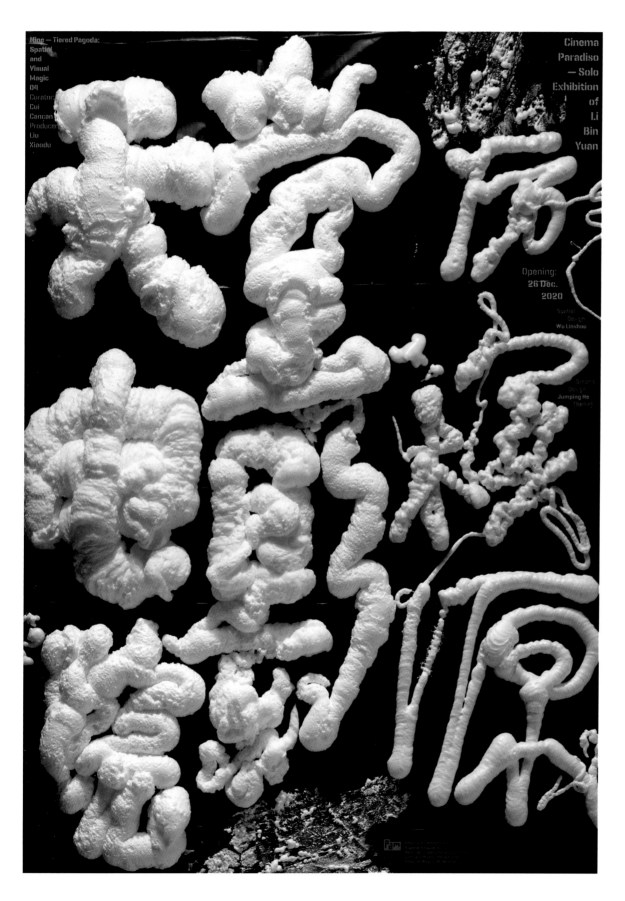

Concept: This poster for the Typomania 2020 in Moscow is a graphic embodiment of a traditional Korean house in letters.

Design
and Art Direction
Byungrok Chae
Seoul

Studio
CBR Graphic Lab

Client
Alexander Vasin

Principal Type
Handlettering

Concept:

Art Direction
Tom Russell

Illustration
David Leutert
Berlin

Agency Producer
Jacqueline Roberto

Production Company
Closer&Closer

Client
Founders
Entertainment
New York

Principal Type
Futura Bold

Dimensions
18 x 24 in.
(46 × 61 cm)

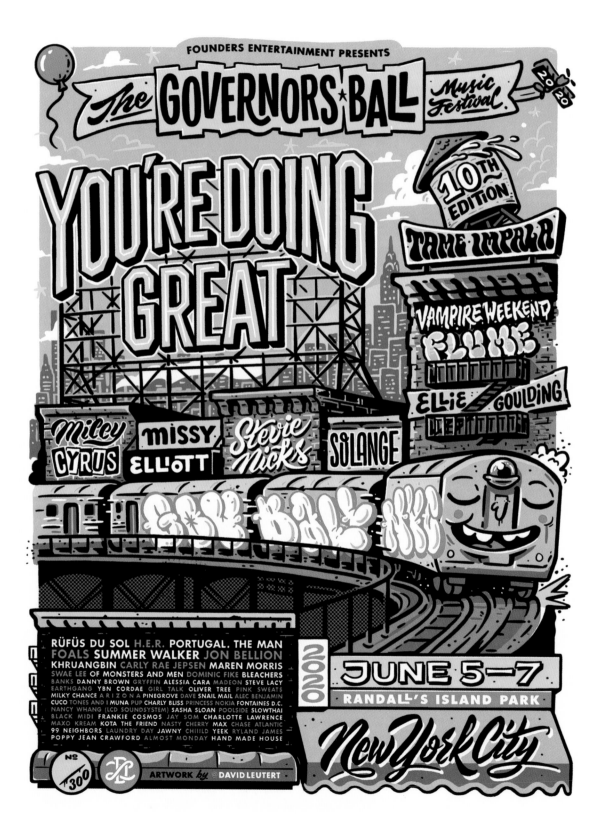

Concept: The brief was simple: to signify the work of Colombian artist Daniel Silva in a poster to promote his exhibition in Tokyo. A Fragmented Garden is Daniel Silva's proposal to show a different way to build a garden. It is composed of 50 Nendo Dango seed units distributed around Tokyo and uses technology and algorithms to come together as a cohesive system. Through a powerful and fragmented typography on the rising sun of Japan, we signify the distribution of the seeds around Tokyo.

Design
and Art Direction
Oliver Siegenthaler
Bogotá

URL
siegenco.com

Design Firm
S&Co

Client
Offline Ventures

Principal Type
Druk

Dimensions
27. 5 x 39.4 in.
(70 x 100 cm)

Concept: *The Intersection* is a show by women celebrating inspiring women. My thoughts went to Ray Eames.

Studio
Marta Cerdà
Alimbau°
Barcelona

Client
W+K

Principal Type
Custom lettering

Dimensions
16.9 x 23.8 in.
(43 x 60 cm)

Concept: La Ferme des Tilleuls is a new exhibition space in a beautiful old house, with performing arts as well, centered around art brut and inviting artists with a social and political angle. We created a new identity. The three blocks represent a giant art brut sculpture in the garden in front of the building. This exhibition, CHECKPOINT, is a collective artistic work by five artists together with young refugees. There are photos and videos, but the central pieces are giant collage maps, and the image on the poster is a detail of one of them. We wanted to give a sense of freedom, roughness, and collage, done by a collective group.

Design
Séverine Dolt

Art Direction
Giorgio Pesce

Studio
Atelier Poisson

Client
La Ferme des Tilleuls

Principal Type
Founders Grotesk

Dimensions
35.2 x 85.6 in.
(89.5 x 128 cm)

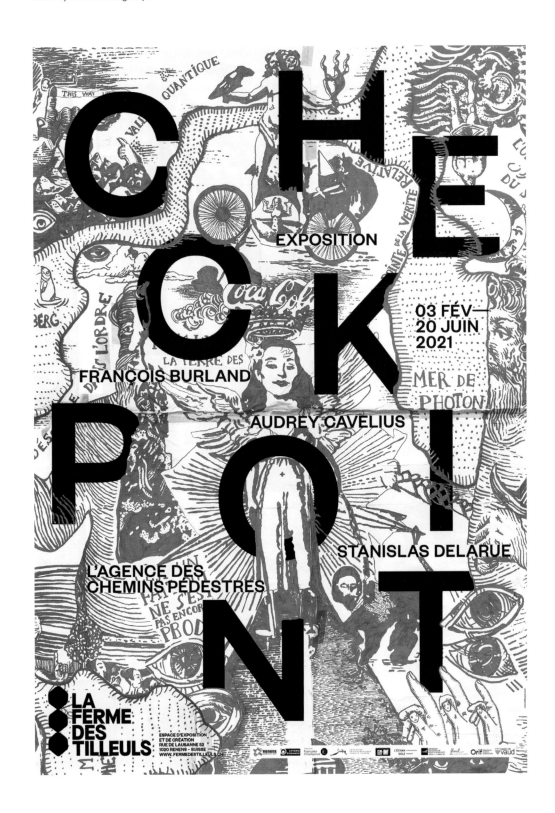

Concept: We fragmented the exhibition theme and kept the core content recognizable while meeting the theme of the exhibition. Holes punched on the poster and all promotional materials, including name tags, flyers, and cards, reflect the exhibition theme, "pieces."

Art Direction
Dawang Sun°
Shanghai

Creative Direction
Hui Pan

Design Studio
T9 Brand

Client
May Art Foundation

Principal Type
Display Dots

Dimensions
22 x 34 in.
(58 × 87 cm)

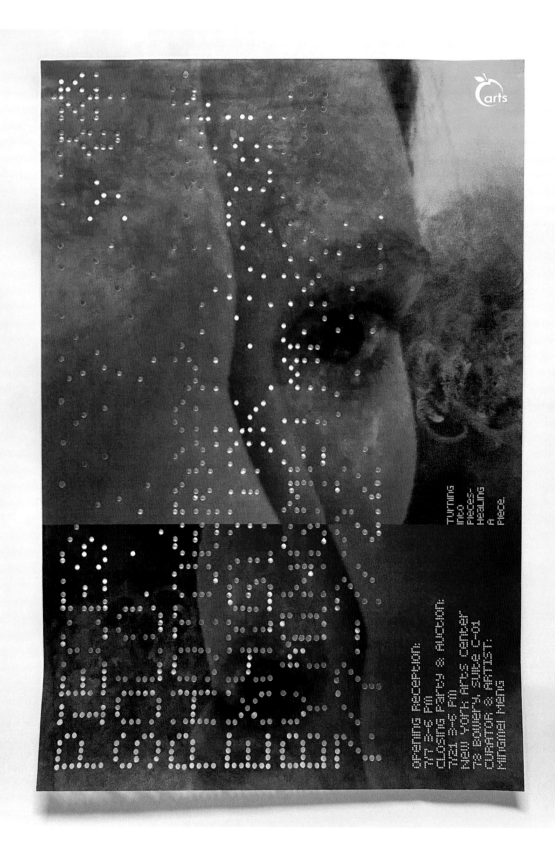

Concept: A set of 3D fonts was designed based on a closed circle. Applying transparent material on the letters allows it to reflect and shine into neon color, which brings youthfulness and playfulness into the design. The four letters of "GAFA" represent "Guangzhou Academy of Fine Arts." The letters were paired in twos and layered together to create an illusion that interfered and merged.

Design
Tian Bo
Guangzhou

Studio
TEN BUTTONS

Client
Guangzhou
Academy
of Fine Arts

Principal Type
Neue Machina
and custom

Dimensions
27.6 × 38.2 in.
(97 × 70 cm)

Concept: Create Theatre Poster is a project to reconstitute and review classic plays. The classics have a universal charm in them. We are fascinated by classics because that teaching still applies to our time. It is our mission to explore it and give it a modern expression. These works are parts of the series: Romeo and Juliet, A Midsummer Night's Dream, Julius Caesar, Richard III, and Antony and Cleopatra. From Romeo and Juliet to Antony and Cleopatra— immature love to adult love—it is the change of love in his works.

Design and Art Direction
Jisuke Matsuda
Tokyo

Studio
Atelier Jisuke

Client
Create Theatre Poster

Principal Type
Georgia Bold,
Helvetica Bold,
Helvetica Regular,
and Hoefler Text
Regular

Dimensions
28.7 x 40.6 in.
(72.8 x 103 cm)

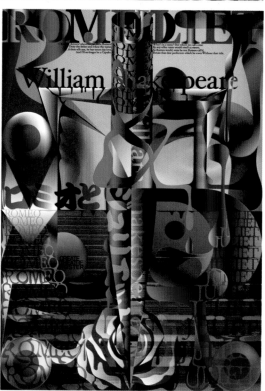

Concept: These words are for elements of nature.

Design
Yan-Ting Chen
Taipei City

Principal Type
Custom

Dimensions
39.3 x 27.5 in.
(70 x 100 cm)

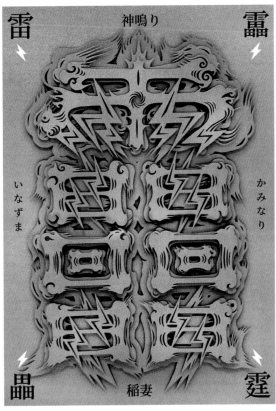

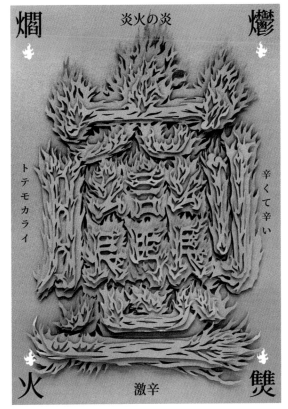

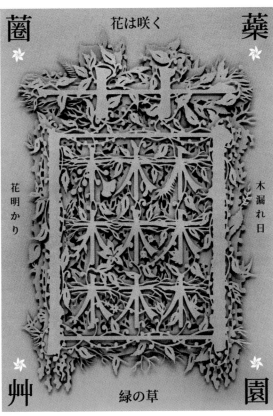

Concept: This shows the history and culture of Vah Thai restaurant while showing the new inheritance of the tradition.

Art Direction
Dan Ferreria
Macau

Creative Direction
Ieong Kun Lam

Design Firm
indego Design

Client
Estabelecimento de
Comidas Vah Thai

Principal Type
Niveau Serif

Dimensions
11.7 x 28.2 in.
(29.7 x 42 cm)

Concept: The main visual of the exhibition was presented in inorganic materials circling the four English letters, D, I, N, and O.

Art Direction
Dan Ferreria
Macau

Creative Direction
Ieong Kun Lam

Design Firm
indego Design

Client
50% TOY

Principal Type
Neue Machina

Dimensions
23.4 x 33.1 in.
(59.4 x 84.1 cm)

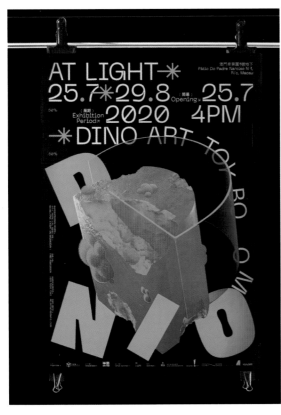

Concept: Inspired by high-fashion magazines, the campaign explores the brilliance behind Dior's creations.

Art Direction
Raymond Lanctot
Montréal

Creative Direction
Louis Gagnon°

Design Firm
Paprika

Client
McCord Museum

Principal Type
Le Jeune and custom

Dimensions
48 × 72 in.
(121.9 x 182.9 cm)

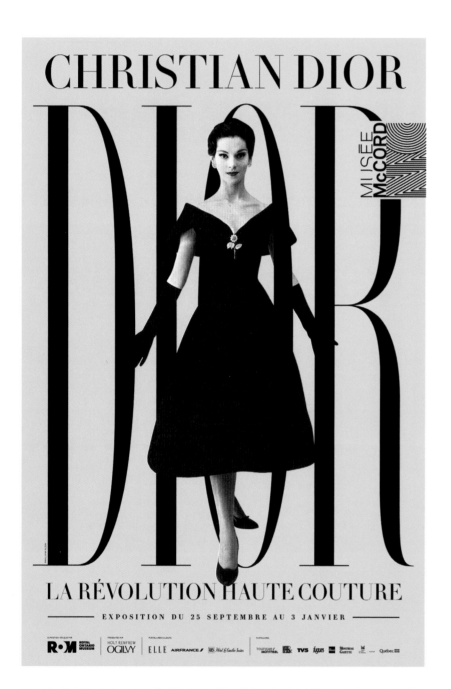

Concept: Musilk is a spontaneous poster design project to express classical music by graphics and typography. The theme of the five posters is Beethoven's Sixth Symphony "Pastoral." Beethoven added a title to each movement of this work to clarify the emotion (rather than the sense of picture) in the abstract music form, which is the first title symphony work in history. I used the German titles of five movements of the symphony as the main element of the poster design and a different type design to convey the emotions expressed by the music.

Art Direction
Siguang Wu
Wuxi, China

Design Firm
HDU23 Lab

Principal Type
Custom

Dimensions
19.7 x 27.6 in.
(50 × 70 cm)

Concept: The Peace & Love mural was created as a message of hope during these uncertain times.

Design
Ben Johnston
Toronto

Principal Type
Custom

Dimensions
12 x 18 ft. (3.7 × 5.5 m)

Concept: Emograms are emojis with letters.

Design
Miklós Kiss
Budapest

Principal Type
Various

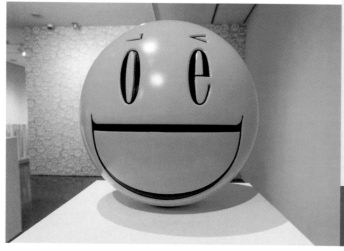

LOVED

LONLEY

SORRY

GOOD

HAPPY

NICE

COOL

CUTE

CRAZY

LUCKY

Concept: Over the past four years, the fabric of our country changed for the worse. Lies and corruption became mainstream. Patriotism became synonymous with terrorism. And the discrepancy between the privileged and the marginalized grew to unthinkable levels. Election Day 2020 would be one of the most important days in every voter's life. I created type-driven social content to inspire people to get out and vote for change.

Design
Blas Madera
New York

Principal Type
Baskerville

Dimensions
15 x 24 in.
(38.1 x 61 cm)

Concept: characters#02 is our second specimag—a blend of Type magazine and a typeface specimen. Our rich archive of collected typeface specimens and Type magazines has inspired us to marry the two into one creative space and share some recent Type-related thoughts and insights while introducing our typeface superfamily NewsSerif.

Design
Jakob Reinhard
and Henning Skibbe
Hamburg

Photography
Bettina Theuerkauf

Creative Direction
Henning Skibbe

URL
charactertype.com

Type Design Studio
Character Type

Principal Type
News Serif

Dimensions
7.9 x 10.2 in.
(20 x 26 cm)

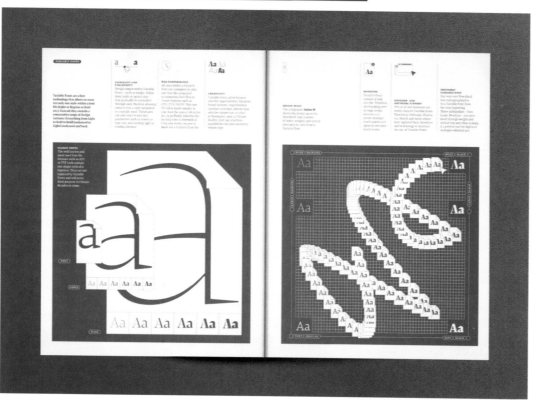

Concept: Ox in the Box is a festive gift set, especially designed and handcrafted to usher in the upcoming lunar new year of 2021 as a self-promotional item for our studio. 2021 marks the year of the ox, a headstrong and driven animal that we've showcased as a spin-off of the "jack-in-a-box" format and mechanism. The outer box sports a barn house silhouette and holds a slim box, which upon opening, an ox leaps out into a 3D form. The ox boasts custom-drawn Chinese typography on all its facets set in rainbow holographic foil printing. The gift set also comes with a set of "red packets," which are usually inserted with money and given out during the festive period as tokens of blessing. The exterior of the red packets displays custom-drawn Chinese characters: 步步高升: an auspicious greeting that means "ascending to greater heights."

Design and Typography
David Ho
Kuala Lumpur

Creative Direction
Joanne Chew

URL
fictionistudio.com

Studio
Fictionist Studio

Principal Type
Custom

Dimensions
8.7 × 5.1 × 1.6 in.
(22 × 13 × 4 cm)

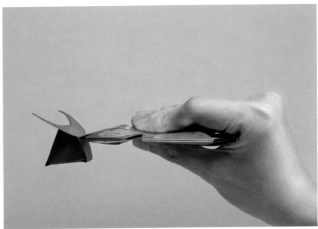

Concept: This is a playful tour through the accomplishments, resilience, and creativity of our customers—Against All Odds.

Design
James Abercrombie,
Chase Curry,
Meg Lindsay,
Chris Sandlin,
and Luke Webster
Atlanta

Art Direction
Ross Zietz

Writer
Austin Ray

Animation
Linda McNeil

Producers
Troy Harris
and Jaclyn Stiller

Creative Team
Chris McGee and
Christina Scavone

Creative Direction
Christian Widlic

Chief Design Officer
Katie Potochney

Agency
Mailchimp

Principal Type
Graphik and
Means

Concept: Layers: MP focuses on Mokpo (South Jeolla Province), known for its mountains, sea, and merrymaking.

Design
Jaei Keem
Seoul

Art Direction
Byungrok Chae

Studio
Layers

Client
Jeonnam
International
SUMUK Biennale

Principal Type
Handlettering

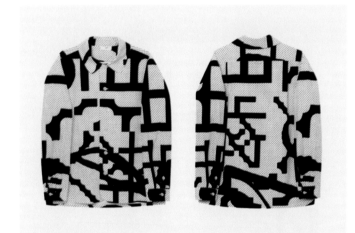

Concept: Bolt is a home appliance repair service.

Design
Minkwan Kim
New York

Principal Type
Bolt and Din

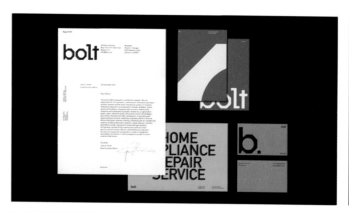

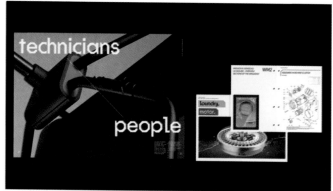

Concept: The rebranding of BRIC was inspired
by the unapologetic voice of the institution.

Design
Chaeyeon Park°
Pasadena, California

Instructor
Brad Bartlett

School
Art Center
College of Design

Concept: Iota Display is a generative modular typeface that represents positive connections between people.

Design
Eun Jung Bahng°
Pasadena, California

Instructors
Simon Johnston
and Roy Tatum

School
ArtCenter
College of Design

Principal Type
Custom

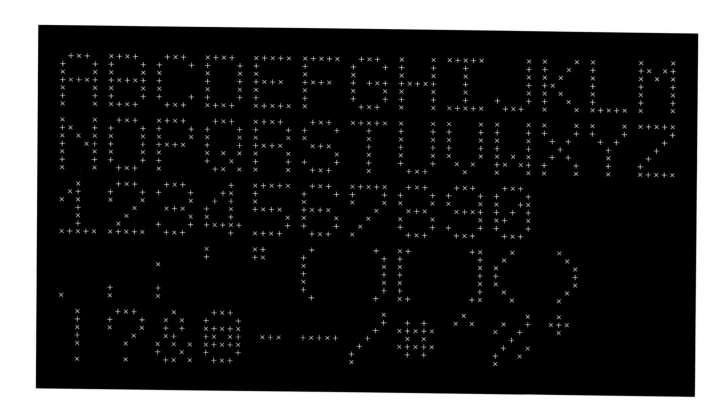

Concept: Liquid Society tells stories about various counterculture phenomena from different time periods.

Design
Ke Wang

Instructor
Brad Bartlett

School
ArtCenter
College of Design

Principal Type
Helvetica Neue

Dimensions
8.5 x 11 in.
(44.7 x 29.4 cm)

Concept: When I visited Fiji in early 2020, Cyclone Sarai tore through its islands. My stay manifested itself into a devastating wake-up call for climate change. 2°C Earth, in turn, began as a rallying cry for our warming world. It took shape in the form of a visual guide that explores five locations around the world whose natural and cultural heritage are threatened by climate change. Created to be visually engaging, auditorily immersive, and easily digestible for audiences disengaged from our climate crisis, this interactive experience hopes to educate and inspire more people to join the collective fight for our future.

Design
Jingqi Fan
St. Louis

Music and Sound
Jingqi Fan
and Stella Stocker

Programmer
Jingqi Fan

Instructor
Jonathan Hanahan

School
Washington
University,
St. Louis

Principal Type
FK Grotesk,
ITC Garamond,
and
Scto Grotesk

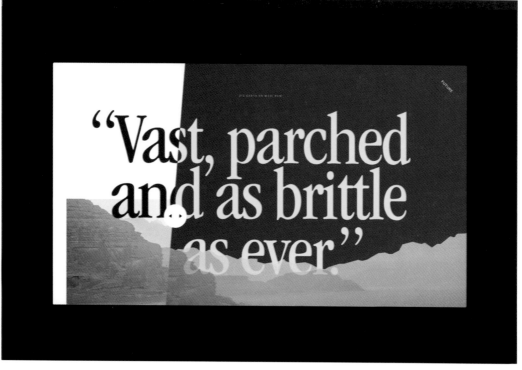

Concept: This hypothetical redesign imagines a new visual identity for Calder: Nonspace, an exhibition held at Hauser & Wirth of monochromatic sculptures by Alexander Calder. The exhibition graphics draw inspiration from the bodies of the artist's famous mobiles, elevating typography as a central design element to a sculptural form. The expressive font Love (designed by VJ-Type) is utilized to allude to Calder's work, its curved strokes and wide counters reminiscent of the frameworks found in his mobiles, all the while portraying the exhibition's concept of new spatial perceptions through the usage of typesetting and negative space.

Design
Amy Fang
Los Angeles

Professor
Willem Henri Lucas

School
University
of California

Principal Type
Love and Whyte

Concept: Marcel Duchamp was one of the most influential artists of the 20th century and one of my all-time favorites. This project was conceived in honor of his memory and his incredible contribution to the avant-garde. Rather than doing him the disservice of imitating his style, I chose for my catalog a concise, modern design.

Design
Inna Ziuko
Berlin

Professor
Svyat Vishnyakov

School
Bang Bang
Education,
Moscow

Principal Type
Neue Haas Grotesk
Display Pro

Dimensions
6.5 × 9 in.
(16.5 x 23 cm)

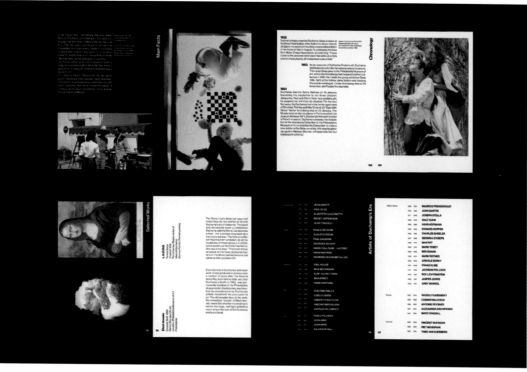

Concept: The mix of fonts reflects the themes of the conference: a grotesque one and one with a futuristic feel.

Design
Sebastian Menting
Münster

Professor
Rüdiger Quass
von Deyen

School
Münster School
of Design

Principal Type
Decima Pro A
and Langulaire

Dimensions
23.3 x 33.1 in.
(59.4 x 84.1 cm)

Concept: This is the story of "Four-Medal Man" Jesse Owens's epic life and achievements through type compositions.

Design
Sebastian Páez
Delvasto

Professor
David Pasquali

School
RM Raffles Milano

Principal Type
GT Haptik, Optimum, and Sharp Grotesk

Dimensions
11 x 12 in.
(28 x 32 cm)

Concept: This is the poster design for the hypothetical event "What About Tomorrow?," representing the idea of new openings.

Design
Vivek Thakker
Baltimore

Instructor
Jennifer Cole Phillips

School
Maryland Institute
College of Art (MICA)

Principal Type
Handlettered
Devanagari,
Neue Haas Grotesk,
and Biryani

Dimensions
22 x 33 in.
(54.7 × 84.6 cm)

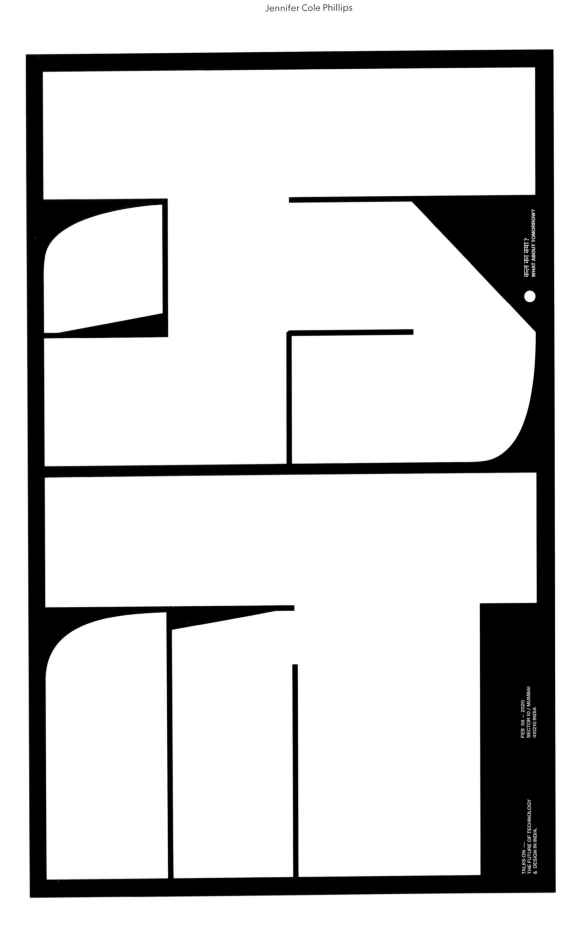

Concept: *Models of Silence* is an anthology of prison writing for an accompanying museum exhibit.

Design
Jack Moore
Pasadena, California

Instructors
Cheri Gray
and Angad Singh

School
ArtCenter
College of Design

Principal Type
Favorit,
Suisse Intl, and
Times New Roman

Dimensions
10 x 14 in.
(25.4 x 35.56 cm)

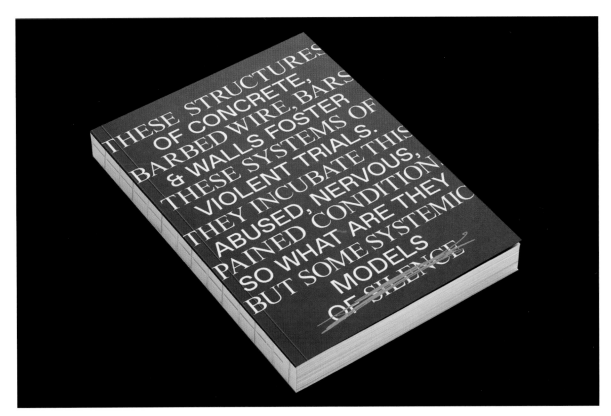

Concept: Seventy years ago, South and North Korea had a war, and lots of families were dispersed. In 1983, Korea's broadcasting company decided to do a live broadcast for people in South Korea who had lost their families during the war. Finding Dispersed Families is a book about that broadcast. The dot on every page represents a birthmark, which means that wherever you are, your family will always be with you, like your birthmark. Dispersed people's names are placed randomly, and as you flip the page, the yellow gradient gets bigger—which means that as you read this book, their memories get clearer.

Design
Woojin Nam
New York

URL
woojinnam.com

Instagram
@woojinnam

Instructor
Chris Rypkema

School
School of Visual Arts,
New York°

Principal Type
Aperçu and
New Century
Schoolbook

Dimensions
8.5 x 11 in.
(21.6 x 27.9 cm)

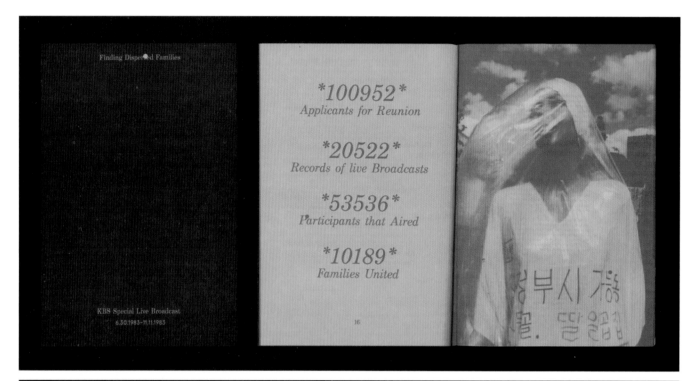

Concept: This project describes the constructed power in architecture from physical containment, mental authority, and surveillance.

Design
Yuan Jiang
Copenhagen

Instructor
Brad Bartlett

School
ArtCenter of Design

Principal Type
Everett, Untitled Sans, and Untitled Serif

Dimensions
7.5 x 10.5 in.
(19.1 x 26.7 cm)

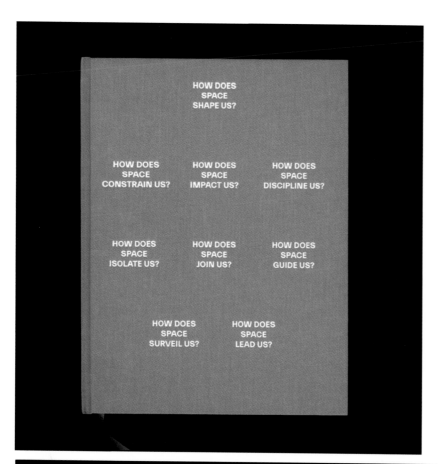

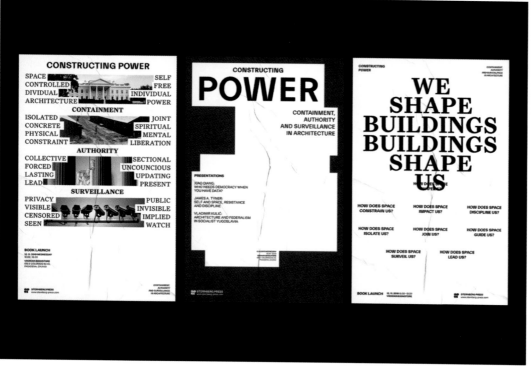

Concept: The Ultimate Guide for Death-to-Be is a speculative farewell celebration planning book.

Design
Nanjin Li
Brooklyn, New York

Creative Team
Xinda Wang

Concept: Chinese Retro is a magazine for people who share an interest in the new Chinese design and photography.

Design
Huiqi Qiu
New York

Photography
Ziyao Chen,
Weishan Hu,
and Betty Liu

Instructors
Justin Colt
and Jose Fresneda

School
School of Visual Arts,
New York°

Principal Type
Noe Display, Omnes,
and Salvaje Display

Dimensions
8.5 x 11 in.
(22 x 28 cm)

Concept: This one-off mini publication dives deeply into Swiss design practice and philosophy from Kasper Florio.

Design
Bao Anh Bui
Singapore

Typography
Duy Dao,
Gabriel Lam, and
Vietanh Nguyen

Type Foundry
Yellow Type Foundry,
Vietnam

Professor
Chen Michael

School
Lasalle College of
the Arts Singapore

Principal Type
Darker Grotesque
and Xanh Mono

Dimensions
6.7 × 9.4 in.
(17 x 24 cm)

Concept: A Big Crush is my 2020 graduation film from the School of Visual Arts.

Design, Animation, and Art Direction
YouTing Lin
New York

Music and Sound
George Warren

Instructor
Robert Kohr

School
School of Visual Arts°,
New York

Principal Type
Helvetica

Concept: Spaces and Stories, Vol. 1, explores four major architectural works around the globe: Casa Estudio Luis Barragán, Nakagin Capsule Tower, La Muralla Roja, and Haus am Horn. Blending architecture and prose, Spaces and Stories crafts new imaginaries for the events that unfold within homes around the world. Each chapter is designed to reflect the ambience and personality of the showcased home and navigates through these spaces through humble, everyday, and familiar lenses.

Design
Philbert Widjaja°
Woodinville,
Washington

School
School of Art
and Art History
and Design,
University of
Washington

Instructor
Jayme Yen

Principal Type
Helvetica Neue

Dimensions
9 x 12 in.
(22.9 x 30.5 cm)

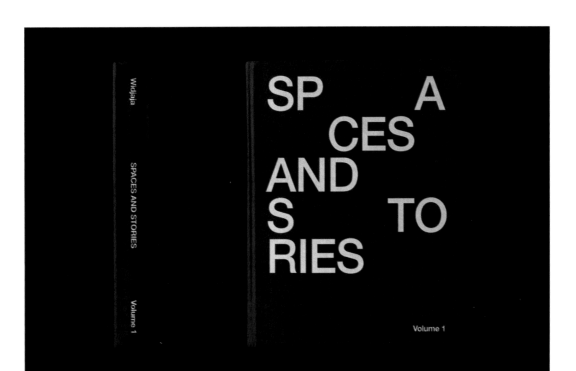

Concept: This project is a personal collection based on Atwood's *The Handmaid's Tale*, in which the author combines "nightmares" of human history. The collection shows both news and book excerpts of events that might have influenced her aside from the story. The composition of several sources with elements such as shadows and overlaps reproduce the aesthetics of an online research with several browser windows open. The book was developed as a master's thesis.

Design
Kristina Hilse
Kiel, Germany

Professors
André Heers and
Annette Le Fort

School
Muthesius University
of Fine Arts
and Design

Principal Type
Arial,
GT Super Display,
Letter Gothic Std,
Minion Pro,
Suisse BP Int'l,
Suisse Works, Times,
and Walbaum

Dimensions
7.9 x 11.2 in.
(20.1 x 28.4 cm)

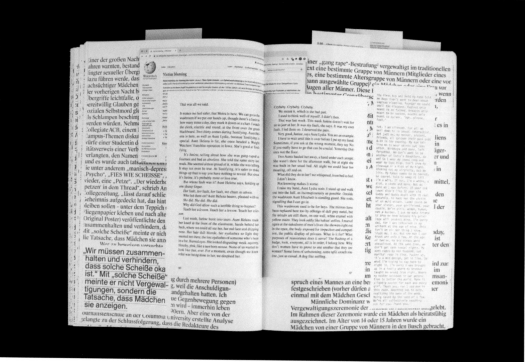

Concept: This interactive typography piece is where type meets order, chaos, and the laws of physics. Coded in p5.js in JavaScript, it was created for a student assignment at MICA for a Generative Typography class. The Chaosifier presently has eight modules, or "phenomena": Fractal, Jellyfish, Mesh, Orbit, Particles, Rain, Space, and Swarm. Each has a mode of order and a mode of chaos. You can try it out yourself at valladares.dev/typechaosifier.

Design
Dev Valladares
Baltimore

Instructor
Dae In Chung

School
Maryland Institute
College of Art (MICA)

Principal Type
Aperçu

1 Order

Type Chaosifier
Fractals

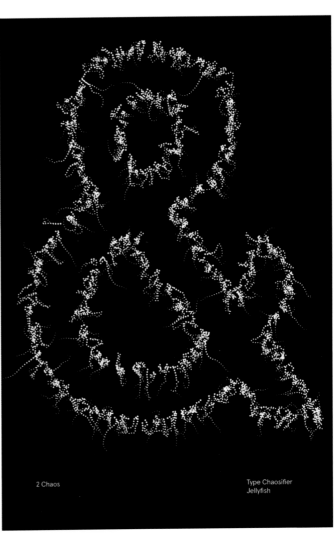

2 Chaos

Type Chaosifier
Jellyfish

Concept: This bachelor's thesis focuses on the design scene in Kyiv, the capital of Ukraine.

Design
Polina Olkhovnikova,
Lera Shaposhnikova,
and
Anastasia Shyshenok
Trier, Ukraine

Professor
Andreas Hogan

Writers
Sofiia Akhmed,
Vladimir Fen,
Bogdana Gelchenko,
and
Kateryna Tkachenko

Typography
Pavel Prannychuk,
Dmitry Rastvortsev,
and
Sergiy Tkachenko

Production
Companies
buch.one
and Kontrastfilm

Supporting Agencies
Looksgreat and
Orchidea Agency

School
University of
Applied Sciences
Trier

Agencies
Sebastian Schubmehl—
Typography and
Graphic Design
and buch.one

Principal Type
Arial
Commune Nuit Debout
Euclid Flex
Explanation Serif
Kritik
Longboy
IBM Plex
Suisse Int'l
Suisse Neue
Suisse Works

Dimensions
8.5 x 12 in.
(21.5 x 30.5 cm)

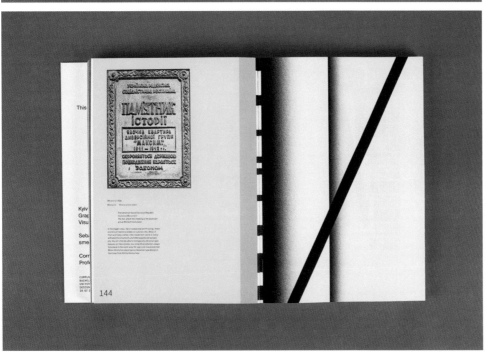

Concept: This specimen was designed for a typeface design course, which was inspired by Richard Wagner's Tannhäuser opera.

Design
Ruslan Abbas
Istanbul

Instructor
Umut Südüak

School
Mimar Sinan Fine
Arts University
Graphic Design
Department

Principal Type
Tannhäuser™ Display
Typeface

Dimensions
24.6 x 35.4 in.
(62.5 × 90 cm)

Concept: *Threshold* examines the relationship between graphic design and liminal spaces.

Design
Shiang-jye Yang
Pasadena, California

Instructor
Brad Bartlett

School
ArtCenter College of Design

Principal Type
Atlas Grotesk
and Druk

Dimensions
8.9. x 10 in.
(22.5 x 25.4 cm)

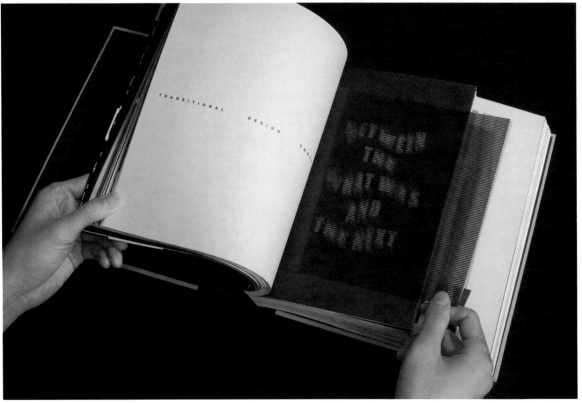

Concept: This set of cards is intended to teach English-speaking users how to form Korean characters, the Hangul.

Design
Jenny Seo Yoon Kim

Professor
Audra Hubbell

School
Washington
University, St. Louis

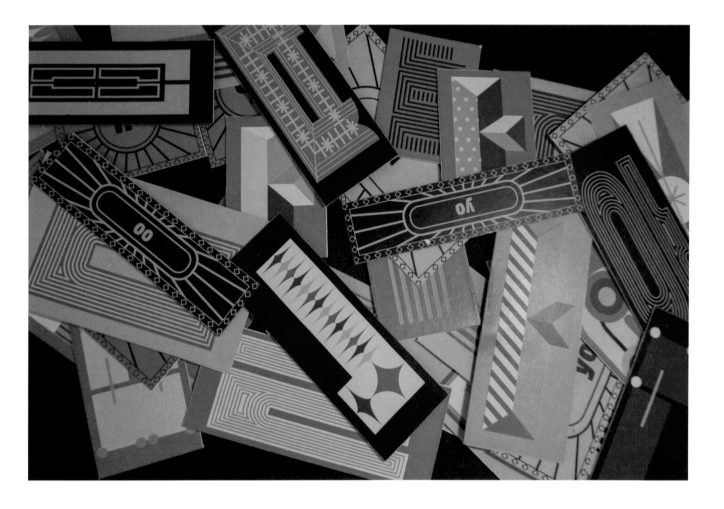

Concept: This series of posters conveys one message, but they all look different in style and design.

Design
Robert Barrese
New York

Instructors
Shawn Hasto
and Anthony Scerri

School
School of Visual Arts,
New York°

Principal Type
Helvetica

Dimensions
18 x 24 in.
(45.7 × 61 cm)

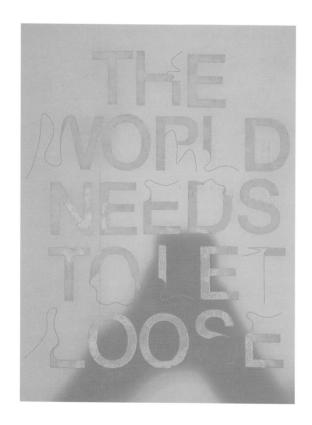

Concept: This is an examination of activism on social media. The message of social media activism lies in the relationship between individual users and the communities the platform can create. Social media activism is transient, but it can create a collective that leads to tangible change beyond the screen. The newspaper as the medium reflects the fleeting nature of social media. Through the use of a clean and utilitarian typeface, large typography, and the bisection of body copy with statistics, the design presents radical ideas in a way that is digestible for the audience.

Design
Phoebe Hsu
Pasadena, California

Instructor
Cheri Gray

School
ArtCenter
College of Design

Principal Type
Suisse Int'l

Dimensions
13.8 x 19.7 in.
(35 × 50 cm)

Concept: This project records my feelings and reflections as an international student during the pandemic.

Design
Xiyu Deng
Valencia, Spain

Instructors
Lorraine Wild and
Michael Worthington

School
California
Institute of Art

Principal Type
Various

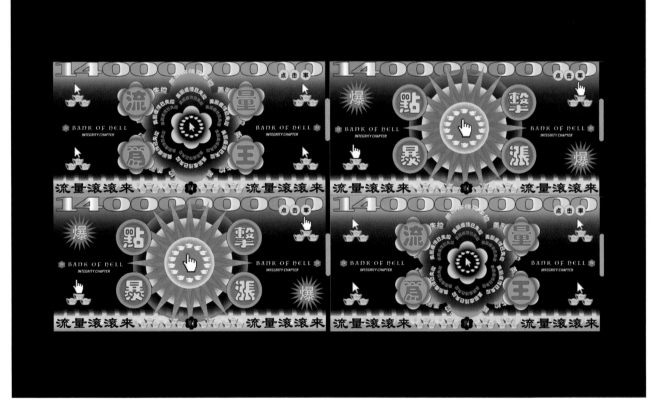

Concept: In an effort to make design fun and happy, I created a magazine called *Wag & Bone* that is dedicated to stories about dogs and their owners. Inspired by the Modern Love section of *The New York Times*, I wanted to create a literary publication that includes essays and analyses on dogs and how they have become an integral part of our lives and our culture as a whole. These stories are meant to bring brevity during a time of chaos and provide comfort to everyone—dog or cat lover. These stories are personal and journalistic, highlighting the fact that dogs are not only our best friends but also family members, confidants, and loyal lifelong companions who stick with us every step of the way.

Design
Ezra Lee
New York

Instructors
Justin Colt
and Jose Fresneda

School
School of Visual Arts,
New York°

Principal Type
Acumin Pro,
Atlas TypeWriter,
Beastly, Calcula STD,
Cimo, Neue World,
and Salvage Display

Dimensions
8.5 x 11 in.
(21.6 x 27.9 cm)

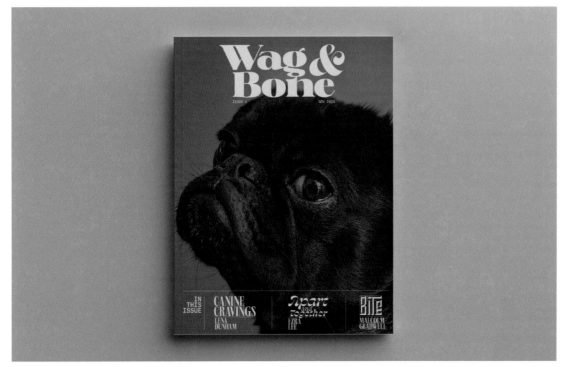

Concept: Roma Publications is a hypothetical rebranding project. Roma is an art publisher and exhibition curator based in Amsterdam. The identity of the hypothetical rebranding is inspired by Roma's diverse body of works. The logo, with a mixture of typeface styles, expresses the modern aesthetic that the publisher primarily presents and the wide range of their published collections. The use of different typeface choices is also cohesively applied to other components of the identity, including ID collaterals and website. Within the identity, brackets are used as a typographic treatment.

Design
Phuong (Chelsea) Le
Pasadena, California

Instructor
Brad Bartlett

School
Art Center
College of Design

Principal Type
GT America Mono,
Helvetica Neue,
Rockwell Std, and
SangBleu Kingdom

Dimensions
24 in x 36 in.
(61 x 91.4 cm)

Concept: This project was inspired by Max De Pree's quote "We cannot become what we want by remaining what we are."

Design
Reagan Copeland
Atlanta

Instructor
Sam Eckersley

School
Savannah College of
Art and Design

Principal Type
Blenny Black

Dimensions
16 x 24 in.
(40.6 × 61 cm)

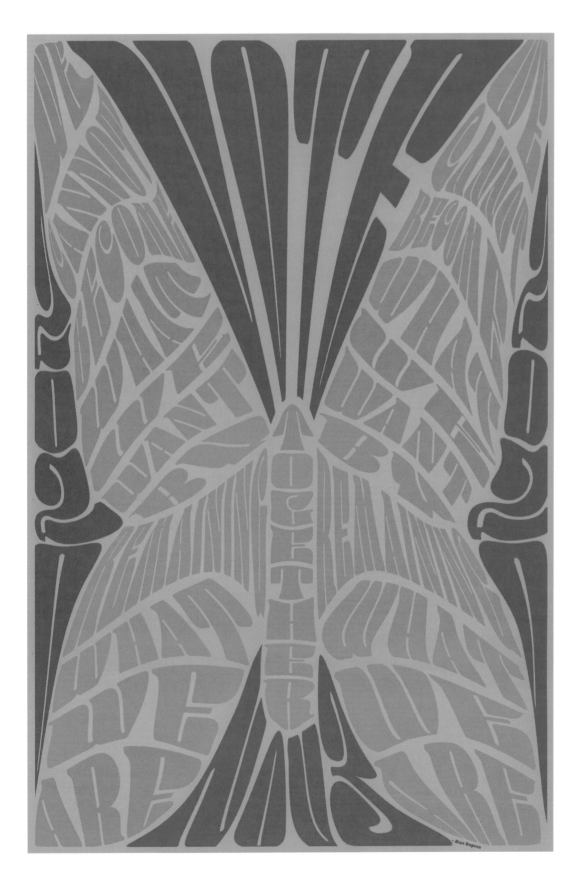

Concept: The identity system was designed for the Plumbers and Gasfitters Employees Union, and the project was intended to reflect the building's Brutalist style on the identity system. The building has a blocky form and includes sharp lines and angles. Therefore, the identity system consists of two columns and two rows of structure, which gives a clean and simplistic approach and creates blocky negative space on the surface. Also, the purpose of the choice of color is to imply raw construction. Overall, the identity system gains a strong mescaline personality and unity with the union's personality.

Design
Gökcan Selem
Melbourne

Instructor
Dominic Hofstede

School
Monash University

Client
PGEU

Principal Type
Untitled Sans

Dimensions
Various

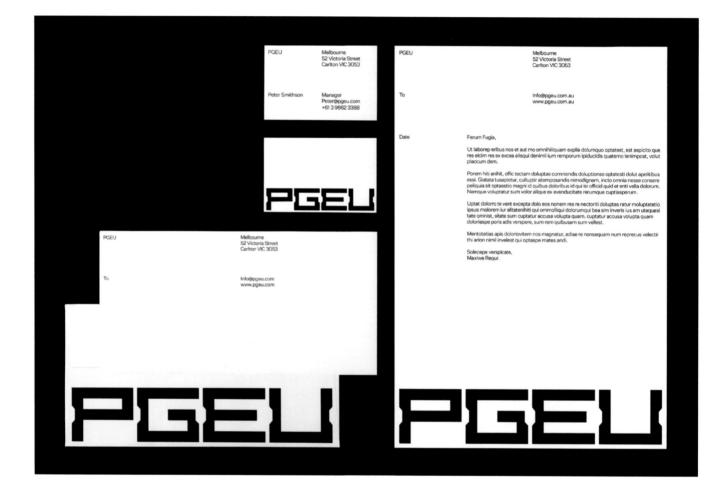

Concept: To promote Jeff Koons's retrospective exhibition at MoMA, the design system and typeface were necessary for the publications. Inspired by Balloon Dog, his most famous work, the typeface was made to emulate his balloon installation. The shape of the typeface that looks inflated and stuck represents the personality of his artwork: funny and playful.

Design
Ji Eun Lee
New York

Instructor
Pedro Mendes

School
School of Visual Arts,
New York°

Principal Type
Neue Haas Grotesk
Display Pro

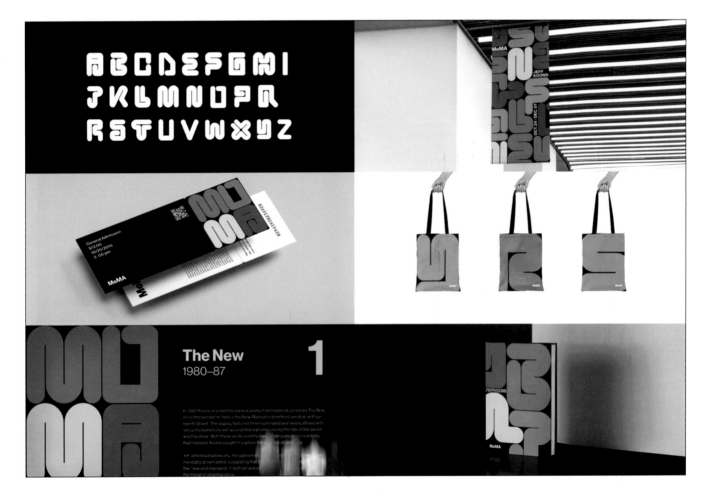

Concept: Smino is an American hip-hop artist, and his music is fun and warm, especially the album *Noir*. This project aimed at designing a fully typographic vinyl record packaging in the theme of surrealism. The typography is bold, expressive, and warped to match the music in the album. A lot of this design was produced by hand and outside the computer to give it a gritty feeling.

Design
Emily Roemer
New York

URL
roemerdesigns.com

Instagram
@roemerDesigns

Instructors
Justin Colt
and Jose Fresneda

School
School of Visual Arts,
New York°,
Masters of Fine Arts
Design (MFAD)
Program

Principal Type
Inknut Antiqua,
Knockout, and
Pitch Sans

Dimensions
12 x 12 in.
(30.5 x 30.5 cm)

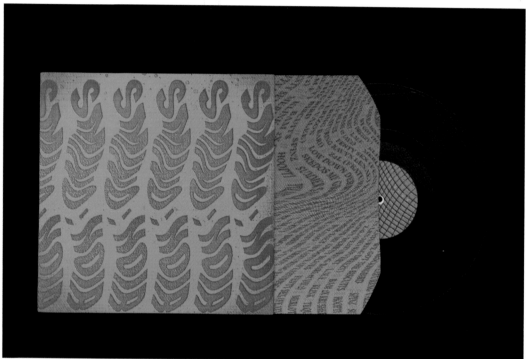

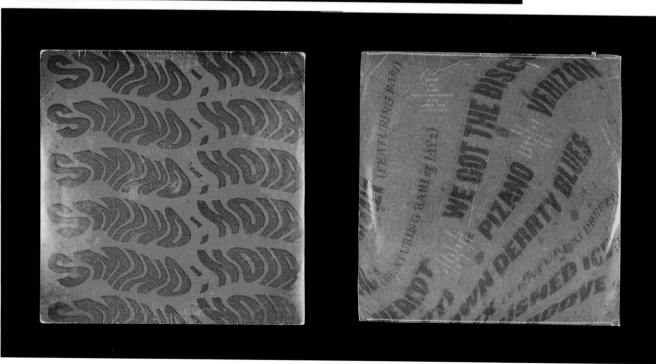

Concept: This is a rebrand of G2E. The new brand name was given to target a broader audience and present a lighter, more engaging feeling.

Design
Eun Jung Bahng°
Pasadena, California

Instructors
Ivan Cruz,
Rudy Manning,
Miles Mazzie,
and Roy Tatum

School
ArtCenter
College of Design

Principal Type
Custom

Concept: This rebranding project is for the Internet Archive.

Design
Yicen Liu
Pasadena, California

Instructor
Brad Bartlett

School
ArtCenter
College of Design

Principal Type
Internet Display,
Media 77,
and Px Grotesk

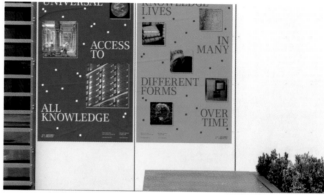

Concept: These are custom-lettered book
covers for L. Frank Baum's timeless children's
series about the magical land of Oz.

Design
Justin Wong
New York

Instructor
Pablo Delcan

School
School of Visual Arts,
New York°

Concept: This is the brand identity for the sushi restaurant Sukiyabashi Jiro.

Design
Minkwan Kim
New York

Principal Type
Neuhaus Grotesk

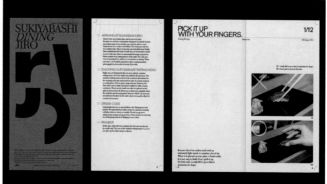

Concept: The new identity for E3 seeks to connect the real world and the virtual world through gaming.

Design
Tong Li
Pasadena, California

Instructors
Gerardo Herrera
and Monica Schlaug

School
ArtCenter
College of Design

Principal Type
Fixture Ultra,
Founders Grotesk,
and Pilat Compressed

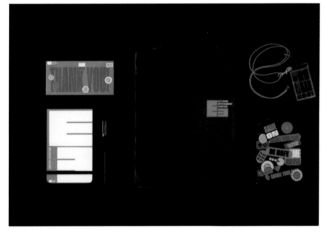

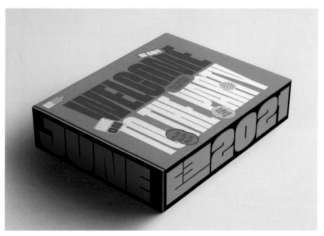

Concept: The poster series showcases each artist's philosophy through customized type for each of their initials.

Design
Yin-Yi Lin
New York

Instructor
Natasha Jen

Client
Museum
of Modern Art

School
School of Visual Arts,
New York°

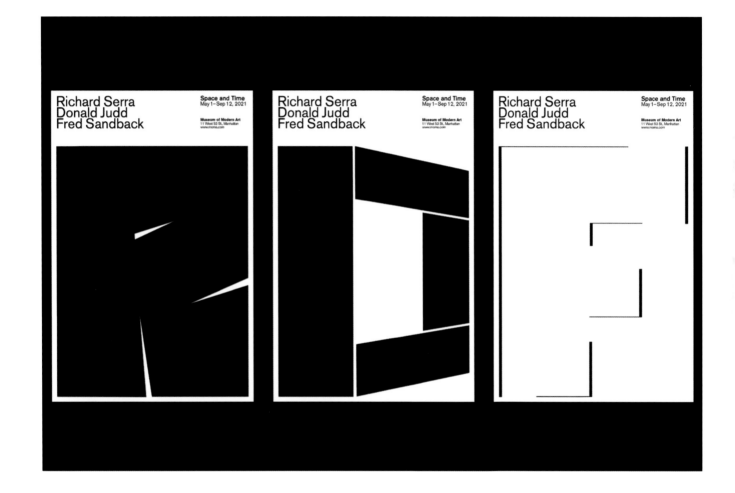

Concept: Hudson is a company that encourages New Yorkers to explore the Hudson Valley in Upstate New York.

Design
Kelly Wang
New York

Instructors
Shawn Hasto
and Andrew Herzog

School
School of Visual Arts,
New York°

Concept: This is a new identity system for EDGE Science Fiction and Fantasy Publishing.

Design
Shirlin Chia Ling Kao
New York

Instructors
Courtney Gooch
and Rory Simms

School
School of Visual Arts,
New York°

Publishing
EDGE Publishing

Principal Type
Aperçu Mono,
Druk Text Bold,
Druk Text Medium,
Druk Wide Medium,
Gosha Sans Bold,
Gosha Sans Ultrabold,
Object Sans Medium,
Object Sans Bold,
and OCR-A

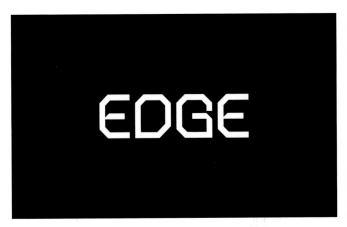

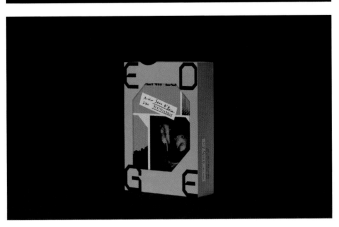

Chair Statement
Meet the Judges

This competition, and this conversation, is part of a relay race. This year—on its 24th run, amid local lockdowns—the TDC's type competition expanded. We were able to have 6 judges instead of 4, hailing from a greater geographical footprint than ever before in the Type Director Club's history. Entries for the competition came from 54 different countries, with winning entries from 49.

This translated to more viewpoints, a wider understanding of different scripts, and an engaged dialogue about what it means to be relevant in the world of type; what it means to provide a valuable contribution. The conversation in the judging room was a learning session, prodding for deeper awareness about cultural subtleties and individual experience. We also witnessed a small but prevalent re-tilting of influence, where at least two of the judges picks are typefaces initially designed for, and thus influenced by, non-western scripts (Masada, Huai). While it is still a smaller slice of the pie, it is simultaneously a mark of a door wedging open.

I've judged numerous competitions, and this is my first time chairing one. I'm inspired and humbled by how not-guaranteed winning is, with many renowned foundries not making the final cut while lesser known and student work is here in the pages that follow. I see it as sign of optimism for those that might otherwise carry a similar skeptical streak, to instead put their best specimen forward and apply. In a year with so much turbulence, and so much lost faith in our institutions, member-driven organizations like the TDC are a chance to collectively unionize toward a world we want to see. Where anyone interested is able to enter, to volunteer, to raise opinions, and to contribute to the letterforms and building blocks that have the capability to connect, and to represent, our global community.

Ksenya
Samarskaya

Ksenya Samarskaya
medium.com/samarskaya
@samarskaya

1

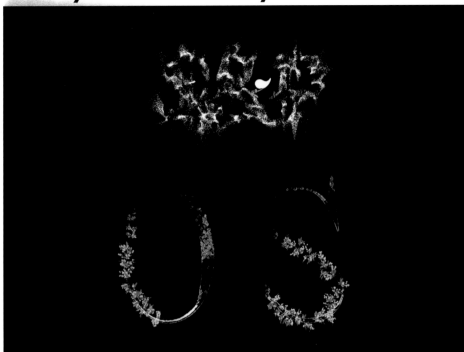

2

Ksenya Samarskaya is a strategic consultant and creative director, passionate about the nuances inherent in our visual and literary culture. Samarskaya has served on the board of AIGA/NY and taught creative practices at Harbour.Space University (Barcelona), IE School of Architecture and Design (Madrid), School of Visual Arts (New York), and the University of the Arts (Philadelphia). She has previously judged competitions for ADC/The One Club, Communication Arts, TISDC, TDC, and the SoTA Catalyst Award.

Samarskaya & Partners is a creative practice with a collaboration model at heart, featuring a rotating team of kick-ass designers, developers, copywriters, and artists, who come together to craft visual identities, brand strategies, marketing initiatives, editorials, and multiscript type design. Clients and collaborators have included Adobe, Apple, Google, IDEO, Intel, Monotype, Rosetta, Snoop Dogg, WeWork, YouTube, and others.

3

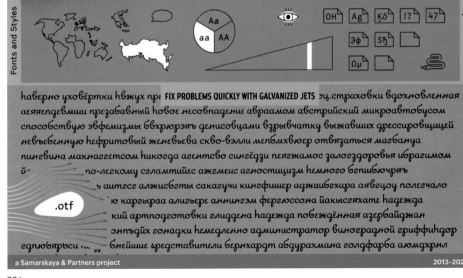

a Samarskaya & Partners project   2013–2021

1
Top:
S&P in salt, viewable at samarskaya.com, programming by Eric Jacobsen
Bottom:
O and S, from THRESHOLDS, in collaboration with Vincent Wagner

2
Dimensional TypeExplorations from Samarskaya & Partners

3
Galvanized Jets. A type proofer from Samarskaya & Partners. Since 2013.

JUDGES

Agyei Archer

Peter Bil'ak

Nadine Chahine

Sandra García

Noël Leu

Ryoko Nishizuka

Agyei
Archer

Peter Bil'ak

Noël
Leu

Ryoko
Nishizuka

Agyei Archer agyei.design @agyeiDesign

1

OLD ENGLISH

ROTUNDA

SCHWABACHER

FRAKTUR

KNOW YOUR BLACKLETTERS

Agyei Archer is a multidisciplinary designer and art director from Trinidad, focusing on commercial work that integrates graphics, type design, and programming. He recently co-founded Unqueue, a mobile app designed to improve retail experiences in the Caribbean. Past clients include Google, RISD, the Government of Trinidad and Tobago, and the Caribbean Mental Health Foundation.

Agyei runs a small studio in Trinidad, and works on type projects that are both referential of the space he's in, and with consideration of the implications for the global Black population as a whole. As a result, he's interested in African Latin language support, but also non-Latin writing systems of colour. Most recently, he completed a digitisation of the Afáka script, the world's only creole writing system, and he's currently working on a variable font project for Google.

2

3

4

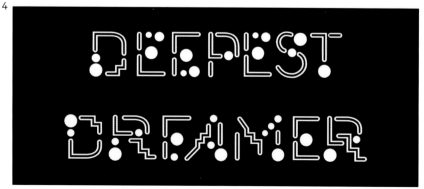

1

2

3

4

Peter Biľak
typotheque.com
@typotheque

1

Greta Sans

*The complete type system for
online and offline publishing.*

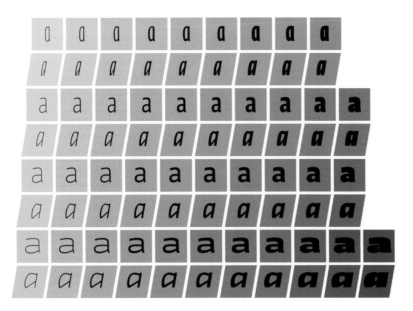

Greta explores a multidimensional
continuum of possibilities. It is a
powerful toolbox capable of dealing
with the most complex typographical
situations. It has been 10 years
in development and comes in 80
styles of Latin alphabet, and also
Cyrillic, Greek, Arabic, Hebrew and
Devanagari support makes it truly
an unprecedented type system,
supporting over 300 languages, and
over 2 billion speakers.

TPTQ.com/Greta_Sans

Peter Biľak works in the field of editorial, graphic, and type design. In 1999 he started Typotheque type foundry, in 2000, together with Stuart Bailey he co-founded art & design journal Dot Dot Dot, in 2012 he started Works That Work, a magazine of unexpected creativity, in 2015 together with Andrej Krátky he co-founded Fontstand.com, a font rental platform. Peter is teaching at the Type & Media, postgraduate course at the Royal Academy of Arts, The Hague.

1
Greta Sans comes in 10 weights which, combined with its four widths (Compressed, Condensed, Extended), create a tremendous range of possibilities. Even the intervals between the styles are an integral part of this unified typeface system.

2
Greta is a powerful toolbox capable of dealing with the most complex typographical situations, supporting Latin, Greek, Cyrillic, Armenian, Arabic, Hebrew, Devanagari, Thai and Hangul (Korean).

3
November is a highly functional typeface inspired by street signage, with extremely large language support covering: Latin, Greek, Cyrillic, Arabic, Hebrew, Armenian, Georgina, Thai, Chinese, Japanese Kana, Canadian Syllabic, Bangla, Devanagari, Gurmukhi, Kannada, Malayalam, Meetei Mayek, Ol Chiki, Odia, Tamil, Telugu, making it one of the largest multiscript typeface available.

4
Slovakia EU presidency stamp, 2016 — A commemorative postage stamp celebrating Slovakia's presidency of the Council of the European Union. The postage stamp depicts Slovakia's forests, which cover more than 40% of the country, and are pine-scented.

2

3

November multilingual type system

from Typotheque.com

November Latin
November Ελληνικά (Greek)
November Кириллица (Cyrillic)
November عربي (Arabic)
November עברית (Hebrew)
November Հայաստան (Armenian)
November ქართული (Georgian)
November ไทย (Thai)
November 中文 (Chinese)
November ひらがな (Japanese Kana)
November ᐸᑎᐅᑕᖕᐊᐅᒃ (Syllabics)

November বাংলা (Bangla)
November देवनागरी (Devanagari)
November ગુજરાતી (Gujarati)
November ਗੁਰਮੁਖੀ (Gurmukhi)
November ಕನ್ನಡ (Kannada)
November മലയാളം (Malayalam)
November ꯃꯤꯇꯩ ꯃꯌꯦꯛ (Meetei Mayek)
November ᱚᱞ ᱪᱤᱠᱤ (Ol Chiki)
November ଓଡ଼ିଆ (Odia)
November தமிழ் (Tamil)
November తెలుగు (Telugu)

4

Nadine Chahine

arabictype.com
@arabictype

1

2

3

4

Dr. Nadine Chahine is an award-winning Lebanese type designer and principal at ArabicType Ltd. She has an MA in Typeface Design from the University of Reading, UK, a PhD from Leiden University, The Netherlands, and a Master of Studies in International Relations from Cambridge University. She has numerous awards including two Awards for Excellence in Type Design from the Type Directors Club in New York in 2008 and 2011. Her typefaces include: Frutiger Arabic, Neue Helvetica Arabic, Univers Next Arabic, Palatino Arabic, and Koufiya.

Nadine's work has been featured in the 5th edition of Megg's History of Graphic Design and in 2012 she was selected by Fast Company as one of its 100 Most Creative People in Business. In 2016 her work was showcased in the 4th edition of First Choice which highlights the work of the 250 top global designers. In 2017, Nadine was selected by Creative Review to their Creative Leaders 50.

1
This poster features a quote by the Palestinian poet Mahmoud Darwish in which he says: The most of what I fear is when treason becomes a point of view.

2
A famous Arab quote that says, if the people ever wanted life, then destiny must comply; and the night must end and the chains must break.

3
Ila Abi: Poster featuring Sawad, a typeface exploration of grief. The word read: to my father.

4
The Arabic word free as a male and female adjective.

Sandra García @tipastype
@wondertype

1

Woun iek Serif

12/14 WOUN IEK REGULAR /BOLD

Mug phidag wautarr gaaisim chi iek phãnum maach wounaan phobor athee chi wautarr khuun GENTE eem khuunau oopiig parãg phobor Kartagena aajem durr LABICCO (labicco aawayan phidag ompaanum dich khirjug eemua kolombia ee kartagena) aajem khuunau ed 2016. Chi wautarr chaain athee waujim thumaam dojãrragam khuun durragam khuunau magwie chaainag ẽsap dau jaujem woun Bladimir Moya aajem, mawia phobor kartagena durr magwie ãandui ich khiirjug oopiig. Mug phidag wautarr gaaisim chi iek phãnum maach wounaan phobor athee chi wautarr khuun GENTE eem khuunau oopiig parãg phobor Kartagena aajem durr LABICCO (labicco aawayan phidag ompaanum dich khirjug eemua kolombia ee kartagena) aajem khuunau ed 2016. Chi wautarr chaain athee waujim thumaam dojãrragam khuun durragam khuunau magwie chaainag ẽsap (...)

14/16 WOUN IEK BOLD/BOLD ITALIC

Mug phidag wautarr gaaisim chi iek phãnum maach wounaan phobor athee chi wautarr khuun GENTE eem khuunau oopiig parãg phobor Kartagena aajem durr LABICCO (labicco aawayan phidag ompaanum dich khirjug eemua kolombia ee kartagena) aajem khuunau ed 2016. Chi wautarr chaain athee waujim thumaam dojãrragam khuun durragam khuunau magwie chaainag ẽsap dau jaujem woun Bladimir Moya aajem, mawia phobor kartagena durr magwie ãandui ich khiirjug oopiig.
Mug phidag wautarr gaaisim chi iek phãnum maach wounaan phobor athee chi wautarr khuun GENTE eem khuunau (...)

Puch chi
AMITAUO
magbamun
www.tipografiawounaan.com
CHI AAYAU JUR
atha chi
phãnum dewam
magwia jaauba agjoo nemig khaa ich khapeenag.
Mamá o papá haz que tu niño elija una letra amiga para contar una aventura con sus amiguitas.

Variables	Gráficos
Escolar	
Regular	
Regular Italic	
Bold	
Bold Italic	
Black	
Black Italic	

Diseño de fuente: Manuel López Rocha, Sandra García Saldarriaga, Óscar Guerrero, Sergio Aristizabal   Ilustraciones: David Espinosa.

Graduated in Graphic Design from the Universidad del Área Andina, Bogota-Colombia. Master in Typographic Design from the Gestalt Studies Center. Teacher with more than 10 years of career. Speaker at national and international conferences, recently in the version of ATypI Tokio 2019 and Letrástica 3, Guadalajara. Winner of the 2018 FONCA Co-investment Grant from the Secretary of Culture of Mexico. She received the international Clap award for font design Xantolo, co-author of the book "Elementype, a practical guide to typographic use." Co-founding partner of Tipastype.

2

3

4

1
Woun Iek font family.
The project consists of a typeface family of 3 weights and a tilt variable, a keyboard and a set of symbols.

2
Emperatriz
A typeface with deep roots in the tradition of Roman Capital letters.

3
Elementype
Elementype is a fast and effective reference book that facilitates the understanding and learning of complex content, through agile and clear graphics and texts.

4
School health in latin america and the caribbean / Questionnaire
Client: Pan American Health Organization

317

Noël Leu
grillitype.com
@grillitype

1

Noël Leu is a graphic designer and co-founder of the Swiss based type foundry Grilli Type. He usually spends a large part of the year traveling the globe to broaden his horizon, getting inspired, and to give lectures about design.

2

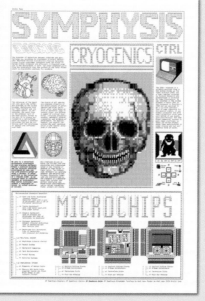

3

1
GT America
Typeface and
newspaper spread
Design by Grilli Type

2
GT Symphisis
Typeface and poster
(cover and back)
Design by Grilli Type

3
GT Maru Emoji font
Emoji colour and B/W font
Design by Grilli Type

Ryoko Nishizuka

1

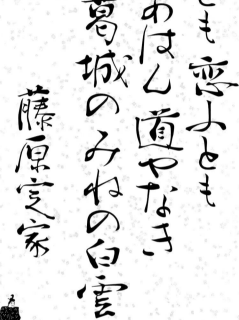

KAZURAKI®

Adobe's Type Engineering team in Japan has created a ground-breaking new typeface that is visually rich and free from the rigid design protocols that have constrained Japanese fonts for decades. Called Kazuraki, this new design serves as an inspiration and model for other CJK type designers and type foundries.

The Kazuraki typeface design was inspired by the calligraphy of 12th century artist and writer Fujiwara-no-Teika, who is considered to be one of the greatest poets in Japan's history. Inspired by Teika's calligraphy, Adobe Senior Designer Ryoko Nishizuk a began creating a new typeface years ago. Her work won the Silver Prize at the Morisawa's 2002 International Typeface Design Competition. Knowing that Japanese type foundries had a strong interest in creating capabilities.

Most Japanese fonts are monospaced, meaning that their glyphs are designed to fit within an imaginary book known as the em-square. On the other hand, Kazuraki is an example of genuinely proportional type that can faithfully represent the calligraphic quality of the typeface inspired by an ancient master. While Kazuraki is clearly not suitable for typesetting text in books, it is expected to be used by designers for what typographers refer to as "display uses." Display use include advertising copy, headlines, greeting cards, movie and book titles, restaurant menus, and so on.

Kazuraki is a special-purpose Japanese font that includes glyphs for the complete set of kana (hiragana and katakana) and punctuation, along with a limited number of glyphs for kanji (ideographs or Chinese characters) .

難くとも恋ふとも

あはん道やなき

君葛城のみねの白雲

藤原定家

プロポーショナルかな書体 －定家仮名源宗伝

かづらき。

ADOBE ORIGINALS   Created exclusively for Adobe by award-winning type designers worldwide. Adobe Originals include new designs as well as revivals of typographic classics.   Tk Adobe Typekit   Available for use on the web and in desktop applications through Typekit.

© 2010 Adobe Systems Incorporated. All rights reserved. Adobe, the Adobe logo, the Adobe Originals logo, Kazuraki and Typekit are either registered trademarks or trademarks of Adobe Systems Incorporated in the United States and/or other countries.

Ryoko Nishizuka received her degree in type design from Musashino Art University in 1995, she joined Adobe in 1997, and is currently a Principal Designer of Japanese Typography. Ryoko was a member of the team that designed and developed the first Adobe Originals Japanese typefaces, Kozuka Mincho and Kozuka Gothic.
She designed the typeface Ryo family, the world's first full proportional OpenType Japanese font Kazuraki, Source Han Sans and Source Han Serif as the Pan-CJK typeface family and Ten-Mincho. She has won several awards including NY TDC, Tokyo TDC and the Morisawa Awards International Typeface Design Competition.

1
Kazuraki is based on the writing style of Fujiwara no Teika (1162–1241), an aristocrat and a distinguished poet. Unlike other traditional Japanese typefaces, Kazuraki is designed as a fully proportional typeface allowing each character to have its own width, and this helps the representation of the dynamic movement of brush strokes.

2
Source Han Sans is a Pan-CJK font co-developed by Google and Adobe. It is a versatile typeface that can be effective for a wide range of uses from long texts to titles.

3
Source Han Serif was born from the same Pan-CJK font project as that of Source Han Sans. In order to improve the readability of the Mincho Style design on digital display devices, its characters are designed slightly larger, and the horizontal strokes heavier.

4
Ten Mincho will be useful for a broad range of settings, such as advertising copy, book titles, and greeting cards. Prominent in the design are the dynamic characteristics of hand-written characters, as well as a stroke formation style that is typically seen in the Kawaraban printed newspapers from the mid- to late Edo period (1603–1863) in Japan.

2

At daybreak I leave Baidi amidst clouds aglow.

朝に辞す白帝彩雲の間
朝辭白帝彩雲間
朝辞白帝彩云间
아침 일찍 구름 낀
백제성을 떠나

3

兰陵美酒郁金香，
蘭陵美酒鬱金香，
蘭陵の美酒はチューリップの香り，
울금향 그윽한 난릉의 좋은 술은

流
流流

4

明朝体 Pan-CJK フォントを実現。

"積もった雪と一緒に Ten 明

貂 山椒の花が落ちる

min てん cho 朝

Adobe Originals Ten Mincho & Text

Adobe Fonts

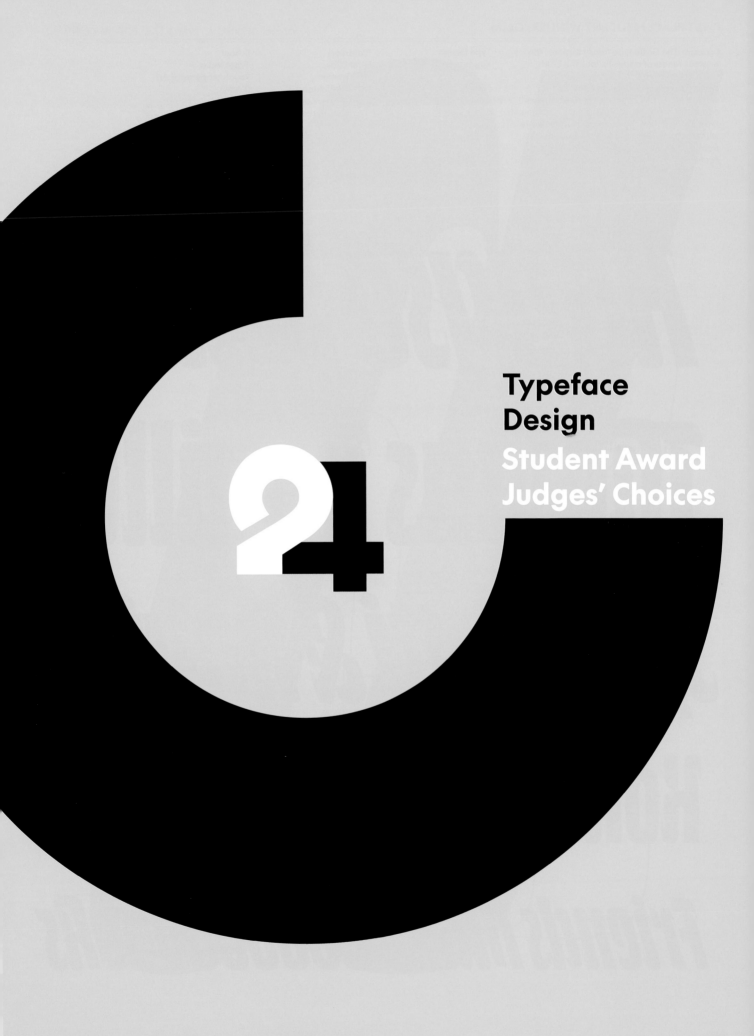

Typeface
Design

**Student Award
Judges' Choices**

It's also one of the most unique designs I've seen in a long time, especially in an era of neo-grotesques and geometrics all trying to be the Next Big Thing.
Agyei Archer

Huai is a triumph of design, and is as politically relevant a typeface as I can think of in these times. Potch created a Thai/Latin type family that does the work of shirking the urge to "Latinise" the Thai, and instead deploys a Latin whose Thai roots are clear in their elegance, rhythm, and the font's charming tone. It's also one of the most unique designs I've seen in a long time, especially in an era of neo-grotesques and geometrics all trying to be the Next Big Thing.

With Thai script, there are two different terminal styles—the Loop terminal style, original forms of Thai glyphs; and the Loopless, which has evolved to best coordinate with Latin sans serif. In recent years, this Thai Loopless style has continued to change to become 'more Latin.' One would go so far as to define these heavily Latin-influenced typefaces as Thai Latinized. This curiosity with shifting influences turns the idea around and explores what would happen if the vernacular Thai scripts actually influenced their Latin counterparts instead.

Huai Latin letterforms have embraced a warm, expressive from vernacular Thai handwritten. Then Huai Thai allows the result from Latin influenced back again. Through the design process of Huai, I came across my own term which I would like to define, an 'Inversion of Thai Latinized'.

TYPEFACES

Type Design
Potch Auacherdkul°
Bangkok

A new bilingual typeface
stands in between Thai scr
Thai script &Latin. Est
อินเวิร์สชั่น}ออฟไทยละตินไน
ระหว่างลายมือและดิจิทัลฟอ
Handwritten street sign

Vazeh Classic Quranic is a wonderful mix of heritage and modernity.
Nadine Chahine

Vazeh Classic Quranic is a wonderful mix of heritage and modernity. The style is strongly grounded in manuscript and calligraphic traditions but the overall design feels contemporary and fresh. My favourite aspect of this design is that the typeface does not sacrifice classical proportions in its pursuit of modernity and this confidently shows the way towards a style of Naskh design that is rooted in heritage but designed with today's aesthetic preferences and sensitivities.

A typeface that is nice to read, having Iranian spirit, containing very legible and recognizable letters, not scaring off the young audience by just looking at it but actually encouraging them to read Holy Quran; a typeface that is invisible, not showing off, and not interrupting the reading rhythm. By studying Neyrizi Naskh script more than ever, we revived the calligraphic elegance. We designed lots of Ligatures for this typeface and also designed 2 to 3 different lengths for letters, joints, and diacritics in order to create the best balance between positive and negative spaces.

TYPEFACES

Typographers
Reza Bakhtiarifard and
Omid Emamian
Tehran

Type Foundry
Maryam Soft

Technical Production
Naser Azarshab

Client
Ofogh Rooydad Co.

Concept
This is a typeface for the Holy Quran that is nice to read. It has an Iranian spirit and is warm, friendly, and legible.

ظَلَّلْنَا | لَيْلَةَ الصِّيَامِ | يُبَدِّلُونَهُۥ

الصَّٰبِئِينَ ← الصَّٰبِئِينَ ← الصَّٰبِئِينَ ← الصَّٰبِئِينَ ← الصَّٰبِئِينَ

إِنَّ الَّذِينَ كَفَرُوا سَوَآءٌ عَلَيْهِمْ ءَأَنذَرْتَهُمْ أَمْ لَمْ تُنذِرْهُمْ لَا يُؤْمِنُونَ ﴿٦﴾ خَتَمَ اللَّهُ عَلَىٰ قُلُوبِهِمْ وَعَلَىٰ سَمْعِهِمْ وَعَلَىٰٓ أَبْصَٰرِهِمْ غِشَٰوَةٌ وَلَهُمْ عَذَابٌ عَظِيمٌ ﴿٧﴾ وَمِنَ النَّاسِ مَن يَقُولُ ءَامَنَّا بِاللَّهِ وَبِالْيَوْمِ الْأَخِرِ وَمَا هُم

فَسَيَكْفِيكَهُمُ اللَّهُ

بَقْلِهَا وَ قِثَّآئِهَا وَ فُومِهَا وَ عَدَسِهَا وَ بَصَلِهَا

329

The quality of the images allows us to "feel" the weight of the ink falling on the paper.
Sandra García

LiebeHeide takes full advantage of Color Font technology and brings us an intelligent font, with multiple iterations between letters, adjusting to what really happens when we write by hand - with errors included - that give the font a human flavor that Font designers have always wanted to capture in a typeface. The quality of the images allows us to "feel" the weight of the ink falling on the paper. The ligatures proposed by the typeface feel natural and necessary. The font brings interesting graphics and icons that give it a warm and friendly extra, the underlined texts are an achievement of typographic engineering, patience and meticulousness.

Congratulations to Liebe Fonts and their project LiebeHeide Color Font for this well-deserved recognition.

Amazingly real looking handwritten messages: LiebeHeide is a bitmap color font that authentically reproduces the writing of a ballpoint pen. A combination of OpenType and color Font technology makes this typographic miracle possible.

LiebeHeide is based on high-res digitized ballpoint pen writings with lots of alternate letters and ligatures. Typical handwriting attributes like symbols and doodles, up to underlines and strikethroughs give this typeface its charm.
To increase performance, the font has 3 different resolutions, so that applications only load the size that is currently needed.

TYPEFACES

Design
Ulrike Rausch

Type Design
LiebeFonts
Berlin

LiebeHeide

a novel color font based on high-res digitized ballpoint pen writings with lots of alternate ❤ letters and ligatures.

Handwriting attributes ~~with~~ like sym~~-~~bols & doodles, ~~as~~ underlines, and strikethroughs give this type-face its ~~pretty~~ charm.

AÁĂÂÄÀĀĄÅÃÆBCĆČÇDĐĎÐEÉĚÊËĒÈĘFGĞĠGH IÍĬÎÏÌĪ JKĶĹĽĿŁĻLCMNŃŇŇŅÑOÓŎÔÖÒŐØÕŒPPQRŔŘŖ SŚŠŞŚßTFŤŢŢUÚŬÛÜÙŰŪŲVWẂŴẄẀXYÝŶŸỲZ ŹŽŻABCDEFGHIJKLMNOPQRSTUVWXYZASRAH§

aáăâäàāąåãæbcćčçdðďđeéěêëēèęfgğĝġhiíĭîïìī ijkķĺľŀłļlmnńňņŋñ oóŏôöòőøõœppqrŕřŗsśšşśßtŧťţ ţuúŭûüùűūųvwẃŵẅẁxyýŷÿỳzźžż abcdefghijklmnopqrsftuvwyzaefghiklmnortuaeiooeflm nsvwyæszszce cer ch er ff ita nn on osí sh ss ta th tt ve ch er ff sh ss th tt 0123456789012345678901234567897/ ½ ¼ ⅛ .,:;…!¡?¿·,·:!?·,·˙˙**#/\(){}[]---—_-„""''«»"'↑→↓←↦←↤ ₵¤$€£¥¢$€+-×=><≈∞%‰%@@&§&§©®℗°†‡ ☆♡♥✓☺☹☺☹_____⚡≡⊙⊘✗⊁⌇≡

In addition to the well-balanced skeleton, dynamic features such as large curved horizontal lines can be seen.
Ryoko Nishizuka

This font is basically a thick Chinese regular script common brush stroke. In addition to the well-balanced skeleton, dynamic features such as large curved horizontal lines can be seen. On the other hand, the shape that the brush makes, such as the corner part and the shape of the start, is suppressed. As a result, the characters are quite bold, but I thought they were highly readable. Congratulations on your award.

Coca-Cola Care Font is based on the inspiration from the trademark font adopted by Coca-Cola Care in the early period after it returned to the Chinese market. By taking advantage of the unique expression of "Care" in the Chinese culture, Coca-Cola China interprets its understanding of the "Care" culture in strokes in hope of providing everyone with a customized font in the digital era.

TYPEFACES

Art Direction
Yin Qiu, Jia Yang,
and Yichao Xu

Production Companies
CoolCharacter, Shanghai
and
FounderType, Beijing

Client
Coca-Cola China /
Shanghai

Extra bouncy strokes

Powerful truning angle

Firm handwriting style

Tight strokes

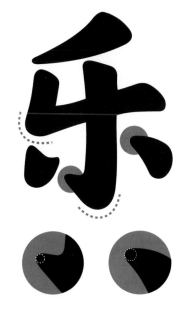

Rounded corner like water drop

可口可乐在乎体
Coca-Cola Care Font

天地玄黄宇宙洪荒日月
盈昃辰宿列张寒来暑往
秋收冬藏闰余成岁律吕
调阳云腾致雨露结为霜
金生丽水玉出昆冈剑号
巨阙珠称夜光果珍李柰
菜重芥姜海咸河淡鳞潜
羽翔龙师火帝鸟官人皇
始制文字乃服衣裳推位
让国有虞陶唐吊民伐罪
周发殷汤坐朝问道垂拱
平章爱育黎首臣伏戎羌
遐迩一体率宾归王鸣凤
在竹白驹食场化被草木

可口可乐在乎体
Coca-Cola Care Font

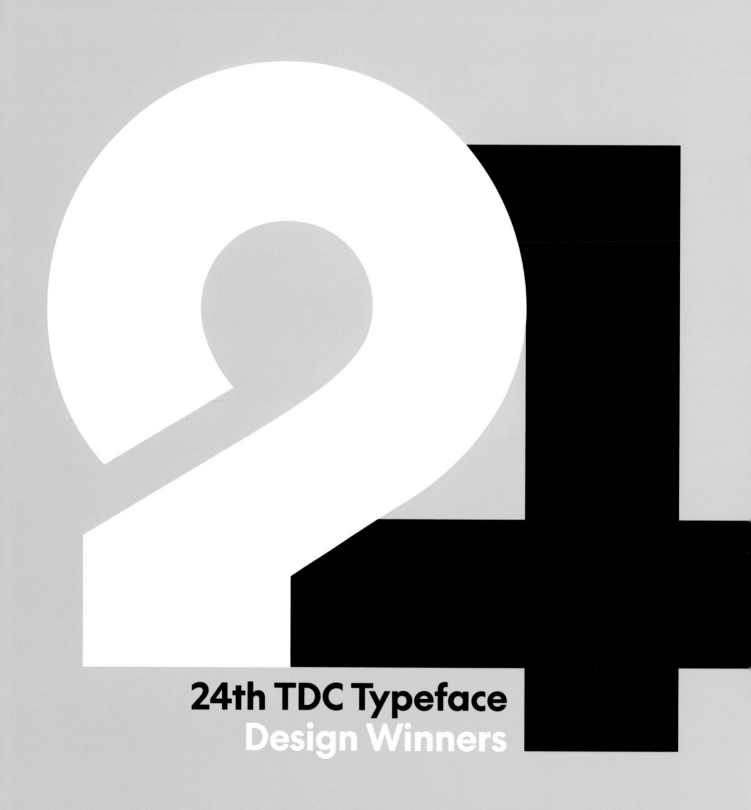

24th TDC Typeface
Design Winners

Concept: Balcony is a display type family inspired by motifs of metal safety grills. The primary purpose of the type family is to create a grill-like pattern when letterforms are placed together. The best way to use this typeface is without leading, as shown in the visuals. The family comes with four weights (Thin, Light, Regular, and Bold) and two stylistic sets, including dingbats. It supports Western and Central European languages.

Type Design
Shaily Patel
and Hitesh
(Rocky) Malaviya
Baroda, India

School
Department of
Applied Art,
Faculty of Fine
Arts, The Maharaja
Sayajirao University
of Baroda

Weights
Bold, Light, Regular,
and Thin

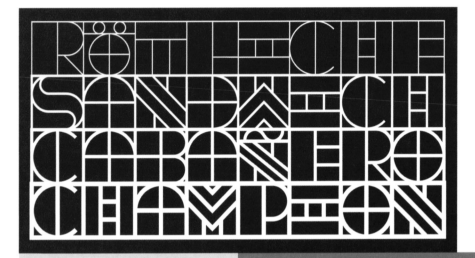

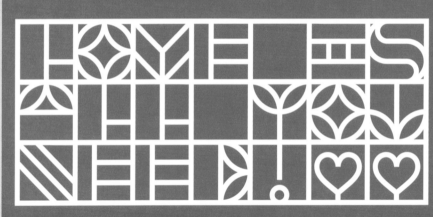

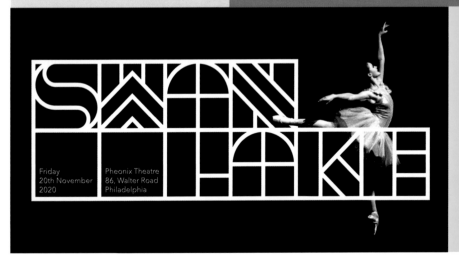

Concept: This is a super-condensed contemporary Devanagari and Latin typeface with unusual yet elegant proportions.

Type Design
Kimya Gandhi

Foundry
Mota Italic

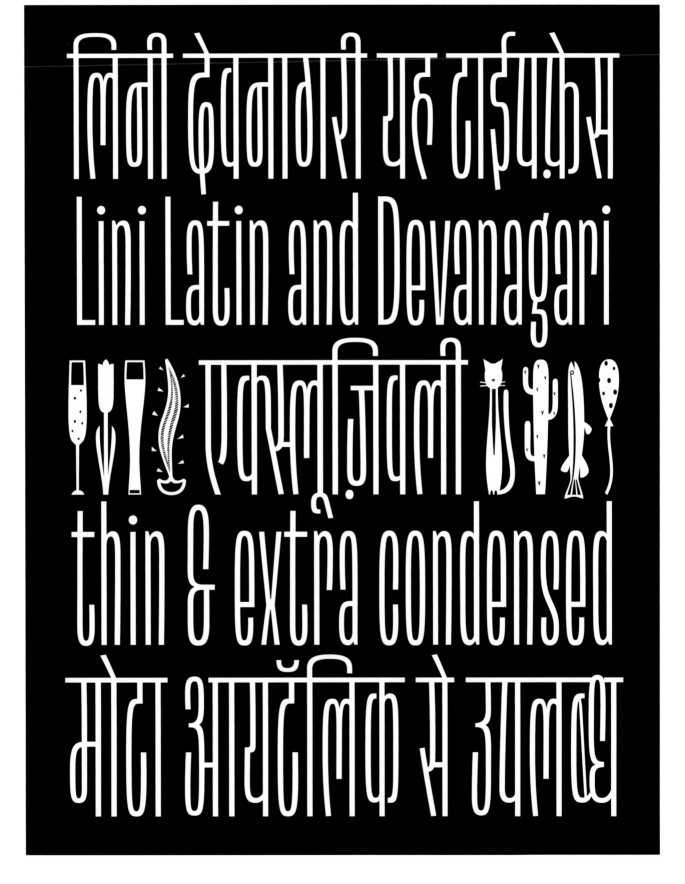

Concept: This is a customized typeface for the Swedish real estate contractor Vasakronan.

Design
Kristian Möller

Creative Team
Isabelle Rudström-
Österlund

Creative Direction
Jonas Bäckman

Design Firm
Familjen Sthlm

Client
Vasakronan

VASAKRONAN SERIF DISPLAY

ABCDEFGHIJKLM
NOPQRSTUVWXYZ
0123456789
abcdefghijklmno
pqrstuvwxyz
"., !?fiflffjfk@¶§&åäö"

VASAKRONAN SERIF TEXT

ABCDEFGHIJKLMNOPQRSTUVWXYZ
abcdefghijklmnopqrstuvwxyz
0123456789
"., !?@¶§&åäö*†‡®™½%‰"

Concept: Hong Kong Beiwei Zansyu is a contemporary type design inspired by Hong Kong Beiwei calligraphy.

Creative Direction
Adonian Chan
Hong Kong

Design Firm
Trilingua Design

Concept: This display typeface with exaggerated serifs and proportions is a refreshing play on a classic style.

Type Design
Etienne Aubert Bonn
and My-Lan Thuong

Foundry
Coppers and Brasses

New Work
Fresh Ink
Frank BARTUSKA

Compositeur Versatile
AS LARGE AS POSSIBLE
Dancing Shoes
Expression Libre

Thick & Thin
SWELLING
Arrondis Intérieurs

BIG BAND
Cool Cats & Kittens
100% Display*

Concept: Lifta is an Arabic, bold, protest typeface for display, available in two styles: Black and Stencil. It was inspired by the Palestinian Resistance posters during the 1970s and '80s, and it is dedicated to all Arab refugees around the world.

Type Design
Omaima Dajani
Jerusalem

Professors
Nadine Chahine
and Daniel Grumer

Agency
ArabicType

حبوا ساعاتكم من وقتنا، و انصرفوا وخذوا ما شئتم من ز
رو و رمل الذّاكرة و خذوا ما شئتم من صور، كي تعرفوا أنّكم
فوا كيف يباني حجر من أرضنا سقف السماء أيّها المارّون
مات العابرة منكم السيف - ومنّا دمنا منكم الفولاذ والنّار -
نا منكم دبّابة أخرى - ومنّا حجر منكم قنبلة الغاز - ومنّا الـ
بنا ما عليكم من سماء وهواء فخذوا حصّتكم من دمنا وانصـ
خابوا حفل عشاء راقص و انصرفوا، وعلينا نحن أن نحرس
هداء وعلينا نحن، أن نحيا كما نحن نشاء أيّها المارّون
مات العابرة كدّسوا أوهامكم في حفرة مهجورة، وانصـ
بدوا عقرب الوقت إلى شرعيّة العجل المقدّس أو إلى تو
يقى مسدّس فإنا ما ليس يرضيكم هنا، فانصرفوا ولنا ما لـ
كم: وطن ينزف شعبا وطن يصلح للنّسيان أو للذّاكرة أيّها المـ
الكلمات العابرة آن أن تنصرفوا وتقيموا أينما شئتم ولكـ
عوا بيننا آن أن تنصرفوا ولتموتوا أينما شئتم ولكن لا تموتوا
ا في أرضنا ما نعمل ولنا الماضي هنا ولنا صوت الحياة الأوّل
ضر، والحاضر، والمستقبل ولنا الدّنيا هنا .. والآخرة فاخر
ن أرضنا من برّنا .. من بحرنا من قمحنا .. من ملحنا .. من جـ

Concept: This is a custom font system for all UK railway overground station signage, commissioned by Network Rail.

Design
Margaret Calvert
and Henrik Kubel
London

Design Firm
Margaret Calvert

Foundry
A2-TYPE

Client
Network Rail

Sign + Text face

Designed by Margaret Calvert in close collaboration with Henrik Kubel Commissioned by Network Rail. Custom font.

Rail Alphabet 2

Designed specifically for signage on UK Railway stations.

1 typeface, 7 fonts

The brief was to design a new typeface that would relate to the original Rail Alphabet used on signs in the 1960s, and to make sure it integrated well with the new wayfinding and pictogram system designed by Spaceagency. The new system of signs, pictograms and typography has a lighter typographic voice than the signs from the 60's and is far more readable than the current dark blue signs with reversed out type. The design process was one of collaboration; Margaret Calvert would draw by hand, and we would work on-screen. With input from

Network Rail, Spaceagency and station architect WestonWilliamson+ Partners, we arrived at Rail Alphabet 2, a highly legible and modern typeface with a clear historical lineage.

Rail Alphabet 2, is a comprehensive digital typeface consisting of 7 fonts; a special weight designed for signs, and three font styles including Italics crafted for all other text settings for print, online and for mobile. Rail Alphabet 2 has sharp junctions, and the proportions are a little narrower than the original Rail Alphabet.

Sign Alphabet

Tighter letter spacing, shorter ascenders (Medium weight)

abcdefghijklmnopqrstuvwxyz
ABCDEFGHIJKLMNOPQRSTUVWXYZ
0123456789&%({[£€$¥@#]}

Character set

506 glyphs in total

ABCDEFGHIJKLMNOPQRSTUVWXYZÆŒŁØÐÞ
abcdefghijklmnopqrstuvwxyzæœłøðþßſıȷfifl
ÁÂÄÀÅÃĂĀĄÇĆČĈĊĎĐÉÊËÈĚĔĖĒĘĜĞĠĢĤÍÎÏİÌĨĬĪĮĴĶĹĽĿŁŃŇÑŅŊ
ÓÔÖÒÕŐŌŔŘŖŠŚŞŜȘŤŢŦȚÚÛÜÙŬŰŪŲŮŴẀẂẄÝŶŸỲŽŹŻ
áâäàåãăāąçćčĉċďđéêëèěĕėēęĝğġģĥíîïıìĩĭīįĵķĺľŀ·ńňñŋ
ħóôöòõőōŕřŗšśşŝșťţŧțúûüùŭűūųůŵẁẃẅýŷÿỳžźż
‚‛‘’‹›„“”·,..;:...?!¿¡¿i(){}[]/_-‐–—―‖«»‹›«»‹›„‚"'""'"
&¶†‡§*™®©℗@ªº#฿₽€$¥£¢ƒ¤·
012345678901234567890123456789°%‰
0123456789 0123456789 0123456789 0123456789
+−×÷=¬~<>±∧≈≤≥∞◊√∫πμΣΩΔℓ℮|{}[]()
←→↑↓↖↗↙↘

Concept: Signifier is a Brutalist response to 17th-century typefaces.

Type Design
Dave Foster

Creative Technologist
Noe Blanco

Foundry
Klim Type Foundry

Signifier.

Type Design
Thomas Huot-
Marchand

Foundry
205TF

Type Design
Hsin Yin Low
and Sueh Li Tan
Kuala Lumpur

Typographer
Pham Đam Ca

Programming
Suppakit
Chalermlarp

Post-Production
Company
Katatrad

Creative Direction
Carina Teo

Client
Grab

Type Design
Studio
hrftype

Type Design
Inga Plönnigs

Foundry
Frere-Jones Type

MAGNET

Magnet Standard Light
Magnet Standard Light Italic
Magnet Standard Regular
Magnet Standard Italic
Magnet Standard Medium
Magnet Standard Medium Italic
Magnet Standard Bold
Magnet Standard Bold Italic
Magnet Standard Black
Magnet Standard Black Italic

**A TYPEFACE FAMILY
CONSISTING OF
TWO SUBFAMILIES
FOR HEADLINE SIZES
AND RUNNING TEXT**

HEADLINE
Upright
Slanted
Backslanted

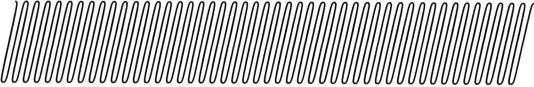

Appendix

2021 TDC Scholarship Recipients

Derrick Mensah Bonsu, KNUST

Ana Valeria Castillos,
The Cooper Union

Dianne Bahram Zadeh Ebrahimi,
Fashion Institute Technology

Pauline Esguerra, Pratt Institute

Jayla Thompson-Bey,
Lincoln University

Bina Thorsen, School of Visual Arts

Xinyi Zhao, Parsons School of Design

TDC Beatrice Warde Scholarship 2021

Ximena Amaya
ArtCenter College of Design,
Pasadena, California

Honorable Mention

Soniya Stella
National Institute of Design,
Ahmedabad, India

Sakinah Bell
Mercy College, New York

TDC Superscript 2021

Sakinah Bell
Mercy College, New York

Honorable Mention

Avalon Garrick
Mercy College, New York

Lisa Marie Montgomery
School of Visual Arts, New York

2021 Student Award Winners TDC67

First Place
Troy Vasilakis
Fashion Institute of Technology,
New York

Second Place
Shuchen Xu
ArtCenter College of Design,
Pasadena, California

Third Place
Akshita Chandra
Maryland Institute College of Art
(MICA), Baltimore

24TDC
First Place Student
Ruggero Magrì
TypeMedia,
Royal Academy of Art (KABK)
Den Haag

International Liaison Chairpersons

CHINA
Liu Zhao
China Central Academy of Fine Arts
Beijing
Liuzhao_cafa@qq.com

FRANCE
Sébastien Binder
ASD Education
17 Rue Deshoulière
44 000 Nantes
sebastien.binder@ad-education.fr

GERMANY

Bertram Schmidt-Friderichs
Verlag Hermann Schmidt Mainz
GmbH & Co.
Gonsenheimer Strasse 56
55126 Mainz
bsf@typografie.de

INDONESIA
John Kudos
Studio Kudos
john@studiokudos.com

JAPAN
Zempaku Suzuki
Japan Typography Association
Sanukin Bldg., 5th Floor
1-7-10 Nihonbashi-honcho
Chuo-ku, Tokyo 104-0041
office@typo.or.jp

POLAND
Ewa Satalecka
Polish Japanese
Academy of Information
Warsaw
ewasatalecla@pjwstk.edu.pl

RUSSIA
Maxim Zhukov
3636 Greystone Avenue
Apt. 4C
Bronx, NY 10463-2059
Zhukov@verizon.net

SOUTH AMERICA
Diego Vainesman
455 East 86 Street
Apt. 11A
New York, NY 10028
diego@40N47design.com

SOUTH KOREA
Samwon Paper Gallery
papergallery@naver.com

SPAIN
Jaume Pujagut, Bau,
Escola Superior de Disseny
Pujades 118
08005 Barcelona
christian@baued.es

TAIWAN
Ken Tsui Lee
National Taiwan University
of Science and Technology
No.43, Keelung Rd.,
Sec.4, Da'an Dist.,
Taipei City 10607, Taiwan (R.O.C.)
leekentsui@gmail.com

THAILAND
Kanteera Sanguantung
Cadson Demak Co., Ltd.
140 Kaulin Building
Thonglor 4 Sukhumvit 55
Klongton Nua, Wattana
Bangkok 10110
kanteera.cadsondemak@gmail.com

VIETNAM
Richard Moore
21 Bond Street
New York, NY 10012
RichardM@RmooreA.com

TYPE DIRECTORS CLUB
The One Club For Creativity
450 W. 31st St, 6th Floor,
New York NY 10001
Tel: 212 979 1900 I Fax: 212 979 5006
tdc@oneclub.org

MEMBERS

Aa

Seth Akkerman 2008
Roman Albertini 2021
Paul Albertson 2021s
Marta Cerda Alimbau 2020
Lisa Amoroso 2015
Jack Anderson 1996
Ana Andreeva 2016s
Christopher Andreola 2003
Allyson Andryshak 2021
Ben Anthony 2021
Ann Antoshak 2020
Hugo Aranha 2017
Agyei Archer 2020
Judith Aronson 2021
Potch Auacherdkul 2018s
Bob Aufuldish 2006
Yomar Augusto 2013

Bb

Frances Baca 2020
Eun Jung Bahng 2020s
Peter Bain 1986III
Andreu Balius 2021
Lindsay Barnett 2017
Arthur Beckenstien 2020
Antonio Mondragón Becker 2020
Pernicias Bedow 2021
Christoph Beier 2018
Patricia Belen 2020
Misha Beletsky 2007
Carlos Beltran 2020
Felix Beltran 1988III
Nima Ben Ayed 2020
Jaamal Benjamin 2019s
Anna Berkenbusch 1989III
Ana Gomez Bernaus 2014
John D. Berry 1996III
Peter Bertolami 1969III
Teresa Bettinardi 2020
Gail Bichler 2018
Michael Bierut 2010
Klaus Bietz 1993
Abe Bingham 2015
David Bingham 2020
Henrik Birkvig 1996
Heribert Birnbach 2007
Roger Black 1980III
Jennifer Blanco 2017}
Thierry Blancpain 2016
Elyanna Blaser-Gould 2018
Susan Block 1989III
Peggy Bloomer 2019
Halvor Bodin 2012
Vlad Boerean 2019
Matteo Bologna 2003
Scott Boms 2012
Christian Booton 2021lc
Jeremy Bowen 2019
Lily Boyce 2018lc
Annabel Brandon 2018
Isabelle Brawley 2020lc
John Breakey 2006
Daniel Brevick 2018
Marisa Ten Brink 2017
Vashenna Brisbane 2017
September Broadhead 2020
Ed Brodsky 1980III
Adrian Brown 2019s
Claire Brown 2019
Craig Brown 2004
Helen Bruno 2021
Paul Buckley 2007
Ryan Bugden 2015s
Van Anh Bui 2020lc
Michael Bundscherer 2007
Nicholas Burroughs 2017

Cc

Susana Cadena 2016
Ronn Campisi 1988II
David Card 2020
Paul Carlos 2008
Edman Carrillo 2021
Scott Carslake 2001
Matthew Carter 1988III
Catherine Casalino 2020
James Castanzo 2008
Mariana Castellanos 2020
Beatriz Castro 2020
Ken Cato 1988III
Jackson Cavanaugh 2010
Eduard Cehovin 2003
Nadine Chahine 2021
Luc Chaissac 2021
Eric Chan 2019
Akshita Chandra 2020lc
Chi Hao Chang 2021s
WenChia Chang 2020s
Spencer Charles 2018
Frank Chavanon 2014
Len Cheeseman 1993III
David Cheung Jr. 1998
Patricia Childers 2013
Todd Childers 2011
Joanne Chin 2020
Janice Cho 2021
Hanju Chou 2019lc
H.Y. Ingrid Chou 2017
Ellen Christensen 2020
Sarah Christus 2020lc
Stanley Church 1997III
Calen Chung 2020s
Scott Citron 2007
John Clark 2014
Rob Clarke 2015
Graham Clifford 1998III
Jeff Close 2017
Doug Clouse 2009
Ed Colker 1983III
Nancy Sharon Collins 2006
Cherise Conrick 2009
Nick Cooke 2001
Luis Albert Valencia Córdova 2019s
Jonathan Correira 2017
Madeleine Corson 1996
Daphnee Cote 2021s
James Craig 2004
Andreas Croonenbroeck 2006
Ray Cruz 1999III
John Curry 2009
Rick Cusick 1989III

Dd

Si Daniels 2020
Susan Darbyshire 1987III
Anselm Dästner 2020lc
Simon Daubermann 2015
Mark Davis 2020
Josanne De Natale 1986
Roberto de Vicq de Cumptich 2005
Christopher DeCaro 2017
Lynda Decker 2020
Anthony deFigio 2020
Liz DeLuna 2005
Constantin Demner 2018
Wenqiao Deng 2018s
Xiyu Deng 2020
Mark Denton 2001
Vonetta De Vonish 2020lc
Mark De Winne 2016
Cara Di Edwardo 2009
Biagio Di Stefano 2017
Fernando Diaz 2016
Lisa Diercks 2018
Chank Diesel 2005
Claude Dieterich A. 1984III
Kirsten Dietz 2000
Joseph DiGioia 1999

Yiyua Ding 2020
Andrea Dionisio 2018
Eric Doctor 2018
Joyce Domingo 2021s
Xiaoyi Dong 2019s
Ross Donnan 2017
Eva Dranaz 2018
Christopher Dubber 1985III
Sara Duell 2021
Denis Dulude 2004
James Dundon 2017s
Patrick Durgin-Bruce 2016
Yavuz Durust 2020s
Mark Duszkiewicz 2017
Simon Dwelly 1998

Ee

Yvonne Eberle 2021
Yvonne Eder 2020s
Evan Eggers 2020
Koray Ekremoglu 2019
Garry Emery 1993III
Manija Emran 2021
Marc Engenhart 2006
Carrie Epps-Carey 2020s
Konstantin Eremenko 2017
Jan Erlinghagen 2020
Joseph Michael Essex 1978III
Manuel Estrada 2019
Florence Everett 1989III
Michelle Evola 2017

Ff

Shuhong Fang 2018
David Farey 1993III
Aron Fay 2019
Lily Feinberg 2014
Robert Festino 2020
Rafael Ferreira 2020s
Robert Festino 2020
Louise Fili 2004
Anne Fink 2013
Kristine Fitzgerald 1990
Louise Fortin 2007
Karlo Francisco 2018s
Tristan Free 2020s
Carol Freed 1987III
Christina Freyss 2017
Dinah Fried 2018
Dirk Fütterer 2008

Gg

Evan Gaffney 2009
Louis Gagnon 2002
Maria Galante 2016
Jovanny Gallego 2019s
John Gambell 2017
Jeremy Garcia 2020
Yasmina Garcia 2017s
Jeffrey Garofalo 2020s
Giuliano Garonzi 2020
Christof Gassner 1990
David Gatti 1981III
Maxime Gau 2019s
Verena Gerlach 2020
Isaac Gertman 2021
Jack Glacken 2020
Lou Glassheim 1947I
Howard Glener 1977III
Valerie Gnaedig 2021
Abby Goldstein 2010
Deborah Gonet 2005
Jason Gong 2021s
Derwyn Goodall 2017
Zan Goodman 2018
Yuliana Gorkorov 2018
Jonathan Gouthier 2009
Justin Graefer 2016
Diana Graham 1984

356

Amit Greenberg 2017s
Joan Greenfield 2006
Becky Greubel 2021
James Grieshaber 2018
Katie Griffin 2020s
Lena Gruschka 2020
Artur Marek Gulbickl 2011
Nora Gummert-Hauser 2005
Meng Guo 2020
Noa Guy 2017
Peter Gyllan 1997III

Hh

Andy Hadel 2010
Allan Haley 1978III
Debra Hall 1996
Tosh Hall 2017
Carrie Hamilton 2015
Drew Hamlin 2021
Lisa Hamm 2015
Yanwen Hang 2019s
Pernille Sys Hansen 2020
Egil Haraldsen 2000
Jesse Harding 2021s
Zelda Harrison 2021
Jon Hartman 2019
Knut Hartmann 1985III
Luke Hayman 2006
Bonnie Hazelton 1975II
Jonas Hecksher 2012
Eric Heiman 2002
Karl Heine 2010
Elizabeth Heinzen 2020
Anja Patricia Helm 2008
Brendan Hemp 2020
Oliver Henn 2009
Andrea Herstowski 2020s
Klaus Hesse 1995III
Cassie Hester 2021
Jason Heuer 2011
Fons M. Hickmann 1996
Bill Hilson 2007
Kit Hinrichs 2002
Masaaki Hirano 2021
Reid Hitt 2015
Serena Ho 2017s
Wing-Sze Ho 2018
Fritz Hofrichter 1980III
Alyce Hoggan 1987
Kevin Horvath 1987
Chengcheng Hou 2020s
Pamela Howard 2019
Paul Howell 2017
Debra Morton Hoyt 2016
Christian Hruschka 2005
Hannah Huang 2020s
Andrea Hubbard 2020
John Hudson 2004
Aimee Hughes 2008
Thomas Hull 2019
Keith C. Humphrey 2008
Ginelle Hustrulid 2021

Ii

Robert Innis 2021
Mayo Inoue 2019s
Sabah Iqbal 2020
Todd Irwin 2016
Danika Isdahl 2021
Yuko Ishizaki 2009
Alexander Isley 2012
Yusuke Ito 2020
Sabah Iqbal 2020

Jj

Donald Jackson 1978II
Torsten Jahnke 2002
Mark Jamra 1999
Janneke Janssen 2019s

Etienne Jardel 2006
Charles Jeffcoat 2021
Yanqiao Jiang 2020s
Song Jin 2017lc
Thomas Jockin 2016
Dean Johnson 2017
Luciano Johnson 2018
Matthew Johnson 2019
Giovanni Jubert 2004

Kk

John Kallio 1996III
Boril Karaivanov 2014
Richard Kegler 2017
Christine Kell 2020
Jeff Kellem 2020
David Kelley 2017
Scott Kellum 2019
Paula Kelly 2020
Russell Kerr 2018s
Jonathan Key 2021
Thoma Kikis 2020
Megan Kile 2020
Doyoon Kim 2020s
Gowan Kim 2021s
Leslie Kim 2017s
Su Hyun Kim 2019
Sung Kim 2019s
Peter Kimmins 2019
Rick King 1993
Dmitry Kirsanov 2013
Amanda Klein 2011
Arne Alexander Klett 2005
Keith Knueven 2020
Akira Kobayashi 1999
Mokoena Kobell2020
Boris Kochan 2002
Anmari Koltchev 2020s
Irina Koryagina 2018
Yuliya Kosheeva 2020s
Nikola Kostic 2019
Johannes Kramer 2020
Markus Kraus 1997
Stephanie Kreber 2001
Ingo Krepinsky 2013
Bernhard J. Kress 1963III
Prem Krsihnamurthy 2021
Sudiksha Krishnan 2019s
Karin Krochmal 2020
Stefan Krömer 2013
John Kudos 2010
Christian Kunnert 1997
Melissa Kuperminc 2020s
Amber Kusmenko 2021
Joshua Kwassman 2019lc
Doah Kwin 2021lc
Oeun Kwon 2019s

Ll

Brandon Labbe 2019
Ginger LaBella 2013
Raymond F. Laccetti 1987III
Karolina Lach 2016
Caspar Lam 2017
Melchoir Lamy 2021
Horacio Lardés 2019
Quang Huy Le 2021s
Binna Lee 2021s
Cindy Lee 2020lc
Diane Lee 2020
Eric Lee 2020s
Gracia Lee 2021
Pum Lefebure 2006
Troy Leinster 22020
Simon Lemmerer 2016
David Lemon 1995III
Brian Lemus 2015
Kevin Leonard 2021
Olaf Leu 1966III
Jean-Bapiste Levée 2019

Aaron Levin 2015
Edwrd Levine 2021
Tom Lewek 2018
Chaosheng Li 2019
Yixue LI 2018s
Lisha Liao 2020s
Jasper Lim 2017s
Karla Faria Lima 2019
Jessica Lin 2017s
Armin Lindauer 2007
Sven Lindhorst-Emme 2015
Shadrack Lindo 2018
Alison Lindquist 2020
Domenic Lippa 2004
Wally Littman 1960III
Angela Liu 2020lc
Xiaoxing Liu 2018
Richard Ljoenes 2014
Margeaux Loeb 2018
Uwe Loesch 1996
Oliver Lohrengel 2004
Utku Lomlu 2016
Kirsten Long 2019
Xin Long 2017
Christian Loos 2019
Tatiana Lopez 2020s
Frank Lotterman 2016
Claire Lukacs 2014
Gregg Lukasiewicz 1990
Abraham Lule 2017
Ken Lunde 2011
Ching-Fa Lung 2019s
Ellen Lupton 2021

Mm

Iain Macmillan 2018
Saki Mafundikwa 2021
Jenny Makarchik 2019
Avril Makula 2010
Nicholas Marabella 2020s
Frankie Margotta 2018s
Crystal Marquez 2020
Bobby C. Martin, Jr. 2011
Emilee Martin 2019s
Frank Martinez 2013
Mike Martins 2019s
Jakob Maser 2006
Abraham Mast 2020
Steve Matteson 2017
Tammie Matthews 2020s
Scott Matz 2011
Ted Mauseth 2001
Andreas Maxbauer 1995III
Douglas May 2021
Elizabeth May 2017lc
Trevett McCandliss 2016
Mark McCormick 2010
Rod McDonald 1995
Olivia McGiff 2019
Daniel McManus 2018
Marc A. Meadows 1996III
Veeksha Mehndiratta 2020lc
Amanda Mei 2021s
Maurice Meilleur 2020
Uwe Melichar 2000
Gloria Mendoza 2021
HopeMeng 2020
Faride Mereb 2019s
Trevor Messersmith 2017
Marnay Meyer 2020
Sarah Mick 2020
Rachael Miller 2020s
John Milligan 1978II
Michael Miranda 1984II
Raven Mo 2020lc
Mary Moffett 2017
Rachel Mondragon 2017
Sakol Mongkolkasetarin 1995
James Montalbano 1993II
Charrel Montalbo 2018
Maria Montes 2017

Pat Taylor 1985III
Shaun Taylor 2015
Kevin Teh 2020
Marcel Teine 2003
Bansri Thakkar 2021lc
Eric Thoelke 2010
Eric Tilley 1995
Laura Tolkow 1996
Liyuan Tong 2019
Andrey Tovcigrechko 2020
Kayla Tran 2020s
Jeremy Tribby 2017
Klaus Trommer 2012
Niklaus Troxler 2000
Adam Trunk 2019
Irene Tsay 2020s
Ling Tsui 2016
Minao Tsukada 2000
Viviane Tubiana 2020
Natascha Tümpel 2002s
François Turcotte 1999
Benjamin Tuttle 2018
Anne Twomey 2005

Uu

Andreas Uebele 2002
Ryota Umemura 2018
Cagdas Ilke Ünal 2018
Milcho Uzunov 2020

Vv

Diego Vainesman 1991III
Oscar Valdez 2017
Victoria Valenzuela 2019
Patrick Vallée 1999
Jarik van Sluijs 2017
Jeffrey Vanlerberghe 2005
Pano Vassiiou 2020
Rozina Vavetsi 2011
Bruno Vera 2020s
Hagen Verleger 2016s
Leo Vicenti 2020s
Christa Vinciquerra 2017s
Franci Virgill 2021
Patricia Vogler 2020
Svenja von Doehlen 2020
Danila Vorobiev 2013
Matija Vujovic 2019

Ww

Frank Wagner 1994
Oliver Wagner 2001
Rosalie Wagner 2020
Allan R. Wahler 1998
Jurek Wajdowicz 1980
Sergio Waksman 1996III
Clark Walecki 2020
Zakk Waleko 2020
Garth Walker 1992III
Dorothy Wang 2020
Yiqi Wang 2020s
Emily Wardwell 2017
Graham Weber 2016s
Harald Weber 1999III
Yoni Weiss 2021
Craig Welsh 2010
Mariano Werneck 2018
Alex W. White 1993III
Philbert Widjaja 2020s
Lutz Widmaier 2018
Christopher Wiehl 2003
Richard Wilde 1993III
Edith Williams 2020
James Williams 1988III
Steve Williams 2005
KC Witherell 2014
Delve Withrington 1997
Janine Wolf 2020
David Wolske 2017

Gloria Wong 2019s
Megan Wong 200lc
Fred Woodward 1995III
Chris Wu 2021
Guanyan Wu 2020s

Xx

Yuchen Xie 2020s

Yy

Zeynep Yildirim 2020
Lori Young 2021
Garson Yu 2005

Zz

Weixi Zeng 2019s
Zhao Zeng 2016lc
Shuo Zhang 2018
Jie Zhao 2020s
Wendy Zhu 2020s
Maxim Zhukov 1996III
Holger Ziemann 2020
Roy Zucca 1969IIII

Corporate Members
Adobe 2014
AEGraphics 2021
Bleacher Report 2019
École de Visuelle Communications 2011
Font Bureau 2015
Lobster Phone 2020
School of Visual Arts, New York 2007
SXM Media 2020

I Charter member
II Honorary member
III Life members
s Student member (uppercase)
lc Lowercase student member
Membership as of July 29, 2021

In Memoriam
Ed Benguiat 1964III
Conny J. Winter1985III

84pt Thin -10

Nāgamangala

84pt Light -10

Chimbarongo

84pt Regular Alternate S,s,a -10

Saint Ghislain

84pt Medium -10

Fürstenwalde

84pt Bold -10

Khagrachhari

84pt Black Alternate a -10

Mozambique

CHARACTER SET